Canadian Social Policy Renewal, 1994–2000

William E. Warriner and Ian Peach

Fernwood Publishing • Halifax & Winnipeg

Printed and bound in Canada by Hignell Book Printing

Published in Canada by Fernwood Publishing
Site 2A, Box 5, 32 Oceanvista Lane
Black Point, Nova Scotia, B0J 1B0
and 324 Clare Avenue, Winnipeg, Manitoba, R3L 1S3
www.fernwoodpublishing.ca

Fernwood Publishing Company Limited gratefully acknowledges the financial support
of the Government of Canada through the Book Publishing Industry Development
Program (BPDIP), the Canada Council for the Arts and the Nova Scotia
Department of Tourism and Culture for our publishing program.

Library and Archives Canada Cataloguing in Publication

Peach, Ian, 1965-
Canadian social policy renewal, 1994-2000 / Ian Peach and Bill Warriner.

Includes bibliographical references.
ISBN 978-1-55266-253-3

1. Canada--Social policy. I. Warriner, Bill II. Title.

HV108.P42 2007   361.6'10971   C2007-903419-5

Contents

Acknowledgements

In writing this book, we have sought to coherently document events to which we were lucky enough to be a party. As government officials, it is often hard to situate our efforts in a broader context and reflect on where our efforts are leading us and the citizens that, ultimately, we work for. The day-to-day demands of keeping the processes of government moving or, as it is sometimes described, "feeding the beast" that is a modern government, make such reflection a luxury. This may be particularly true for officials responsible for keeping the intergovernmental processes that are so important to policymaking in a federation like Canada functioning. Thus, our first acknowledgement must be to those with the foresight and commitment to establish the Saskatchewan Institute of Public Policy and ensure that it provides policy practitioners who are so inclined the opportunity to catch our breath, reflect, and share our knowledge, our experience and our analysis with others. Our sojourns at the Institute as Government of Saskatchewan senior policy fellows and, in Ian's case, director, made the writing of this book possible.

Our second acknowledgement must be of those who made social policy renewal in Canada happen. We have both had many valued colleagues over the years; often, it is the quality of those relationships that makes success possible in the face of difficult odds. We must also express our deep respect and gratitude for the Ministers and First Ministers, who demonstrated their commitment to making good social policy and fostering intergovernmental collaboration throughout the years that we document. The privilege of having been able to work with our fine elected men and women and watch them work with one another has done much to overcome the cynicism about politics and politicians that is so much a part of the "malaise of modernity" in developed democracies. Those social policy advocates, members of the "third sector," who were involved in social policy research and advocacy during these years must also be recognized as having performed a vital service to Canadians. Without the unfailing commitment of these people, whatever their roles or backgrounds, there would not have been a story for us to tell. We are also pleased that several of these people agreed to provide "reflections" pieces, which contribute to the richness of our story with their own words.

A thanks is also owed to Bob Stirling, not only for providing us with his insightful foreword, but for all of his editorial advice throughout the writing of this book. His wise counsel and encouragement are greatly appreciated. Lastly, we want to thank publisher Errol Sharpe and the staff at Fernwood Publishing, whose careful work has taken us from manuscript to book. Thank you all for making our work, and our lives, richer.

Foreword

Robert Stirling

We live in times when it is very difficult — not impossible but very difficult — for ordinary citizens to ferret out the truth about important public events. The picture is too often incomplete and fuzzy. By contrast, this book by Bill Warriner and Ian Peach brings into better focus a recent period of Canadian social policy and the politics of Canadian federalism.

The implementation of social policies has been no less impenetrable than that of other areas of public policy. Government budgets are shrouded in obscurity. Finding accurate data on tax expenditures in some provinces can be a challenge. It is equally difficult to work your way though governments' resource taxation and royalties; typically they are a labyrinth of exceptions and concessions that may, or may not, have encouraged development but certainly benefit resource companies. The Canadian Centre for Policy Alternatives and its provincial affiliates create "people's budgets," which give a clearer picture of government finances, but the challenge is huge.

In the same vein, this work by Warriner and Peach does us a useful service. It clarifies the social policy process. It takes us behind the postmodern cacophony of media stories, public relations spins and personalities to show us more deeply the structures and processes of Canadian federalism and, using a case study, how policy is formed in such a system.

"Fuzziness" is a methodological issue so some brief comments on the methodological implications of this careful study are in order.

Social and political amnesia may show epochal tendencies, but for the last three or four decades it has been on the increase. The problem of knowledge is not one confined to the masses. Scientists, experts, officials and academics have struggled over what constitutes knowledge and how it is formed. How has our way of thinking changed, particularly in the social sciences, that area that especially informs social policy and trains social policy practitioners? Indeed, we have seen a major upheaval in our methodologies and in the way we generate knowledge.

It used to be, when we were confronted with obscurity, confusion or competing claims, that we asked for "just the facts." For much of the last century, positivism had the franchise on facts, particularly in the United States. This approach to knowledge insists that reality lies exclusively in the empirical realm. Positivist social scientists spend a lot of time getting their measurements right, that is, valid and reliable, without exercising much thought about what might be going on in the deeper structures beyond the realm of observations. Indeed, they deny that such a deeper reality exists. This approach appeared to produce a straightforward foundation for knowledge — it had to square with observations.

Positivism explained things by describing them — a cause was simply the regular occurrence of two or more things together. But some spun elaborate theories or causal explanations nonetheless. Parsons (1951) often used obscure concepts to theorize that society was a functioning system, superior to its individual people, and with a tendency to maintain a steady state, perhaps a will to live. While not logically entailed in Parsons' structural functionalism, it is a short leap to claim that leading nations in the world, such as the United States, must be functioning pretty well and deserve to be modelled as exemplars of healthy societies (Hoselitz, 1960; for a critique see Frank, 1967). As well, it trained a host of policy practitioners for the United States and other governments and arguably informed American policies during the Cold War and beyond (Buxton, 1985).

Positivism brought forth its critics. Underclass representatives noticed that its grander theories centred the ideas of the ruling class. Feminists showed how they privileged the lives of men, underdevelopment theorists how they legitimized imperialist powers and regions, African-Americans and other dominated ethnic and racialized groups how they legitimated the rule of whites, or more precisely, dominating groups. In the face of positivism's claim that it was value free, not only were the theories shown to be biased, they were shown to play a role in maintaining ideological hegemony in capitalist and other unequal and divided societies.

In the hands of postmodernists such as Foucault, this critique revived an old suspicion. If the foundations of knowledge in the tradition of positivism were not possible, then, foundationalism itself became suspect. From this perspective, claims cannot be true or false. Instead, we hold claims because we are committed to them, think they are important, like them or they are part of our moral upbringing. For Foucault (1980), knowledge and power are closely associated. There are knowledges that dominate and colonize subaltern "others." This, in turn, brings into existence resistance and other knowledges. It is not a matter of one or the other knowledge being true. In the postmodern view, all knowledge is relative; we must be suspicious of explanations, the social policies that they spawn and even the state that puts them into practice.

The postmodern approach has a subtle attraction. It deconstructs grand theories, showing how their "totalizing" explanations and "universal" causes are contradictory and oversimplifications. It may even appear to be liberating when it unmasks the privileged status — or truth — of conventional and official knowledges, thereby legitimating the voices of colonized and dominated peoples. But this is a backhanded form of liberation. On this account, all forms of oppression are equally important and have an equal right to be heard and accommodated. Further, in practice, those giving voice to a particular oppression are competing against others. Each becomes suspicious of the others' claims. Grounds for adjudicating between claims become limited and tend toward force rather than respectful, reasoned and democratic discourse. Instead of building liberatory solidarity among dominated peoples, it breeds individualism and ineffective isolation. It surely frustrates the work of democratic policymakers, who must search through shrill voices and quiet voices to find truly important needs. After all, things *are* caused, and some causes *are* more important than others. Social policy formation must get the order of causes right if it has any hope of being effective.

According to Jameson (1991), postmodernism fits well with the current stage of multinational capitalism dominated by the global marketplace and speculative finance. With it come the decentring of the subject as an autonomous agent and the end of collective projects. Even the common national language by which such projects could be framed is replaced by micro languages and the micro politics of identities — racial, ethnic, gender, religious and others. Market alienation grows to the point where we consume the image, the spectacle or the pseudo-event and we scarcely know use-value, only exchange-value. Amin (2006) shows how postmodernism makes the development of resistance to liberal globalization both difficult and uncertain.

As the neo-liberal ideology began to legitimate the end of the Keynesian welfare state and downsized government, a process that Warriner and Peach describe well in chapter one, people increasingly became suspicious of government, of experts and bureaucrats, of other social groups, of each other. With no convincing way to judge competing claims, new forms of fundamentalist religious faith became a substitute, leading on the world stage to what Achcar calls "the clash of barbarisms" (Achcar, 2002).

Neo-liberalism began to be reflected in state policies in the mid-1970s but by the 1980s and 1990s it was in full bloom. Curiously, the civil servants that put the National Child Benefit into place didn't seem to notice! Or more likely, and no less important, they were able to peer through the ideological fog to stay focused upon two central elements of Canadian reality: the importance of social programs and the unacceptably high number of children in poverty, and threats to Canadian federalism.

In her "Reflection" at the end of chapter six, Martha Friendly remembers her persistent question: "Is this as good as it gets?" Not only is this a useful question in the campaign for better social programs, it is an important methodological question as well. For one thing, it expects some evidence; what proportion of children are in poverty, what are the conditions under which children grow up, and so forth. What is more, the question recognizes that we need to do some deep theoretical thinking in order to figure out the evidence and to understand the experience; what is child poverty, what caused it to be like this, what are its fundamental tendencies? Finally, the question is asked within a certain political, economic and cultural context. It is value-laden, as are those of us who ask it. It does not expect that the answer will be outside society or value-free or that the answerer, attempting some "God trick," will step outside of social conditions to proclaim the truth on child poverty. Rather, it expects that, using our powers of observation and reason and drawing upon our best social practices of dialogue, criticism, reflection and restatement, we will arrive at a true understanding of child poverty, its causes and tendencies, that will allow us, collectively, to improve the situation. If our understanding turns out to have been wrong, then the question expects that, collectively, we will fix it. The question does not expect that "anything goes" for an answer, even though social commentators may sometimes, perhaps increasingly, proffer answers on minimalist standards of reason and observation. It expects an answer that is true.

Martha Friendly's question also has a certain dialectic embedded in it. On the pessimistic side, as the authors show in chapters one and two, child poverty and the condition of Canadian federalism could be much worse. With the rise of transnational corporations, "free" trade and more thorough-going global competition, what is to stop the rise in poverty and the withering of the state? When workers and, arguably, farmers and parts of the middle class, were (and are) pitted against each other globally, it was hard to see how the "race to the bottom" had any way-stations on the way down. On the optimistic side, the question demands our commitment, our human agency and our hope to make things better.

As the story unfolds during the 1980s and 1990s, a core group of government officials might also have been asking "Is this as good as it gets?" The processes of globalization in its current version took hold, growth in the low end of the wage scale stagnated, income disparities widened, and Canada's child poverty rate grew. Similarly, the politics of federalism in Canada took a hit; the federal government, often unilaterally, cut domestic programs and offloaded costs to the provinces, and a Quebec referendum to separate came very close to passing. An unlikely force, Canada's provinces and territories, which in the past and since have not often agreed or even regularly talked to each other, attempted to correct the situation. They constructed intergovernmental structures and processes for developing and considering alternative proposals, negotiating and reaching conclusions for action. This in itself offered a new version of Canadian federalism, one in which the provinces could develop and advance a national agenda as opposed to a conflicting collection of provincial and territorial agendas. They found ways to engage the federal government in this process. The National Child Benefit was the first program to appear from this new ensemble. The National Children's

Agenda also benefited from it. The Social Union Framework Agreement, while pursued vigorously, showed some of the weaknesses of the new mechanisms. But, I will let the authors tell the story!

What can be said of the study that follows? To my mind it is neither postmodern nor positivist. Certainly it relies upon observations and experience but, unlike positivism, the explanation doesn't end there. More in the tradition of critical realism (Archer, Bhaskar and Collier, 1998; Danermark et al., 2002), the authors have given us a reasoned explanation by which we can begin to understand observations about poverty rates, the intricate workings of assistance delivery systems, the web of intergovernmental structures and meetings, and more.

Not paralyzed by competing claims, the authors peer far down into the causal processes of the Canadian political economy to show us where alleviating child poverty fits in. It is, fundamentally, a wage supplement, a way-station of sorts for low-income working families who are dealt a very poor hand by the forces of globalization. Of course, it is also a wage subsidy to employers who are unable or unwilling to pay wages sufficient to bring families out of poverty.

Still, it is at root a social program focused upon helping families with children to mitigate the effects of poverty. Done adequately, it assures them decent shelter, food and education, and it helps children to grow up in environments where their human potentials have some reasonable chance of being realized. These are use-values. No doubt, using some alienated arithmetic, money values could be attached to them, but it would give us merely a vague appearance of deeper human needs. These use-values are justified not by the inhumanity of the markets but because they are fundamental to the human condition and essential to the collective well-being of human societies (Polanyi, 1957).

Perhaps Medicare and public health, public education, public housing and transportation, and other parts of our state-supported social services and public infrastructure can be seen in the same light. If, traditionally, we have tried to mitigate the effect of global markets by demanding better wages and working conditions, a higher minimum wage or, in agriculture, higher commodity prices and marketing boards, the authors' analysis suggests an alternative politics of resistance, demanding a stronger state with stronger social services and infrastructure, and joining forces internationally with those who have similar interests. Is this a return to the post-World War II "welfare state" or is this something new? Can such a state be financed without a revolt by capital and if not, what then? It is well beyond the scope of this study to answer such fascinating questions, but it ought to make us think about them.

Finally, unlike positivists or postmodernists, Warriner and Peach do not offer legitimation to imperial projects, corporate domination or the interests behind globalization. On the contrary, their study offers a critical analysis of these forces at work in important economic and political corners of Canadian society. In that sense, it is a product of the social conditions in Canada. It is value-laden. It examines its object of study from a certain standpoint. It is written by two experienced and respected civil servants and policy practitioners, so, of course, it takes that standpoint. But, more broadly, it addresses poverty and federalist policy formation from the standpoint of those who resist domination and globalization. Notably, against those of us who have been dumbed down, are suffering political amnesia or are lulled into complacency and the attitude that "there is no alternative," this study shows that things can be done, changes can be made, new structures can be put in place. It is a story about how people acted to bring about change and conserve important collective values. The subject is not decentred in this narrative.

Critics may dismiss the National Child Benefit and the National Children's Agenda as inadequate. It is true that programs to "eliminate" poverty can be more pastiche than real and defences of Canadian federalism can be merely spectacle and media speak. But Warriner and Peach demonstrate that this was not true for the National Child Benefit, National Children's Agenda and the Social Union Framework Agreement. Of course, programs may not live up to their expectations; conditions change, the challenges and effects of global markets intensify. This does not mean that suspicion will suffice or that despair is convincing. It simply means that the programs and Canadian federalism, once again, need to be strengthened.

Postmodern cynicism is not helpful here. We can take some comfort in knowing, at least, that when push comes to shove, there still is a cadre of democratic civil servants who know how to put social programs in place and make Canadian federalism work. We need to encourage these people and train more of them for future crises and struggles. This book will help with that task.

—Bob Stirling, Professor Emeritus, University of Regina

Chapter One

The Social Policy Environment

Social policy refers to the arrangements of communities in respect of their general welfare. How are goods and services distributed? How are claims on the social product established? How is the social order maintained? How is public health and well being enhanced? The development of social policy involves the complex, dynamic and evolutionary expression of contending interests that are typically mediated, although not necessarily controlled, by political authority and reflected in legislation. As a consequence, the investigation and discussion of particular elements of social policy, or specific aspects of social policy development, are informed by a review of the general social, economic, political and historical context.

This chapter considers the historical perspective and discusses some of the important, overarching social and economic factors that have conditioned social policy development in general and have influenced the current development of social policy in Canada. The main points are that social policy is a function of state mediation of contending class interests; that there are recurring themes that are the expressions of these different interests; and that the current economic environment and global economic forces are driving social and economic adjustment. These factors are not always obvious in the practical development of specific social policy responses, but it is helpful to keep this perspective in mind when considering the fundamental nature of social policy and the circumstances contributing to its development.

The development of the capitalist economy has been accompanied by an increasing level of state regulation of the whole process of production. In its regulation of the production process, an important concern of the state is the maintenance and reproduction of the labour force, including both employed and unemployed workers and their families. Government regulations affect the process of production directly, through the imposition of labour standards legislation, and, indirectly, through social welfare legislation. The importance of social welfare legislation is indicated by the dramatic increase in government expenditures directed to social welfare programs and by the influence that such policies and programs have had on society. To identify the major themes of social policy and to get a sense of the role of social policy in the current context, it is instructive to briefly review the origins of social welfare legislation in relation to the general dynamics of capitalism and to consider the development of social policy in relation to the ongoing development of the modern capitalist economy.

Poverty and Relief

The origins of modern social policy in societies influenced by the British tradition can be traced to the Elizabethan poor laws of 1601 and their revisions over the following two centuries. These laws established a system of land taxation known as the "poor rates," which financed parish administered programs to provide employment and economic assistance for the poor. The parish authorities were empowered to create employment through public projects or private contract, facilitate employment by subsidizing wages, pressure the unemployed to seek employment and provide relief without the obligation of employment (Rimlinger, 1971: 19). The poor laws' residence regulations inhibited labour mobility and thereby provided a stable labour reserve, maintained through taxes and charity, that could be employed by local agricultural and manufacturing interests. In addition, wage subsidies depressed wages, benefiting larger employers at the expense of landed taxpayers (Mencher, 1967: 29, 99).

The industrial revolution changed everything. With the growth and development of productive capacity, the transition to urban industrial manufacturing and the introduction of advanced agricultural techniques, the poor laws became an obstacle to economic development. Urban manufacture, and industrial development generally, was hindered by a relative shortage of wage labour and residual competition from rural manufacture, which was propped up by the system of poor relief wage subsidies. At the same time, the surplus rural population and the associated need for poor relief increased the tax pressures on rural landowners (Mencher, 1967: 100–103; Rimlinger, 1971: 37–38). Redesigning poverty legislation was in the interests of both industrial and landed capital.

The *British Poor Law Reform Act* of 1834 rejected the concept of social responsibility for social welfare and strictly limited access to poor relief. The objective of the Act was to provide assistance only to indigent persons, those either unable to work or provide for their subsistence through employment. It was not intended for the relief of poverty resulting from market forces (Rimlinger, 1971: 53). Assistance to able-bodied workers was restricted to that provided through the "workhouse" system, which had been designed to be so unpleasant as to deter all but the most destitute from seeking public relief. In addition, the Act rationalized the administrative apparatus of poor relief and encouraged the free movement of labour (Mencher, 1967: 97, 121–27). All of this contributed to the concept of poor relief eligibility that distinguished between the "deserving" poor, who were unable to work, and the "undeserving" poor, who were able to work but were unemployed or underemployed.

Throughout this period, the process of industrialization generated a relative surplus population, a labour reserve, which could not be adequately maintained by the restrictive provisions of the existing poor relief legislation. In addition, the excesses of unregulated production had degraded social well being to such a degree that it necessitated the introduction of regulatory legislation. By the last quarter of the nineteenth century, the pressing need to develop more appropriate employment and welfare policies was evident. The appalling social and economic conditions of workers and the poor were widely documented and reported through a proliferation of public investigations, and social protest and disorder had become increasingly intense (Gilbert, 1966: 26–39).

The dynamics of this period led eventually to the modern approach to social welfare legislation. Competition, conditioned by the initial measures to regulate production, and the demands of an increasingly organized labour force encouraged the development of advanced technological and organizational measures to enhance productivity. Increasingly, industrial development required the ready availability of a stable, efficient, educated and generally modern work force. This encouraged the development of a whole range of social policy initiatives.

With the rapid industrial development of the late nineteenth century, the inadequacies of the poor relief system became more significant as the poor became recognized not only as a potential resource but also as a threat to social order. The liberal reform movement argued that extensive poverty diminished labour resources, decreased productivity, encouraged social instability and was generally disadvantageous to the national economy. Some social reformers emphasized the benefits of social welfare to ensure the "national efficiency" required to advance imperial objectives. The concept of national efficiency had a sustained effect on British social policy and led to the development of a "national minimum standard" of subsistence (Gilbert, 1966: 60–101).

In Canada, social policy was influenced by British experience and legislation. As in Britain and other industrializing nations, the negative effects of unregulated industrialization necessitated social protection, and the liberal reform movement that emerged in reaction to the impacts of industrialization influenced the development of social welfare legislation. The social and economic consequences of industrialization also advanced trade unionism and encouraged several government and other investigations into the working and living conditions of the emerging industrial labour force. For example, the 1887 Canadian Royal Commission on the Relations of Labour and Capital identified certain employment practices that were responsible for antagonistic industrial relations. In particular, the Commission reported that all wage earners in subordinate positions were paid "barely enough to supply sufficient of the necessaries of life for the proper maintenance of a wife and family" (Labour Commission, 1889: 117). The Commission's observation regarding the insufficiency of wages to support the needs of families identifies a central issue and a recurring theme with respect to the development of social policy in support of families and children.

Industrialization, War and Social Policy

In the late nineteenth century, with the rise of monopolies and the domination of finance capital, the intense rivalry between the capital interests of different nations led to increased protectionism and, eventually, to world wars. Attempts to establish institutions to regulate and moderate international relations followed. After World War I there was the Treaty of Versailles, the League of Nations and the International Labour Organization (ILO). Following World War II there was the United Nations and the Bretton Woods Agreement, leading to the creation of the World Bank (WB), International Monetary Fund (IMF) and the General Agreement on Tariffs and Trade (GATT). These institutions created a framework for the conduct of international economic relations. They provided protections for national autonomy by establishing controls over the movement of money. As a result, interest rates could vary without affecting capital flight, and nation states could deficit spend and implement other Keynesian measures without the negative financial consequences associated with unregulated capital flows. The capacity of national governments to implement social policies, which today would be labelled as initiatives to "enhance human capital," was a beneficiary of these arrangements.

In the aftermath of both the world wars, much attention was directed to reconstruction, economic development and social policy initiatives associated with advanced industrial development. James Rice and Michael Prince observed that the events of the 1940s were "epoch-making for social security in many countries" (2000: 55). It was during this period that the general approach and fundamental elements of the welfare state emerged. During World War II, governments had marshalled national economic and social resources, and the enhanced economic role of governments had been legitimated within the Keynesian economic perspective (Rice and Prince, 2000: 57, 64). Post-war reconstruction plans were strongly influenced by the 1942 Beveridge report, *Social Insurance and Allied Services*, in Britain, and other directional reports that advocated a comprehensive approach to social policy, including major social security and welfare initiatives and the establishment of a "social minimum" entitlement to security and welfare.

This approach to social policy reflected public attitudes and was widely accepted in post-war society. There was "broad ideological consensus regarding the role of the state in ensuring domestic employment, price stability and social safety nets" (Kell and Ruggie, 1999: 1). As a result, governments were well positioned and intellectually oriented toward the development and implementation of a range of social policy initiatives. Active government involvement in economic regulation and social programming resulted in programs such as the Family Allowance, expanded welfare benefits and services, Unemployment Insurance, public health care, retirement income insurance, regional economic development, Crown corporations and infrastructure development.

However, by the 1970s, the controls of the IMF, WB and GATT had become a fetter on the global economic activity of multi-national corporations. Neo-liberalism emerged, resulting in deregulation, free trade and privatization. In 1973 exchange rates were allowed to float, and by the late 1970s through the 1980s, with Thatcher and Regan in the lead, all the major economies dismantled their capital controls. Also during this period, trade was liberalized through the establishment of the World Trade Organization (WTO).

Globalization of the market economy in the absence of an effective supra-national governance structure to regulate the relations between labour and capital, and the associated intensification of economic competition, has encouraged a "race to the bottom" and promoted a mal-distribution of costs and benefits. This has contributed to increasing income inequality, undermined population health and well-being and presented challenges for economic and social adjustment (Grinspun, 1993: Burtless et al., 1998). In addition, the competitive consequences of international trade liberalization and market integration have made it difficult for governments to maintain social policy initiatives to protect or promote population health and well-being. Increasing rivalry by governments for economic development investment and job creation and pressures to maintain or increase the competitiveness of national enterprises have constrained the use of labour legislation and other social policy measures to address the detrimental effects of intensified competition and economic restructuring. Government interventions to increase productivity and enhance competitiveness and the limited implementation of effective labour force adjustment measures have contributed to the deterioration of living standards, especially for low-skilled workers and their families

The big advances in social policy thus occurred in the aftermath of the two world wars, not so much because social programs were introduced during or immediately after the wars, although some programs did originate then, but because the change of economic and social conditions associated with the wars shaped the approach to social policy and precipitated initiatives that led to the program accomplishments of later years. On this point it has been noted that "the demands of war and its resultant social impact opened the way for reforms long advocated by labour, women and social organizations" (Moscovitch and Drover, 1987: 23–24). In general, social policy initiatives that were identified during and immediately following the wars achieved substantial public support and also often political recognition and commitment. However, social policy reform is typically a lengthy process involving the peculiarities of political dynamics and even popular proposals often required many years to achieve legislative approval and implementation.

This overview of the trends in social policy development is as true for Canada as for other developed countries. In Canada, there was much concern about the social policy needs of post-war reconstruction and economic development. Union membership had almost tripled between 1911 and 1919, and organized labour was determined to press for improved working and living conditions. In 1919 a greater number of workers were engaged in more strikes and other actions and more days were lost as a result of strikes than in any year previous. A significant portion of the agriculture and small business sectors, also beset by economic difficulties, became increasingly active in demanding social reform. In addition, women's organizations and other social welfare movements pressed for social change (Moscovitch and Drover, 1987).

During the turbulent post-World War I period the Liberal Party (in opposition) found it advisable to advance a social reform platform. In 1919 the Liberal Party elected W.L. Mackenzie King as party leader. In his book, *Industry and Humanity: A Study of the Principles Underlying Industrial Reconstruction*, published the previous year, King argued in favour of protective labour legislation and accepted the British Labour Party proposal for a government regulated "national minimum" of social conditions (Bryden, 1974: 65–66).

In 1919, concerns over the post-war deterioration of industrial relations prompted the federal government to appoint the Royal Commission on Industrial Relations. Among the Commission's recommendations was the proposal that an expert board be commissioned to conduct an immediate enquiry to effect the early implementation of legislation to establish government insurance against unemployment, sickness, invalidity and old age (Department of Labour, 1919: 19). In response to the Commission's report, the federal government convened the National Industrial Conference of the Dominion and Provincial Governments of Canada. The conference included representatives of business and labour and discussed matters concerning industrial relations, labour law and the labour related features of the Treaty of Versailles (Canada, 1919: i).

While several social policy proposals were identified following World War I, only a few, such as the mothers' allowances in Manitoba (1919) and Ontario (1920), were actually implemented (Moscovitch and Drover, 1987). Other popular proposals, such as Unemployment Insurance, were not actually implemented until the 1940s and 1950s. The only major national program of the period was the *Old Age Pension Act* of 1926, which mandated federal-provincial cost matching to provide modest pensions to eligible citizens aged seventy years and older.

In Canada, World War II advanced the process of industrialization, increased demand for an educated and trained labour force, and conditioned the need for complementary social security measures. Following from the Beveridge Report, the 1943 *Report on Social Security for Canada* by Leonard Marsh proposed a comprehensive set of social security programs based on both social insurance and social entitlement principles. It addressed employment risks, such as unemployment, and universal risks, such as old age, sickness and disability. Both the Beveridge and Marsh reports recognized that a major cause of poverty resulted from wage levels that for many workers were insufficient to meet the needs of families with children. The Marsh report stated that "the starting point of all social security discussion is the level of family income or… wages" (Marsh, 1975: 18). Both reports advocated children's allowances to augment the wage system and assist low-income families with children (Guest, 1991: 109–13).

During the period from about 1940 to 1970, the orientation of the social security system in Canada changed from primarily the provision of economic relief in exceptional circumstances involving economic hardship, toward a more comprehensive approach that involved universal entitlement and social insurance as well as means-tested economic assistance. In reviewing the development of the welfare state, Armstrong observed that "In the quarter century following the Second World War, then, Canada developed a series of programs, services and regulations that established rights based on a notion of collective responsibility. They grew out of demonstrated needs and of demands for change. They acknowledged that many Canadians faced risks over which they had little control and for which they could not individually provide" (Armstrong, 1997: 52).

While some social programs, such as Family Allowance, social housing, Unemployment Insurance and the guaranteed income supplement, were introduced during or immediately after World War II, other programs, such as assistance for disabled persons, the federal Old Age Security program, Unemployment Insurance, the Canada Pension Plan, the Canada Assistance Plan and Medicare were not actually implemented until the 1950s and 1960s. Programs such as Unemployment Insurance and old age security were implemented incrementally and adjusted periodically over a long period of time in a way that reflected the developing role of the federal and provincial governments in their provision and administration of social security programs.

It should be noted that, in practice, the cost of producing labour and the provision of basic needs is shared between public services, which provide welfare, education and health care, and private means, which are the source of wages and other incomes. The degree to which the support of individuals and families is shared between public services and private means is determined by social, economic and historical circumstances. In effect, public measures to subsidize the maintenance and reproduction of labour can be understood as the partial socialization of the wages system. In effect, social consumption expenditures, also referred to as the "social wage" serves to "socialize some of the costs of the labour force" and, in part at least, contribute to "the general social reproduction of labour" (Moscovitch and Drover, 1987: 24).

The details and process of implementing the social programs of the welfare state had much to do with economic circumstances, political contingency, division of federal and provincial jurisdictions, and the dynamics of federal-provincial relations. Nevertheless, throughout this period, the general vision and approach for social policy development was consistently associated with increasing involvement of the federal government (Rice and Prince 2000: 79–81). Federal conditional transfers and cost shared programs enabled the federal government to intervene in areas of provincial jurisdiction and impose federal criteria and national standards (Laurent and Vaillancourt, 2004: 1–4).

Modern Canadian Social Policy

During the 1960s, and 1970s, the government of Canada, like governments elsewhere, became concerned with the extent of poverty. In 1965, the federal government initiated measures intended to facilitate employment and address poverty, and the following year, the Canada Assistance Plan was introduced to expand federal cost sharing of social assistance and other social services programs. It was intended that this would enable provinces to improve coverage for social assistance, including income support for the working poor, and increase access to training for the unemployed.

In 1968, a Special Senate Committee on Poverty was established to investigate the nature of poverty in Canada. The Committee's 1971 report, *Poverty in Canada*, focused on the working poor and identified insufficient wages as a major source of poverty. Notably, the Senate Report was critical of the Canada Assistance Plan and proposed the establishment of a guaranteed annual income plan. Other reports of the time, including *The Fifth Annual Review* of the Economic Council of Canada, *Income Security and Social Services*, *The Report of the Royal Commission on the Status of Women* and *The Real Poverty Report*, also expressed concerns about low wages and the welfare system, and identified elements of inequality associated with race, gender and region (Guest, 1991: 166, 173). In 1970, the federal white paper, *Income Security for Canadians*, raised concerns about the financial sustainability of social programs, questioned the practice of universal coverage and proposed revisions to the Family Allowance and old age pension programs that would target benefits in relation to income (Guest, 1991: 175).

In 1973 the federal government initiated a joint federal-provincial review of the Canadian social security system. The white paper associated with this initiative, *Working Paper on Social Security in Canada*, proposed an approach to developing a more coordinated and integrated federal-provincial approach to social security programming. This review was comprehensive and addressed five policy areas, including: community employment, social insurance, income support and supplementation, social and employment services, and federal-provincial cooperation. A central focus of the review was the issue of income adequacy (Guest, 1991: 190). Of particular interest is the structure and process that was created to conduct the review. The review established intergovernmental "working parties" of federal and provincial officials, reporting to deputy ministers and Ministers of Welfare, to address the main issues related to community employment, income support and supplementation, and social and employment services. This approach was quite effective in facilitating intergovernmental collaboration and it provided a model future initiatives.

With respect to the central issue of income support for the poor, the review resulted in the creation of two important proposals: 1) an income support program, to provide a needs-based income for persons not in the labour force, including disabled persons, mothers with young children and persons unable to find employment; and 2) an income supplement program, primarily to increase the incomes of low income families with children (Guest, 1991: 191–92). These discussions encouraged several provincial governments, including British Columbia in 1973, Saskatchewan in 1974 and Ontario in 1975, to introduce income supplementation programs.

The national social security reform initiative of the 1970's might have reduced welfare to a more residual role. However, after prolonged efforts it was not possible to achieve a national consensus on the income support and supplementation proposals, and in 1978 the federal government proceeded unilaterally with the Refundable Child Tax Credit. This program involved a programmatic shift and, in effect, a transfer of resources that involved a significant reduction in the Family Allowance. Together, the reduction of the Family Allowance and the implementation of the Refundable Child Tax Credit served to progressively target benefits to lower income families. The Refundable Tax Credit approach is particularly notable because it involved creative and proactive use of the tax system to transfer income to low-income families. In particular, the program demonstrated the feasibility of using emerging computer technologies and data processing capabilities to achieve redistributive objectives through the tax system in ways that were not previously possible.

Since the 1970s, the growth of international trade, the reduction of trade barriers, the establishment of multilateral trade agreements and the strengthened institutionalization and regulation of trade practices have become central features of economic and social development. Trade advocates identify a positive relationship between trade and economic growth. The various benefits attributed to trade include increased efficiency and national wealth, and improvements in employment incomes, population health, environmental protection, human rights and other aspects of social wellbeing. It is known that "trade creates arbitrage in the markets for goods, services, labour and capital" and the associated price convergence is believed to be the source of gains from trade (Rodrik, 1997: 12, 29). However, opponents of unrestricted trade and international market integration question the basic assumptions of the trade argument, noting that "propositions on the effects of free trade may fail in the presence of large capital movements, exchange rate imbalances, market failure, unemployed resources or significant intrafirm trade" (Grinspun, 1993: 113). From this perspective, the downward harmonization pressures of international competition encourages a "race to the bottom" in labour, social and environmental standards and generally causes the deterioration of population health and well being (Burtless et al., 1998). In particular, the combination of free trade and unfettered capital mobility allows corporations to move and establish production anywhere, and the resulting competition among nations causes a deterioration of employment incomes, labour standards, social welfare and environmental protection.

Although there is wide divergence of opinion, it is clear that the impact of increased international trade and competition have significant implications for social policy. Although free trade and market deregulation may generate economic growth in the aggregate and produce substantial benefits for large corporations, the benefits are not evenly distributed. Changing trade and market patterns have economic and social impacts that require transition and adjustment. For many workers and their families free trade has meant job losses, job insecurity, unsafe working conditions, declining social services and stagnating wages.

In considering the implications of increased international competition on Canadian social conditions, Richard Splane has observed:

> The turbulent world economy has adversely affected Canada, contributing to regional tensions and to deficit financing by both federal and provincial governments. These, in turn, have militated against the allocation of resources to social programs and to measures for reducing unemployment. Unemployment of the national work force has exceeded ten percent during most of the period and has been extremely high in both Atlantic and Pacific regions and among such groups as the youth and native people. The percentage

of the population living below the poverty line has increased, and with the provinces failing to provide adequate social assistance and to extend, or even maintain, their community and personal social services, increasing numbers of Canadians have had to resort to food banks, soup kitchens and other demeaning forms of aid for their survival. (Splane, 1987: 224)

Throughout the late 1980s and 1990s, with the pressures of international competition, repeated budget deficits and growing public debt, there was a fundamental shift in the attitude of policymakers and governments that altered the established approach to social programming. In summarizing the change in the approach to social policy, Keith Banting has noted that throughout the post-war period,

> the prevailing assumption was that a welfare state would comple-ment the market economy; it would be an instrument of automatic countercyclical stabilization, it would ensure an educated and healthy work force; and it would provide the complex social infrastructure essential to an urban economy.... [however] A resurgent conserva-tive critique insists that the modern welfare state and its associated taxes undermine growth by stifling entrepreneurship, distorting the incentive structure, interfering with the operation of labour mar-kets, and reinforcing dependency among the recipient population. (Banting, 1987: 185)

On this directional change, Havi Echenberg has observed that "a tectonic shift in economic and social behaviour was evident, made possible and necessitated by a globalization of the economy...[and] has led to an equally profound shift in how social programs are designed and what policy instruments are selected" (Echenberg, 2004: 15).

During this period, government debt increased to unsustainable levels as federal and provincial governments repeatedly adopted deficit budgets. It has been argued that these deficits resulted primarily from tax expenditures rather than from increased spending on social programs. For example, in 1984 alone, over $18 billion in financial aid, including $7.5 billion in direct income transfers and $11 billion in tax concessions, was provided to corpora-tions operating in Canada (Ternowetsky, 1987). Nevertheless, the approach of both federal and provincial governments to address persistent deficits and increasing debt was to introduce cost reduction measures that significantly decreased the progressivity of public financing and social transfers. Changes to the income tax system reduced the number of tax brackets from ten to three and decreased the tax liability of those in the highest income categories. At the same time, partial de-indexation of the tax brackets increased the taxes, relatively, for middle- and low-income earners. The federal government also introduced the Goods and Services Tax (a regressive tax) and changes to the Unemployment Insurance system that decreased protection for workers and shifted the costs of labour market adjustment to workers, employers and provincial social services. In addition, successive federal budgets "radically reduced federal transfers for provincial social and health programs and, in the process, put an end to the 'cooperative federalism' that built the post-war social security system in Canada" (Battle and Torjman, 1995a: 3).

The income distribution effect of the tax system and the impact of government income support measures are of particular interest. From 1951 to 1991 the proportion of federal revenue from personal income tax increased from about 26 percent to over 50 percent, while the share of corporate income tax declined from over 40 percent to under 30 percent (Yalnizyan, 1993: 14–16). Data from the Statistics Canada Survey of Consumer Finances for the period 1973 to 1991 show that the distribution of family pre-tax income from wages and investments declined for the lowest quintile of families from 5.5 percent of all income to 3.3 percent, while the wage and investment income of the highest quintile increased from 38.2 percent of all income to 42.4 percent. Interestingly, when government transfer payments and retirement income are added, the distribution of family pre-tax income was somewhat less severe, with a decline in the share of income for the lowest quintile of families from 7.1 percent of all income to 6.1 percent, while the proportion of income for the highest quintile increased from 37 percent to 39.2 percent (Yalnizyan, 1993: 3–5).

As noted above, the course of social program development in Canada has been profoundly affected by the constitutional division of powers and the course of federal-provincial relations, a phenomenon which continued throughout the 1990s. The *Constitution Act, 1867* anticipated neither the mobility of capital and people that accompanies a modern developed economy nor the development of the welfare state and, as such, is poorly suited to the efficient development of a national welfare state. As a consequence, the course of social policy development has been accompanied to varying degrees by federal-provincial negotiation and agreement and unilateral federal action and intergovernmental conflict. Quebec's challenge to the legitimacy of the federal government's leadership in social policy has been the most prominent, though not the sole, influence on the course of social policy development in Canada. The particular source of conflict has been the federal government's use of its spending power to avoid the impediments of the constitutional assignment of most social welfare jurisdictions to the provinces.

The 1990s began on a note of federal-provincial conflict caused by a federal decision to restrict spending on social policy. In 1990, the federal government introduced measures to restrict federal cost-sharing for provincial social programs by establishing a "cap" on the Canada Assistance Plan that limited increases in transfer payments under the program to 5 percent for the "have" provinces of Ontario, Alberta, and British Columbia. In addition, changes to the *Unemployment Insurance Act* eliminated government financing, decreased benefits and increased contributions. The Child Tax Benefit replaced the Family Allowance and Child Tax Credit and benefits were partially de-indexed (Yalnizyan, 1993: 14–16). The Conservative government's surreptitious approach to reducing social security and welfare benefits came to be referred to as "social policy by stealth" (Battle and Torjman, 1995a: 10).

Throughout the 1980s and into the 1990s there was an increasing need for welfare support. Contributing factors included the increase of single-parent families and the economic vulnerability associated with restricted income potential and increased child-care requirements, and increasing international competition with its downward pressure on employment and wages, especially for low-skilled workers. In addition, the demand for social assistance was increased by reductions in Unemployment Insurance benefits. Yet national capacity to respond to this need was weaker than ever, due to financial and political circumstances in the country. It became increasingly apparent that established social security programs were structurally inappropriate for addressing the employment dislocation and adjustment issues that had emerged. This understanding was reflected in the decisions of the First Ministers Conference on the Economy in 1992. The First Ministers reviewed the discussion paper *Effective and Efficient Social Programs* and established the Income Security Reform Initiative, an exercise that involved five assignments, including that Labour Market and Social Services Ministers develop strategies to address "disincentives to work and training" in income support programs. This particular assignment was to investigate structural and systemic barriers to employment and economic independence. It included identification of possible measures to address the "welfare trap" that encouraged workers, especially single parents, to remain on social assistance rather than accept low-wage employment.

Federal participation in the Income Security Review was weak, interprovincial work on assigned projects progressed slowly, expectations declined and the federal-provincial review produced few results. In January 1994, it was superseded by the federal Social Security Reform initiative, which proposed to review major social programs, including the Canada Assistance Plan, Established Programs Financing, Unemployment Insurance, and other income support and employment development programs. This initiative was a major attempt by Human Resources Development Canada (HRDC) to engage the provinces and territories, social policy organizations, community groups and the public in a national discussion on the future direction of Canadian social policy. The highlights of this initiative are reviewed in chapter two.

Chapter Two

The Social Security Review Initiative

The Federal Agenda

Our economy is in disarray. We are now entering our third year of double-digit unemployment, and it is expected to remain above 10 percent until 1995. Over a million Canadian children live in poverty. Many of our national institutions have been shaken. Our cultural and social fabric has been weakened. For an overwhelming number of Canadians, hope for tomorrow has turned to fear for the future. (Liberal Party of Canada, 1993: 9)

Following the 1993 federal election, the new Liberal government faced a number of factors that challenged and constrained its national policy agenda. The successive failures of the constitutional discussions had created uncertainty around national unity. The federal deficit and debt imposed serious constraints on the range of feasible policy options. The rise of regional populism and of strong regional parties (the Bloc Québécois and Reform Party) in Parliament reflected regional tensions and grievances. An increasingly complex and dynamic international context presented new demands and obligations. In addition, the general public was disillusioned about the capacity of government to address economic security.

Within this environment, the federal government attempted to advance a policy agenda that would balance the demands for government action on job creation with the need to show progress on deficit reduction. The new federal government framed its top policy priorities around the issues of job creation, economic renewal, and deficit reduction. It moved quickly on job creation through its infrastructure program. It endorsed the North American Free Trade Agreement and the General Agreement on Tariffs and Trade, removed internal trade barriers and introduced measures to reduce overlap and duplication in federal and provincial programs. It initiated several specific measures to raise revenue and announced a series of reviews on the following issues: social security reform, foreign and defence policy, the Goods and Services Tax, the surface transportation system, and trade and competitiveness.

Early in its mandate, the federal government initiated the Efficiency of the Federation initiative. This involved an internal program review to determine appropriate areas for federal involvement, measures to improve administrative efficiency and a re-definition of federal-provincial responsibilities in order to reduce overlap and duplication. The intent of the exercise was to review the coverage, design and administration of relevant programs and to make them more effective, affordable and accessible. An important part of the review was to determine which order of government was best suited to deliver particular programs and services. The Efficiency of the Federation initiative included or was associated with several major policy reviews, including the 1994 Social Security Review.

Provinces were particularly concerned about the federal government's intention to reduce its deficit because it would likely involve offloading program costs to provinces and reducing financial support and transfers. The provinces wanted to ensure that the federal government would sufficiently consult and coordinate with provincial governments. However, most provinces, largely influenced by an interest in jurisdictional disentanglement and decentralization, were willing to participate in federal initiatives, including negotiations for an agreement on internal trade, the Efficiency of the Federation exercise, the reform of fiscal transfer arrangements, labour force development and job creation initiatives, and the review of social security programs (Saskatchewan 1994; Western Finance Ministers, 1994).

The Social Security Review Process

I am asking the House and our colleagues in the Senate, our counterparts at the provincial and territorial level, members of the business and labour sectors, the leaders of our communities — indeed, each and every Canadian — to throw off old ideas, to put aside vested interests, and begin thinking of the kind of ground rules we need in Canada to restore fairness, hope, and a sense of security.
(Axworthy, 1994: 1105)

In late January 1994, the federal Minister of Human Resources Development Canada (HRDC), Lloyd Axworthy, announced that the federal government would be undertaking a major review and overhaul of Canada's social security system. The Social Security Review would address income-support and labour-market programs, including all related federal-provincial programs. The main federal programs that were to be reviewed and reformed included Unemployment Insurance, training and employment programs, the Canada Assistance Plan (CAP), Established Programs Financing (EPF), the Canada Student Loan Program and the Child Tax Credit. Other social programs, including health care, social housing and the retirement income system, would also be reviewed, but under different processes. Other initiatives, including the federal program review exercise, federal-provincial negotiations on reducing duplication, internal trade negotiations, the national infrastructure program, the Aboriginal self-government agenda, the review of major fiscal transfers and the national unity issue, all contributed to the overall reform environment. (Saskatchewan, 1994; Government of Canada, 1994).

The broad goal of the Social Security Review was to develop a social security network that would make meaningful connections between programs, reward effort and offer incentives to work. The main objectives of the review included the following:

- meeting basic labour market needs;
- restructuring Unemployment Insurance and the Canada Assistance Plan to create a new form of "Employment Insurance";
- facilitating the school-to-work transition through a range of training options;
- broadening education and training assistance for life-long learning;
- enhancing support and care provisions for children;
- redefining the distribution of work and rules of the workplace;
- ensuring equality, independence and full participation for individuals with disabilities;
- seeking a better balance between job creation incentives and payroll taxes;
- ensuring basic security for the needy;
- redefining intergovernmental responsibilities and strengthening coopera- tive arrangements; and
- designing new ways to deliver services and avoid duplication.

In developing a social security reform package, the federal government planned to consult with representatives of national organizations and com- munity groups, including, among others, those relating to business, labour, women and First Nations. It also intended to engage in extensive federal- provincial discussions to define issues, explore options for reform and test solutions. The government proposed that reform measures could include federal-provincial agreements, joint ventures and pilot projects. In undertak- ing the review, HRDC contracted a small task force of "independent experts" to provide advice on social security policy and program design issues and to assist in the development of an "action plan." Also, the Standing Committee on Human Resource Development would facilitate the reform process by conducting nation-wide consultations on the discussion paper, producing a final report and drafting legislation by late 1994 so that reforms could be implemented beginning in 1995.

Early in the review process, the federal minister met with his provincial counterparts to discuss provincial concerns and seek provincial involvement. The ministers established a federal-provincial working group to review the scope of the review, consider issues regarding duplication in social programs and coordinate implementation of pilot projects.

The federal government set explicit fiscal parameters for the review, including changes to Unemployment Insurance to save $2.5 billion, and a budget reduction of $1.5 billion in federal transfers to provinces through Established Program Financing and the Canada Assistance Plan. The federal government also established an $800 million fund for the Strategic Initiatives Program, through which pilot projects could be initiated as a means of testing different policy and program options. Despite federal efforts to portray this program as a new initiative, funding for projects was to be redirected from existing social programs. In effect, provinces would be required to negotiate participation in federal-provincial projects in order to receive funding that they would have otherwise received in support of existing programs. The federal government also proposed new, three-year labour force development agreements that would enable the continuation of training purchases by the federal government while the review was being conducted. The federal proposal offered provinces the option of assuming responsibility for managing and delivering some federal training programs.

The Standing Committee on Human Resource Development tabled an interim report in March 1994 that identified three broad priorities to be addressed in the federal action plan: 1) the increasing financial pressures on Canadian families, and the unacceptably high number of Canadian children living in poverty; 2) the challenges facing Canadian youth and the need for more effective support, particularly in making the transition from school to work; and 3) the needs of unemployed and underemployed adults, particularly those coping with major shifts in the economy (Standing Committee on Human Resource Development, 1994). The interim report also recommended the following eight principles to guide the social security review:

1. The social security system must serve people, first and foremost, and be sensitive to their individual needs and circumstances throughout their lives.
2. Social assistance and social services must be readily available to all those in need.
3. Social security should be designed to enhance human dignity and provide the optimal combination of income support and social services to enable all Canadians to be integrated into the mainstream of our economic and social life.
4. Reforms must reflect the fact that, for most people, meaningful employment is essential to an individual's dignity and self-respect, and basic support services, such as education, training, child care, housing and special needs, must take this into account.

5. Federal and provincial social security programs and policies should work together so as to better serve the needs of individual Canadians. Canadians are insisting on a new constructive spirit of cooperation between federal and provincial governments.

6. The social security system should be financially sustainable, and all federal-provincial financial arrangements should be stable and predictable and not subject to unilateral change by either level of government.

7. The social security system should recognize that caring for families and individuals is a shared responsibility. The system must be comprehensive, flexible and holistic in its approach, investing in people and providing family support. It should be used as a preventive tool, not merely a reactive one.

8. The restructuring of social services should be coordinated with government employment strategies to ensure that such measures as training programs will result in meaningful employment for participants.

The Social Security Review did not proceed as planned. A proposed April meeting at which the federal minister was to brief provincial ministers on the contents of the federal action plan was cancelled as a result of concerns expressed by the province of Quebec, and supported by others, that there had been insufficient time to properly conduct the review on a federal-provincial basis. The planned public release of the federal action plan, scheduled for May, was delayed. The proposed action plan was eventually downgraded to a "discussion paper."

In June, the federal minister distributed a confidential outline of the Social Security Review for discussion with provinces. This document identified four broad categories for reform: employment, learning, security and governance. It briefly outlined some possible options for each area but was generally vague. The orientation of the paper suggested that the federal intentions include making support contingent on participation in training and employment programs, providing financial support directly to individuals rather than transfers to provincial governments, greater targeting of programs, increasing funding for child related programming, improving opportunities for disabled persons and shifting program costs to workers, employers and provincial governments (HRDC, 1994a).

By this time, the entire review process was in a highly uncertain state. The federal minister had encountered political pressures to keep his Cabinet colleagues fully informed on the full range of political and policy issues that were being considered. Several federal ministers, including the Prime Minister, had increasingly become concerned that management of Social Security Review issues not be allowed to complicate relations with Quebec in the run up to the upcoming election in that province. In addition, it became apparent that the federal government would increasingly seek to engage provinces on a bilateral basis and possibly narrow the scope of the review to those policies and programs that could be undertaken by the federal government without consent of the provinces.

Federal-Provincial Relations

It is time for the provinces and territories to collectively assume a more cooperative leadership and coordination role with respect to their common national agenda in their areas of responsibility. (APC, 1994)

Most provinces were hesitant to provide unqualified support for the federal Social Security Review, especially since there was no clear indication of how provinces would be involved in the decision-making process or the nature of the reforms that would be proposed by the federal government. Provinces were also concerned that the federal government would take unilateral action while claiming that provinces had been consulted. Provincial governments expressed the view that the process should be managed on a federal-provincial basis, with ongoing consultations, and that the review should be as broad as possible and examine all aspects of the social security system, including job creation policies.

From an intergovernmental relations perspective, there were three critical issues that emerged early in the process. First, the federal government had organized its review to target three groups: 1) youth, 2) children and families and 3) employable working-age adults. People who were regarded as "unemployable" were not discussed in the context of the target groups, and there was no mention of Aboriginal peoples. This target-group approach implied a shift in federal involvement in labour market training, which could alter existing federal and provincial roles and affect funding arrangements to universities and training institutions. Basically, HRDC would pay for the tuition of individuals rather than purchase "training seats" as a block from institutions. It was anticipated that this would result in federal funding being directed toward individuals and away from Established Program Financing. This prediction has come to pass: in recent years provinces have experienced a real decline in federal transfers.

Second, an imbalance had evolved through the 1980s between provincial revenue capacity and expenditure responsibility. With the establishment of federal social policy expenditure ceilings, it was anticipated that the review would result in further federal offloading and reductions to the federal share of social spending. Reductions had already occurred with changes in

Unemployment Insurance. The provinces were concerned that the federal government would withdraw from the Canada Assistance Plan, leaving the funding of the social safety net to the provinces.

Third, the federal position was that the issues of program ineffectiveness and inefficiency were related to federal-provincial overlap and duplication, and that disentangling the roles and responsibilities of the two orders of government was fundamental to the overall reform of the social security system. Framed in this manner, the principle of shared jurisdiction was undermined. This created potential difficulties in the establishment of cost-shared programs, the application of federal criteria and the establishment of national standards.

Nevertheless, provinces generally acknowledged the need for reform, the most vocal advocates being Newfoundland, New Brunswick, Prince Edward Island, Manitoba and Alberta. These were also the provinces most concerned with the affordability of existing programs. The provinces of Ontario, Quebec, British Columbia, Nova Scotia and Saskatchewan, while generally supportive of the need for reform, continued to be cautious over the extent to which the review would be federal-provincial in its orientation.

Ontario supported federal objectives on internal trade and the reduction of overlap and duplication, but it also continued with its Ontario First policy and expressed its concerns over the federal cap on Canada Assistance Plan payments. Ontario showed little interest in the national social security review and indicated that the provincial social policy agenda would not be compromised or redirected by developments at the national level.

The Quebec government was generally not prepared to collaborate on intergovernmental initiatives based on the federal agenda. However, Quebec was interested in pressing for its traditional demands regarding jurisdictional "disentanglement" and decentralization of programming in areas of provincial jurisdiction. In particular, Quebec took the position that labour market training programs should be devolved entirely to the province and that it would not engage constructively in the reform process until substantial progress had been made on the transfer of labour market programs.

The Atlantic Provinces, Manitoba and Alberta took the view that reform should focus on removing disincentives to work and developing stronger training and human resource development programming. Thus, benefits to employable people should generally be conditional on enrolment in training programs. British Columbia supported federal aims regarding the reduction of overlap and accepted the need for social security reform. However, the interest of British Columbia centred on the disentanglement of federal-provincial roles in social security. The province was opposed to the federal internal trade agenda.

At the Western Premiers' Conference in May of 1994, the Premiers agreed that "child poverty remains a national disgrace and creative actions must be taken to ensure that parents and young people do not fall into the trap of the 'working poor' or welfare dependency" (WPC, 1994). The Western Premiers called on the federal government to commit to a decision-making partnership in respect to the review, and they endorsed a set of principles for federal-provincial relations that had been advanced by Western Finance Ministers. Some of these principles addressed the issue of social security reform and reflected an agreement that the reform of social security programs must eliminate barriers to employment and provide real opportunities and incentives for all persons joining the work force; provide adequate and innovative training so that Canadians could meet the challenges of the global economy; and recognize and respond to the needs of children and families in poverty, the aged and persons with special needs. The position is important to note because it initiated the use of the Western Premiers' Conference as a policy instrument for elevating the discussion on child poverty. In the following years, the Western Premiers would repeatedly use the forum of the Western Premiers' Conference to prioritize social policy objectives, especially to advance discussion of children's issues at the national level. In contrast, the Atlantic Premiers focused their attention on regional economic issues.

At the Annual Premiers' Conference in August 1994, Premiers asserted, "It is time for the provinces and territories to collectively assume a more cooperative leadership and coordination role with respect to their common national agenda in their areas of responsibility" (APC, 1994). The Premiers also agreed on the need for discussions with the federal government on social policy reform and, in that context, they endorsed the following principles, which Provincial Ministers Responsible for Social Services and Income Security had identified as critical to the success of social policy reform:

- The reformed social security system must continue to support Canadians most in need and reinforce Canada's record as a compassionate society.
- Fiscal arrangements between the federal government and the provincial and territorial governments should treat Canadians with fairness and equity.
- Reform must be the product of genuine federal-provincial negotiations and joint decision-making.
- There must be no fiscal offloading from the federal government to the provinces and territories.
- The reformed system must provide meaningful opportunities to assist people to become more self-sufficient and to live with dignity and independence.

- The federal government must respect provincial and territorial jurisdiction, promote administrative efficiency and elimination of overlap
and duplication while assuming its fundamental role in the Canadian
federation by providing adequate funding directly to the provinces to
exercise their own responsibilities. (APC, 1994: 9)

This statement signalled the more proactive role on national social policy
reform that would be undertaken by provinces the following year. Still, there
was no anticipation of the outcome of the federal Social Security Review. The
objective was simply to assert the collective provincial position on social policy
and the provincial defence in respect of any threats to their jurisdiction.

The Social Security Review Discussion Paper

> *The status quo is not an option. Changes in our economy, in our families,
> in our workplaces, in our communities, and in the financial standing of our
> country are too dramatic to allow us to tinker at the edges of social policy and
> programming. The fact is that Canada's social security system needs to be fixed.*
> (HRDC, 1994b)

In October 1994, HRDC released a discussion paper, *Improving Social Security
in Canada*. This document was augmented by the following technical papers
dealing with specific federal proposals: The Context of Reform, Reforming
the Canada Assistance Plan, Income Security for Children, Child Care
and Development, Persons with Disabilities, Unemployment Insurance,
Employment Development Services, Federal Support to Post Secondary
Education, and Guaranteed Annual Income.

The discussion paper proposed the following principles to guide social
policy reform: creating opportunity, investing in people, mutual responsibility,
preventing future problems, putting people's needs first, greater fairness and
affordability. The paper addressed three major objectives: 1) working, which
included employment development services, Unemployment Insurance,
financing Unemployment Insurance and employment development, and
the needs of working parents; 2) learning, which included financing for
postsecondary education and supports for life-long learning; and 3) security,
which included reform of the Canada Assistance Plan, income support for
low-income families with children, employment services for social assistance
clients, and income and other supports for persons with disabilities.

The general approach of the discussion paper in addressing social security issues included the following:

- a focus on affordability, cost reduction, limiting expenditures, deficit reduction and "budgetary predictability," including limitations to the Canada Assistance Plan and Established Program Financing transfers, and Unemployment Insurance reductions (but not direct or explicit tax reform);

- concentration of resources on seniors, children, disabled persons and persons with long-term labour force attachment, including targeted support and increased funding to address child poverty and improve opportunities for disabled persons;
- increased integration of training/employment and financial assistance for active income support programming, including making income support contingent on participation in training and employment programs;
- increased harmonization of federal and provincial programs, including delineation and possible redefinition of federal and provincial roles and responsibilities, and reduction in overlap and duplication in federal and provincial programs and services;
- reallocation of federal funding away from transfers to provinces toward transfers to individuals; and
- transfer of program costs and decision-making from the federal government to individuals, workers, employers, communities and provincial governments. (HRDC, 1994b)

Like previous assessments of the social security system, the Social Security Review paper identified barriers to employment and training. This refers to facets of the social security system that result in people who leave social assistance to take up employment being worse off financially. It also suggests that Unemployment Insurance and social assistance should be tied more directly to labour market participation, meaning that benefit recipients should be required to take employment or training. The discussion paper offered only a limited acknowledgement of the insufficient economic activity and growth that had resulted in persistently high levels of unemployment and underemployment. Rather, the paper advocated training as the main response to unemployment. This remedy may have been helpful in addressing labour force adjustment issues, but it was inadequate for dealing with the fundamental difficulties in creating employment under the prevailing economic circumstances.

The review proposal for child benefits did address the fact that the incomes provided by low-wage and minimum-wage employment had declined in real terms and were insufficient to maintain a family, especially a single-parent family. In effect, the cost of maintaining a family, and of maintaining and developing the labour force, had shifted to a significant degree from the wages system to the social security system (broadly defined). However, the social security system had been designed to provide only temporary, limited and residual support and was not suited to the provision of permanent income subsidization for large numbers of low-income workers and their families. The proposal for a National Child Benefit would provide a partial solution to this situation and at least provide some ongoing income assistance to low income families.

Armstrong (1997) noted that the document reflected the general ideological shift that supports targetted, needs-based, welfare programming rather than the universal, social insurance approach. She further observed that "there is talk of allowing all Canadians to meet their needs, the stress is on 'the most vulnerable' rather than on the 'public responsibility for individual economic security' which had been the concern of the Dominion-Provincial Conference" (Armstrong, 1997: 52).

The main proposals outlined in the Social Security Review discussion paper included the following.

Established Program Financing

In accordance with the 1994–95 federal budget, Established Programs Financing (EPF) entitlements would grow at the same rate as the gross national product minus 3 percent. The discussion paper proposed that the cash portion of this support for postsecondary institutions be redirected to provide for a system of expanded student loans and grants to individuals. In 1996–97, the component of the Established Program Financing transfer for postsecondary education was frozen at 1993–94 levels.

Canada Assistance Plan

The 1994–95 federal budget announced that starting in 1995–96, the Canada Assistance Plan (CAP) payments to the provinces would be frozen at 1994–95 levels. In 1996–97, the CAP would be frozen at 1993–94 levels. These limitations would reduce federal expenditures by approximately $500 million. It was anticipated that existing and possible future constraints on CAP funding would decrease the ability of provincial governments to deliver social programs and respond effectively to the needs of low-income persons. Consequently, provinces opposed the termination of open-ended cost sharing through the CAP.

Proposals included in the Social Security Review discussion paper included short-term improvements to the CAP to allow provinces to better address such priorities as child development services; possible replacement of CAP with block funding and redirected federal funding to achieve agreed national goals; and identification of priority areas including improving child benefits, independence for persons with disabilities, child care and child development, child support payments and continuing support for social services. It appeared inevitable that social security reform would require significant adjustment to fiscal arrangements. The concern for provincial governments was that new fiscal arrangements could result in greater provincial responsibility for financing income security and other social service programs.

Employment Development Services

The discussion paper identified measures for improving existing human resource development programs, including enhanced needs assessment and counselling, better labour market information, improved basic skill training, more relevant and cost effective institutional training, a greater role for employers in workplace training and direct employment measures (incentives for hiring unemployed workers). In addition, the federal government would discuss with the provinces means to improve access to employment services for social assistance recipients, persons with disabilities and persons outside the labour force. Interim measures would be provided through federal-provincial labour force development agreements. For example, the Canada-Saskatchewan Labour Force Development Agreement, signed in November 1994, provided for such initiatives as co-location pilot projects; joint planning process; work/study options; enhanced career counselling and placement services; and improved labour market information.

Unemployment Insurance

The paper proposed two possible approaches to Unemployment Insurance reform: 1) providing basic insurance for occasional claimants and lower, income-tested "adjustment insurance" benefits for frequent claimants; and 2) increasing the time persons must work to get benefits and/or reducing the length of time people can draw benefits and/or lowering benefit amounts. In both cases, the income support component would be reduced and funds would be reallocated to employment development services, primarily training. This was consistent with the general agenda of the federal government, which had previously introduced cuts to the Unemployment Insurance program and directed funds to training. The paper also considered the possibility of coverage for non-standard employment and alternative financing.

Provincial governments were concerned that cuts to Unemployment Insurance could result in increased demand for social assistance. In addition, the shift to support for employment and training programs could result in a decrease in federal funding of training, especially in provinces with relatively low numbers of frequent and long-term Unemployment Insurance clients.

Child Care Development

The discussion paper expressed commitment to the development of child-care services that would promote child development and support parental employment. Proposals included new funding for child-care spaces, encouraging the development of non-profit child care, redesigning dependent care allowances to meet child development objectives, improving subsidies, creating new spaces for underserved groups, providing incentives for employers to create work-related child care, improving access and increasing programming for Aboriginal families, including child development and family resource centres within new child-care programs and harmonizing child-care services with Aboriginal Head Start programs.

Income Security for Children

The paper identified priority areas with regard to income security for children. Proposed options included increasing the Child Tax Benefit for low-income families, enhancing the Working Income Supplement of Child Tax Benefit and improving child support payment enforcement. The proposal to increase the Child Tax Benefit was widely supported and eventually defined the policy direction that would lead to the National Child Tax Benefit.

Persons with Disabilities

The discussion paper identified options that could be explored to enhance disability-related programs and services. It proposed that these initiatives be funded through the redirection of resources resulting from reduced Unemployment Insurance expenditures. The paper noted the importance of shared funding and administration between governments, corporations and communities in order to increase training and employment opportunities. The paper recognized a need to enhance the independence of persons with disabilities and improve access to federal labour market programs.

Postsecondary Education

The paper proposed a new approach to funding postsecondary education that would involve redirecting the cash portion of EPF from support for institutions (through the provinces) toward a system of expanded student loans and grants to individuals. The paper also proposed an income-contingent loans repayment plan and the use of registered retirement saving plans to finance education and training.

Labour Market Training

The paper proposed federal-provincial discussions regarding school-to-work transition, making learning portable, learning and new technology, and international educational opportunities. Control of labour force development programming was a particularly important issue for Quebec, which persistently addressed jurisdictional concerns and emphasized its position that labour market programming should be devolved entirely to the province.

The Parliamentary Standing Committee on Human Resource Development

Canada's network of social benefits, rights, and responsibilities — our social security system — is integral to our country's fabric and vital to our nation's future.
(Standing Committee on Human Resource Development, 1995)

The Parliamentary Standing Committee on Human Resource Development conducted public consultations in November and December 1994. Formal federal-provincial consultations and negotiations were anticipated but failed to occur. The committee's report, *Security, Opportunity and Fairness*, was tabled in the House of Commons on February 6, 1995. The Report contained 52 recommendations under three broad themes: Caring for Canada's Children; Investing in People; and Enhancing Security and Fairness. Key recommendations included the following:

Working Income Supplement

The Committee recommended that the Social Security Review proposal for a Working Income Supplement should be implemented to help increase the economic benefits of employment over welfare. The Working Income Supplement could be implemented unilaterally by the federal government and, by reallocating $200 million within the federal Child Tax Benefit, it would not involve incremental costs. Some social policy analysts were critical of the Working Income Supplement approach citing its narrow target, limited benefits, disconnection with family size and distorting interactions with other programs. It was argued that a more integrated, broader-based child benefit would be needed to address these issues.

Child Tax Benefit

The committee recognized the potential of such an approach to supplement the earned income of low-income families with children, and thereby provide a work incentive, and recommended that the federal government work with the provinces and territories to create a new integrated benefit for children of low-income families. The committee favoured a Child Tax Benefit design, in which social assistance spending on children would be combined with federal tax benefits to create a new program for children in all low-income families, whether the family's source of income was from wages, welfare or Unemployment Insurance. The committee did not address costs, aside from mentioning reallocation of existing tax benefits for children and social assistance for children. However, it was estimated that an adequate National Child Benefit program would cost up to $2.2 billion more than the existing tax benefit arrangements. Some funding could be found from the CAP and provincial social assistance expenditures on children's basic benefits, but additional resources would be needed. The Child Tax Benefit was a more comprehensive approach than the Working Income Supplement, but it was in competition with the existing Working Income Supplement program, to which the federal government had a significant policy, programmatic and financial commitment.

Child Care

The committee observed that federal financing for child care under CAP, as a welfare service, was not adequate and that federal funding for child care was further complicated because it was dispersed over a number of departments and programs. It recommended that the federal government discuss with the provinces and territories the development of a more coordinated approach to child care. This proposal was consistent with earlier indications of the federal government's intentions to separate child care cost sharing from CAP arrangements. The recommendation called for a broader approach but did not make a clear proposal on what should be done in a new arrangement. The committee did not address major issues regarding informal care, taxation and inequities in the level and kind of public support.

Unemployment Insurance

The committee recommended that the government reduce Unemployment Insurance benefits and/or increase eligibility requirements. In making this recommendation, the committee observed that such an adjustment would ensure income support through the entire working year, particularly for those seasonally employed, and would support enhanced employment development services. Provinces expressed concern that reductions in Unemployment Insurance benefits would result in larger social assistance caseloads and increased social assistance costs at a time when other federal measures had already reduced support to provinces for social assistance. In addition, they anticipated that changes to Unemployment Insurance eligibility would provide a disincentive for seasonal employment in forestry, fishing and trapping.

Reforming the Canada Assistance Plan

The committee recommended that the federal government initiate discussions with the provinces and territories on changing CAP to a block-funded program with more flexible provisions that would enable federal funding for preventive measures and programs to encourage greater independence and self-sufficiency. It encouraged governments to make the reduction of child poverty a fundamental goal in these discussions. Provinces supported increased flexibility in cost-sharing social assistance programs, but some provinces were concerned that changes could reduce the level of federal funding and weaken national program standards. Provinces were united in the view that options for changing cost-sharing arrangements should be subject to federal-provincial discussions.

Collapse of the Social Security Reform Initiative

There is a reality out there that even the most committed social philosopher and proponent has to take into account. (Axworthy, quoted in Kennedy, 1995)

Social policy is subject to social, economic and political factors. Early in the Social Security Review process the initiative became the subject of an internal Cabinet debate with regard to fiscal policy and the commitment to deficit reduction, and in relation to national unity objectives and the Quebec separatist agenda. This debate came to a head in the context of preparations for the 1995 federal budget. In early February, media statements by the Minister of Human Resources Development Canada and the Prime Minister conveyed mixed messages about the future of the Review. Both the *Globe and Mail* and *Ottawa Citizen* reported that the Human Resources Development Minister had advised the review committee that social policy reform would be subject to budget cutting and that deficit reduction imperatives would "require spending cuts and make it difficult to immediately finance some proposed reforms, such as training programs for Unemployment Insurance and welfare recipients and enhanced child benefits for poor families" (Kennedy, 1995).

The federal commitment to social policy reform was subsequently reaffirmed following a Liberal caucus meeting on February 2, when Prime Minister Chrétien indicated that the government remained committed to reducing the budget deficit, but that it also intended to proceed with the planned review and reform of social programs The minister also expressed continuing support for social policy reforms, stating, "the reform of our social agenda is as much a part of the equation as reforming our fiscal system" (Campbell and Gray, 1995).

Nevertheless, the impression persisted that the federal government was further narrowing the parameters for social policy reform. It had become clear that fiscal considerations, particularly the perceived need for deficit reduction, had taken priority over social policy and that social security reform was off the agenda, at least until the government was comfortable that reform could occur within its deficit reduction target. It was also considered likely that the scope of any new reform process would be much more limited. In this context, the pending 1995 federal budget became a critical document.

The Social Policy Review initiative had created very high expectations. Canadians had been consulted, issues had been identified, papers had been written, options had been developed and commitments had been made. In particular, on the issue of child poverty, there was a considerable degree of support for the integration of federal and provincial programs through a National Child Benefit. So, it was a shock and a disappointment for advocates when the review lost momentum and the implications of the federal government's fiscal restraint measures and the impact of the 1995 federal budget became apparent. Perhaps an even greater surprise was the subsequent initiative of provincial Premiers in asserting leadership and advancing an interprovincial agenda for national social policy renewal.

Chapter Three

The 1995 Budget and the Council on Social Policy Reform and Renewal

Canada will, in the millennium, be largely defined by its social infrastructure both in its own right and because an appropriate social infrastructure will be an integral part of competitiveness in the new global economic order. (Courchene, 1994: 339)

The Policy Environment

In the last decade especially, the sheer relentless force of technological, economic and social change has shaped our lives and our livelihoods. Government policies and approaches have been too slow in responding. (HRDC 1994c: 7)

The economic, social and political environment has been increasingly defined by a competitive international economy. The forces of economic development that transform industries, sectors, markets, products and production processes also affect the social and political realms and have substantial adjustment implications for the social infrastructure, including education, training, health care, social security, employment creation, transportation systems, environmental regulation and other public services. In general, economic restructuring is associated with employment dislocation leading to increasing economic insecurity and inequality and creating pressures for adjustment measures and social policy reform.

In Canada, increased economic insecurity and growing inequality during the late 1980s and early 1990s confirmed that there was a real and pressing need for social policy reform and restructuring. In 1993, about 17.4 percent of all Canadians had incomes below the poverty line, an increase of 24 percent from 1980; 14.8 percent of Canadian families had incomes below the poverty line; 20.8 percent of Canadian children lived in poverty; and almost 60 percent of single-parent mothers with children had incomes below the poverty line. The national unemployment rate had increased from 6.2 percent in 1971, to 7.5 percent in 1981, and to 10.4 percent in 1994. The annual cost of Unemployment Insurance had increased from 7.3 billion in 1972 to 18.3 billion in 1993 (in constant 1993 dollars). Expenditures for social assistance, nationally, had more than tripled, from $4.1 billion in 1972 to $15.1 billion in 1993 (1993 dollars). At the same time, the proportion of government expenditures to service the deficit had increased substantially (HRDC, 1994c).

Social programs designed to address exceptional and temporary economic difficulties were inappropriate for addressing the more generalized economic insecurity that had emerged. Thomas Courchene observed, "The notion that welfare was largely to support the disabled (or unable to work) while UI was to tide able-to-work persons over the business cycle has long since been displaced by the fact that reliance on both UI and welfare is structurally driven and that the rolls increasingly comprise the able-to-work" (1997).

By the mid-1990s, the lack of effective social policy responses to changing conditions contributed to a general deterioration in social well being and increased social and economic insecurity. There was substantial public concern about unemployment, poverty and other social issues, and there was broad support for the fundamental objectives of Canadian social programs and for maintaining basic social and economic security. However, there was also heightened pressure for governments to lower their budget deficits. Public statements, including presentations to the Parliamentary Task Force on Human Resource Development, referred to the need for fiscal responsibility and accountability and to the necessity of connecting social benefits with social responsibilities. Pat Armstrong noted, "Conscious of how critical these programs are to Canadian identity and Canadian values, policymakers vociferously claim a commitment to ensuring equity and accessibility, while stressing the need to lower the deficit by reducing social spending. This seemingly contradictory purpose is to be achieved by shifting from access based on rights to programs targeted at those who are most deserving and most in need" (Armstrong, 1997: 54–55).

The impact of economic restructuring was exacerbated by government fiscal restraint. Throughout the 1980s and into the 1990s, deficit budgets restricted federal and provincial social policy development and encouraged the reduction of federal involvement in important areas of social programming. In particular, the federal government repeatedly implemented measures to transfer programming costs to provincial governments. Such measures included reducing or eliminating federal transfers; restricting the rate of growth in federal transfers; altering cost-sharing arrangements; imposing new conditions on federal programs; and withdrawing from the provision of services for which provinces would become responsible. For example, labour force development, employment creation and "passive" income support programs were cut or eliminated and replaced with "active" adjustment programs, such as those stressing skills training and retraining and "employability enhancement." The cost of these new programs was shifted and onto employers, workers and provincial governments.

In 1994, the federal government implemented a review in an attempt to improve the relevance, effectiveness and efficiency of government programs, and to reduce government expenditures. Part of this review, the Efficiency of the Federation initiative, was introduced to implement administrative reform measures and to restructure federal-provincial roles and responsibilities. This initiative was largely unsuccessful in addressing major issues, and the federal government subsequently adopted unilateral measures through a "rebalancing" agenda that involved budgetary withdrawals affecting forestry, mining and recreation, and included renegotiation of partnership arrangements in areas such as labour market programs, social housing and immigration.

These actions exacerbated an already tense intergovernmental environment. In the aftermath of two failed attempts to amend the constitution in a manner that would secure Quebec's authority over important areas of public policy, Quebec nationalism was on the rise. In 1994, the Parti Québécois, under the leadership of a former Quebec civil servant, Jacques Parizeau, once again came to power. Parizeau wasted little time in re-establishing Quebec's position for sovereignty by introducing a draft bill in December 1994. The bill stated that after a successful Quebec referendum, an agreement would be pursued with Ottawa whereby Quebec would receive power to "make its own laws, raise its own taxes, and conclude its own treaties." In comments made to the U.S. Ambassador to Canada, James J. Blanchard, Parizeau expressed his views of Quebec's promising international future:

> We'll be an independent country with a seat in the United Nations, but we'll keep the Canadian currency and passport. We'll have our own army, air force, and coast guard, but we'll remain good allies in NATO and NORAD. And, of course, we'll be part of NAFTA. (Blanchard, 1998)

In addition to Quebec's challenges to the federation, Alberta and British Columbia had begun to express a critique of the federal government that has come to be termed "western alienation," both through their provincial governments and through the western Canada-based federal Reform Party.

As federal funding declined, the legitimacy of federally enforced standards was increasingly questioned, and significant momentum emerged in support of increased decentralization in social programming. Provincial governments began to object to the use of federal spending power and other means to establish, interpret and enforce criteria for provincial social programming. At the same time, provinces recognized that without some form of common standards, a patchwork of social programs could emerge and the social safety net could be weakened (Intergovernmental Officials 1995). The effect of the federal government's unilateral budgetary decisions on its ability to secure provincial cooperation in joint policy areas was predictable. Worse, however, was about to come.

The 1995 Federal Budget

There are times in the progress of a people when fundamental challenges must be faced, fundamental choices made — a new course charted. For Canada, this is one of those times. (Martin, 1995: 1)

The 1995 federal budget forcefully expressed the federal position and clarified outstanding issues regarding social policy and fiscal restraint. The budget focused on fiscal restraint measures, including program cuts and transfer reductions that would shift costs and political pressure to provinces. This included the introduction of the Canada Health and Social Transfer (CHST); Unemployment Insurance reform, creation of the Human Resources Investment Fund and reduced funding for federal health programs. The budget dramatically altered the social policy environment and unilaterally redefined the main elements of the federal Social Security Reform agenda. Further consideration of previously identified policy alternatives was suspended, and the context of discussions on social policy reform was set within federally established fiscal parameters. Notably, this Budget was referred to as "a devolution of power to markets (privatization, deregulation, contracting out, etc.) and a decentralization to lower levels of government" (Courchene, 1997: 14).

The federal government characterized the budget and its implications for social security programming as an appropriate balance between affordability and flexibility. Provincial governments regarded the budget as a deficit reduction exercise that would transfer costs to provinces. National advocacy organizations, such as the National Anti-Poverty Organization, the Charter Committee on Poverty Issues, the National Action Committee on the Status of Woman and others, were concerned that federal cost cutting and restructuring through the CHST would undermine the social security principles and protections that had existed under CAP and fundamentally alter the nature of social programming in Canada.

Canada Health and Social Transfer

Effective 1996–97, the CHST was a new structure of federal-provincial fiscal transfers that combined CAP transfers for welfare and social services with EPF transfers for health and postsecondary education into a single block fund. This consolidation would shift responsibility for social programming to provincial governments and reduce federal transfers to provinces by approximately $7.3 billion over the following three years. Thomas Courchene referred to the CHST as "an appealing vehicle for federal deficit shifting" (1997).

The federal government suggested that with the CHST, provinces would no longer be subject to federal expenditure rules and would be able to pursue innovative approaches to social security reform without having to consider cost-sharing requirements. According to the budget, "restrictions attached by the federal government to transfer payments in areas of clear provincial responsibility should be minimized." The document also noted that federal expenditures would no longer be driven by provincial decisions, as they had been under CAP. The new arrangement would "end the intrusiveness of cost-sharing" and "reduce federal-provincial entanglement."

In implementing the CHST, the federal government would continue to enforce the provisions of the *Canada Health Act* (universality, comprehensiveness, accessibility, portability and public administration). In addition, provinces would continue to be subject to the CAP requirement to provide social assistance without minimum residency provisions. However, the CHST would not be subject to other requirements that had existed under CAP. Instead, the federal government would initiate federal-provincial discussions, led by HRDC, to develop a set of shared principles and objectives. The federal Department of Finance would negotiate an allocation formula for the new transfer program. Federal-provincial discussions would also be required on the retirement income review, Unemployment Insurance reform and the Human Resources Investment Fund.

Provincial governments expressed concerns that, although the CHST increased flexibility, the reduced funding would make it more difficult for them to sustain social services, health and education programming. Decreased federal funding would mean that provinces would need to review and possibly redesign social programs and spending priorities. In addition, it is worth noting that the Act to implement the 1995 federal budget gave the federal government power to reduce or withhold part or all of any cash transfers to provinces for failure to comply with federal conditions and criteria. Provinces recognized that, since EPF had not been subject to federal criteria, the new block funding actually increased the proportion of transfers over which the federal government could potentially exercise control.

New principles or criteria that might be associated with federal transfers could result in enforceable conditions that would constrain the ability of the provinces to implement provincial priorities and to introduce innovative responses to local conditions. Provinces were also concerned that new federal standards could create unreasonable expectations for provincial programs and that, as with the *Canada Health Act*, these would be unilaterally interpreted and enforced by the federal government (Intergovernmental Officials, 1995; P/T Council on Social Policy Reform and Renewal, 1995).

Although most provinces were unwilling to accept federally enforced national standards as a means to direct or control provincial social security policies and programs, there was some interest among provinces in developing a set of mutually acceptable principles that could provide a degree of national conformity. For example, provinces generally supported the publicly funded national health-care system and affirmed their commitment to the principles of the *Canada Health Act*, but they opposed unilateral federal interpretation and enforcement of the Act. In addition, provinces would need to respond to federal-provincial discussions on principles and standards and had an interest in working together to develop an interprovincial consensus on national principles (Intergovernmental Officials, 1995).

Unemployment Insurance Reform

It was the federal view that many individuals, industries and regions had become dependent on Unemployment Insurance (UI) income support and that the cost of financing the program had added significantly to payroll taxes and discouraged new hiring. According to the federal budget, UI was undermining the employability of Canadians and discouraging adjustment to changing economic conditions. Reform of the program was intended to direct funds away from aspects of the benefit structure that created dependence and toward initiatives that made people more employable (Martin, 1995). According to the Budget Plan, reform measures, combined with anticipated strong economic performance, would reduce UI program expenditures by a minimum of 10 percent. In 1996–97, expenditures would be reduced by $700 million, with $200 million from administrative reform and $500 million from benefit reductions. In addition, the surplus in the UI account would be allowed to rise above $5 billion and would be redirected toward enhanced employment development services and possible premium reductions. Proposed legislation would enable more flexibility in expenditures for "developmental uses," such as training and employment services for people who were not UI claimants. The federal government had already cut training previously funded through the Consolidated Revenue Fund and had shifted responsibility for training unemployed workers to the UI fund. The proposed changes would eliminate federal financial contributions to UI and further shift the cost of training to employers and employees. It was expected that HRDC would consult provinces on proposed UI changes, including benefit levels, eligibility criteria, employment services, employment and training services, premium rates and program administration. It was also anticipated that the reduced income support through UI would result in increased demand for social assistance.

The changes to the UI system were regarded as consistent with the general transition from a universal, social-insurance, rights-based, collectivist approach toward a more targeted, welfare, individualist, needs-tested approach. Pat Armstrong noted that "in spite of the recognition that unemployment is structural, indeed because it is structural, more of the responsibility has been shifted to the individual and rights have become even more circumscribed.... the effect is to reduce collective responsibility for unemployment and to make

UI payments more contingent, based on need rather than rights" (Armstrong, 1997: 54–55).

Human Resources Investment Fund

The budget established the Human Resources Investment Fund, which would include programs funded through the Consolidated Revenue Fund, including student loans, child-care initiatives, Canadian Jobs Strategy, Strategic Initiatives, Vocational Rehabilitation for Disabled Persons, Pathways and the Social Assistance Recipient Accord. According to the federal government, the Human Resources Investment Fund would focus on assisting the unemployed find jobs, combating child poverty and providing assistance to those who need help most. Planned initiatives included emphasis on employment development services (assessment, counselling, literacy and basic skills training, workplace training and experience, child-care support and earnings supplementation); improved national labour market information; a national workplace strategy to facilitate labour market adjustment; and assistance to persons with disabilities.

The Human Resources Investment Fund would result in reduced federal expenditures by implementing significant reductions in and terminations of numerous federal programs, including reductions in the Canadian Jobs Strategy; a moratorium on new spending under the Strategic Initiatives program; reductions in federal cost-matching under the Social Assistance Recipient Accord; restricted federal support for training for persons with disabilities; termination of the Agriculture Employment Service; reduced funding for Labour Force Development boards; and reductions in labour force adjustment programs. In addition, HRDC would combine Employment Centres and Income Security Offices, reduce the number of Human Resource Centres and transfer program responsibilities for training and employment development to provinces. The consolidation of programs and services were expected to save $600 million in 1995–96 and $1.1 billion in each year thereafter. As part of the overall funding reduction, in 1995–96, federal Consolidated Revenue Fund financing for labour market programs would be reduced by $160 million. With the introduction of the Human Resources Investment Fund in 1996, federal funding for labour market programming would be further reduced by $800 million in 1996–97 and by $100 million in 1997–98.

As a result of these federal reductions, provinces would be pressured to provide replacement programs and services. In addition, the federal reductions would jeopardize the capacity of public training institutions to deliver skills training, apprenticeship training and adult basic education.

Health

According to the federal budget plan, Health Canada expenditures would be reduced by $70 million over three years. The reductions would not include Established Programs Financing for health transfers to the provinces. Many programs would be reduced, with some of the savings reinvested to address priorities such as enhancements to the public health intelligence network, breast cancer research, prenatal nutrition and the Aboriginal Headstart program.

The departments of Health, Agriculture, Fisheries and Oceans and Industry would co-operate, in consultation with the food industry and the provinces, to improve the effectiveness and cost efficiency of the federal component of the Canadian food inspection system. Additional cost-recovery measures would be implemented and administrative costs reduced. New fees would be charged by Health Canada for licensing pilots and air traffic controllers, quarantine, de-rat certificates, services to occupational and environmental health services clients, drug evaluation approvals and medical device approvals. Funding for the Medical Research Council would be reduced by 10 percent over three years, and funding for the Patented Medicine Prices Review Board and the Hazardous Materials Information Review Commission would be reduced by 15 percent.

The budget proposals also indicated that funding for the Tobacco Demand Reduction Strategy would be reduced by 30 percent; grant programs for seniors (Seniors Independence, New Horizons and Ventures in Independence) would be consolidated into a single program with reduced overall funding; grant programs for children (Community Action Program for Children, Pre-Natal Nutrition program and Aboriginal Headstart program) would be either delayed in implementation and/or reduced in funding; emergency health services would be rationalized; Health Canada laboratory space and services would be merged and rationalized; and funding through the Medical Services Branch for some First Nations health services (off-reserve home care, special-care homes and resident fees) would be eliminated.

The difficult fiscal circumstances of provinces were exacerbated by the reduction of federal transfers and direct cuts in federal programming, and it had become increasingly difficult for provinces to sustain health-care services. This situation was reflected in interprovincial discussions regarding the comprehensiveness criteria of the *Canada Health Act* and the call to define "medically necessary or required" for purposes of interpreting the Act. Through a narrow interpretation of comprehensiveness, provinces could reduce costs by providing coverage for a more limited range of services.

Some provinces, including Alberta and Ontario, promoted the idea of relaxing federal criteria and increasing provincial flexibility to restructure their health-care systems. Other provinces, including Saskatchewan and Newfoundland, expressed concern that diminished national standards would weaken the social security system and lead to a two-tiered health-care system. Nevertheless, there was significant provincial interest in at least considering the establishment of a commonly accepted definition of medical services essential to the health and well being of Canadians (Saskatchewan, 1995).

1995 Annual Premiers Conference

Social policy reform represents one of the most significant challenges facing the nation.... Provinces and territories are determined to speak with a common voice on the essential elements in the national debate on social policy reform. (APC 1995a)

The 1995 Annual Premiers' Conference was held in St. John's, Newfoundland on August 23–25. Premiers discussed the key economic, social and intergovernmental issues facing Canada, but the main focus of the conference was the implications of the federal budget and the need for social policy reform and renewal. The Conference was influenced by a degree of tension and uncertainty regarding national unity issues and the upcoming Quebec referendum on sovereignty, the consequences of the federal budget for provincial social programs and growing public concern about government fiscal problems and budget deficits. In addition, substantial momentum was building among provinces to redefine the policy roles of provincial and federal governments and to diminish the application of the federal spending power in areas of provincial jurisdiction, especially health and social services. Several provinces, however, recognized the challenge that they would confront in displacing the federal government as the legitimate voice for national policy in the eyes of the Canadian public.

With respect to social policy, the main issues included negotiation of the CHST allocation formula and principles/objectives; the impact of reduced federal transfers (funding cuts, offloading, devolution) and implications for provincial program redesign; provincial policy development on retirement income reform; and federal-provincial consultation on the federal program review initiative, including UI reform and the Human Resources Investment Fund (Intergovernmental Officials, 1995).

The general environment leading into the conference was reflected in the following statement by Saskatchewan Premier Roy Romanow:

> Recent federal announcements, such as those contained in the last budget, will significantly reduce the amount of money available for income support, child care, health and education programs.... It is therefore falling on provincial governments to exercise the national leadership required. The task now facing Canadians and

their governments is to work together to reform social programs that provide long term stability and affordability while continuing to protect the most vulnerable in our society.... It is my hope that the Premiers can achieve a broad consensus on the fundamental values and principles to guide the future development of social policy in Canada. Notwithstanding the various perspectives and approaches represented across provinces, I believe that our social programs must continue to reflect a Canadian sense of shared values. (Romanow, 1995)

The Premiers undertook a follow-up process that would demonstrate provincial/territorial leadership in protecting the fiscal integrity and future ability of governments to play a positive role in the social and economic lives of Canadians; preserving those elements of Canadian social policy that give expression to Canadians' collective identity; and opening discussions with the federal government on how best to meet the challenges of fiscal reform and social policy renewal.

Common Discussion Paper and Conference Follow-up

A working group of intergovernmental officials from Newfoundland, Nova Scotia, Saskatchewan, Alberta and British Columbia (with the involvement of the other provinces and territories) prepared a background report entitled *Canadian Social Policy Reform and Renewal: Challenges, Issues and Concerns*. This paper identified the key factors contributing to the social policy environment, reviewed the central social security programs, identified the values and principles of Canada's main social programs and discussed the main issues emerging from the federal social policy agenda, as expressed in the 1995 budget. The first section of the report briefly described the social and economic context of Canadian social policy and identified several prominent factors contributing to the need for social policy reform. The main factors included the existence of a well developed social safety net based on fundamental principles; economic restructuring and related labour market implications, including increased unemployment and the need for education and training; changing family structures and social values, including increased frequency of single-parent families and increased family poverty; diminishing fiscal capacity, large government debt and reduced expenditures for social programs; and demands for increased government efficiency and effectiveness. The second section of the report addressed the federal government's approach to social policy reform. In particular, it noted that the federal government had unilaterally introduced fiscal restraint measures, reduced financial support for social programming and shifted costs to provinces and territories, and that the federal orientation on social policy and declining federal funding raised serious questions regarding the fundamental principles and objectives of Canadian social policy and the prospects for maintaining national standards. The report concluded that federal budget reforms had effected fundamental change to the financing and structure of federal programs and that the changes affected not only provinces but also the infrastructure of the social system. It was also noted that the federal social policy agenda was proceeding without provincial involvement (APC, 1995b).

The Premiers also considered a Newfoundland discussion paper entitled *Some Ideas for Follow-up to Premiers' Discussion on Social Policy Reform.* The paper reviewed the environment surrounding social policy reform and concluded that there was a need for provincial coordination on negotiations with the federal government; Premiers need to demonstrate leadership in social policy reform; the reform process must ensure programs are affordable; and reform must be responsive to public need. The paper cited the 1994 Annual Premiers' Conference agreement affirming the timeliness for "provinces and territories to collectively assume a more cooperative leadership and coordination role with respect to their common national agenda." The paper proposed a follow-up process to further pursue interprovincial work in advance of discussions/negotiations with the federal government. Several options for follow-up were identified, including a First Ministers' Conference, a Special Premiers' Conference and the creation of a Ministerial Council on Social Policy Reform. The paper argued that, in demonstrating commitment to cooperative leadership, it was important that Premiers agree on a broad "principles-based" consensus statement outlining the essential elements and underlying values of social policy reform from the perspective of provinces and territories. The paper proposed a Premiers' statement that would include a set of principles to guide the development of social policy in Canada. It was suggested that these principles would address affordability and fiscal responsibility; commitment and comparability; shared responsibility; national standards; adequacy and accessibility; equity and fairness; prevention; active intervention; dignity and independence; federal programs for Aboriginal peoples; gender equity; and the roles of families and communities (APC, 1995c).

Outcomes of the Annual Premiers' Conference
The final communiqué for the 1995 Annual Premiers' Conference reflected the Premiers' agreement that "social policy reform represents one of the most significant challenges facing the nation." Premiers expressed their intention to "improve cooperation and take on a leadership role with respect to national matters that affect areas of provincial and territorial jurisdiction, and... speak with a common voice on the essential elements in the national debate on social policy reform." The Premiers urged the federal government to work cooperatively with provinces to clarify roles and responsibilities and to

improve the efficiency and effectiveness of social programs across Canada.

The Premiers reiterated their concerns about continuing federal efforts to shift costs for Aboriginal social services to provincial and territorial governments; expressed unanimous support for a publicly funded national health system; reaffirmed their commitment to the principles of the *Canada Health Act*; and directed Ministers of Health to consider the development of a definition of the "medical services essential to the health and well-being of Canadians." Most importantly, the Premiers agreed to establish a Ministerial Council on Social Policy Reform to develop an interprovincial approach to federal-provincial negotiations on social policy reform. The Ministerial Council quickly became the main vehicle that the provinces and territories used to assert a new, more active role in defining the course of national social policy reform.

Saskatchewan Position at the Premiers' Conference

In preparing for the Premiers' Conference, Saskatchewan intergovernmental affairs officials recommended that Saskatchewan's position on social policy reform reflect the following:

- Canada's social programs are a fundamental aspect of our national identity and must be maintained. The Canadian system of social security, Medicare and education has contributed much to our economic strength and social progress.
- Canada's social security system has been instrumental in moderating the trend toward increasing inequality and economic insecurity. However, new approaches are required to address current circumstances. There is a real need for social policy to be reformed and strengthened.
- Economic growth and employment creation must provide the basis of social policy reform. Increased employment will reduce social expenditure requirements while increasing the resources to improve health, education and social service programming.
- National social policy must be fashioned in light of the constitutional obligations of both orders of government. Under the constitution, governments' social programs must provide equal opportunity for all Canadians, promote the well-being of all, and provide essential public services.
- Cooperation between governments is vital to ensure a comprehensive and integrated approach to social policy reform. The federal government plays an important role in maintaining a national social policy framework. It is important that provinces work together with the federal government in a serious and meaningful national initiative of social policy reform (APC Briefing Note, 1995d).

1995 Western Premiers' Conference

The 1995 Western Premiers' Conference was held in Yorkton, Saskatchewan, from October 31 to November 2. The Western Premiers took the opportunity to reinforce the positions they had endorsed at the Annual Premiers' Conference. The high priority items included the Western Finance Ministers' Report, social security reform and national unity. The Western Premiers endorsed the Western Finance Ministers' Report and its main message that, while the federal government must get its fiscal house in order, it was unacceptable to pass a significant portion of its fiscal problems onto provinces through reductions in cash transfers for social programs. The Premiers strongly supported the view of Western Finance Ministers that there should be no further cuts in cash transfers until the federal government had reduced spending on its own programs by an amount comparable to reductions in cash transfers to provinces and territories for social programs. The Western Premiers unanimously recommended that attempts to restructure and renew the country must include renewed fiscal arrangements as a first priority. In addition, the Premiers affirmed their strong commitment to the Ministerial Council on Social Policy Reform and Renewal as the leading forum for developing new national approaches to Canada's social programs. They agreed that it is unacceptable for the federal government to unilaterally prescribe structures and standards for social policy while abandoning its commitment to support social programs with adequate, stable and predictable funding (WPC, 1995). The Western Premiers' Conference also presented an opportunity for the western representatives of the Ministerial Council on Social Policy Reform and Renewal to meet informally and discuss the work of the Council in general terms. Saskatchewan and Alberta intergovernmental officials used the occasion to draft a set of principles on social policy reform that would provide the basis for interprovincial discussions in the development of a statement of principles for consideration by the Ministerial Council.

Ministerial Council on
Social Policy Reform and Renewal

The Ministerial Council on Social Policy Reform and Renewal was established by the provinces and territories to develop a common approach to the proposed federal-provincial discussions and negotiations around the CHST and generally oversee the reform process from the provincial-territorial perspective. Premiers agreed that the council could provide a vehicle for interprovincial leadership in social policy reform; allow for the effective coordination of positions in advance of negotiations with the federal government; provide a forum for the integrated and coordinated discussion of social policy reform issues; and potentially serve as a basis for a more permanent intergovernmental consultative forum in the social policy sphere. The specific mandate was to 1) lead interprovincial consultations on the positions provinces were likely to take in the CHST negotiations; 2) develop positions that could be collectively advanced to the federal government; and 3) develop an interprovincial policy statement on the principles and underlying values that should guide social policy reform generally, and, in particular, the development of the CHST.

The Ministerial Council was comprised of one ministerial representative from each province and territory and was chaired by the Minister of Social Services for Newfoundland, as the lead province for the 1995 Premiers' Conference. The existing Interprovincial Committee of Intergovernmental Affairs Deputies would assist the work of the Council and the two discussion papers tabled at the Annual Premiers' Conference would inform the work of the Council. It was intended that the existing interprovincial sector Committees of Ministers for Social Services, Health, Education, Labour Market, Finance, Women and Social Housing would contribute to the overall process and provide necessary technical support.

The Ministers of Social Services, Health, and Education all met in September of 1995. Ministers of Social Services agreed to develop an action plan that would provide a vision for the future of social services and "define roles and responsibilities and develop key principles to guide social services programs." The Ministers of Education reviewed the impact of cuts in federal transfer payments for postsecondary education and agreed that they would work through their respective Cabinets and the Ministerial Council on Social Policy to raise their concerns and develop appropriate strategies.

The Health Ministers approved preparation of a vision statement on health-care policy, to be entitled *Toward a New Vision for our National Health Care System*. This statement would include vision and goals; broad program components; clarification of federal and provincial roles and responsibilities; a continuation of efforts to clarify the parameters of the *Canada Health Act*; and reiterate the need for sustainable (adequate, stable, predicable) funding for the future health system.

The first meeting of the Ministerial Council was held in Winnipeg in October 1995. The Council Ministers reviewed a draft "statement of principles" and discussed draft recommendations related to health, social services, education and labour market programs. These recommendations were very preliminary and the Ministers created a task team of officials to undertake a major rewrite and draft a "framework document" that would facilitate intergovernmental discussions on social policy reform, which would be the Council's Report to Premiers. The task team was comprised of intergovernmental affairs officials representing the lead province (Newfoundland), a large province (Ontario), a small province (Saskatchewan), a Western province

(Alberta) and an Eastern province (New Brunswick). The Council Ministers specifically requested that Saskatchewan be included. The task team was assisted by representative officials from the areas of Social Services, Health and Education. The officials met in St. John's in November and developed a draft paper that was subsequently reviewed and refined by intergovernmental officials from all provinces at a meeting in St. John's immediately following the task team consultations.

In December, the Ministerial Council met in Calgary to review the report to Premiers. All provinces, except Quebec, endorsed the report. On December 22, 1995, Newfoundland Premier Tobin forwarded the Ministerial Council Report to the Premiers. The Premiers approved the report and on March 28, 1996, released it publicly. They forwarded a copy to the Prime Minister and proposed that First Ministers discuss how to work collectively to improve and protect Canada's system of social programs at their forthcoming meeting in June.

Ministerial Council Report to Premiers

The Council report included a statement of principles and twenty-two recommendations that provided a comprehensive framework for federal-provincial discussions on national social policy reform (see <http://www.exec.gov.nl.ca/exec/PREMIER/SOCIAL/ENGLISH.HTM>). It proposed a delineation of federal and provincial roles and responsibilities, and other measures to reduce overlap, improve efficiency and enhance accountability. The statement of principles reflected four central themes: 1) social programs must be accessible and serve the basic needs of all Canadians; 2) social programs must reflect individual and collective responsibility; 3) social programs must be affordable, effective and accountable; and 4) social programs must be flexible, responsive and reasonably comparable across Canada.

The report cast the discussion in the context and language of cooperation, coordination and sharing responsibilities, rather than maintaining the divisive and adversarial approach of centralization versus decentralization. Of primary importance that governments adopt a comprehensive approach to social policy reform, in the sense that governmental review should recognize the inter-relatedness of social programming and address the need for fundamental restructuring. This position was reflected in the report's general orientation and conclusion, expressed through the recommendations, that effective social policy reform would require a rational delineation of federal and provincial roles and responsibilities.

The report proposed criteria for clarifying federal and provincial roles and responsibilities in the social sector and the establishment of a mechanism for settling differences and monitoring progress. These objectives would be further advanced through federal-provincial discussions and eventually lead to the Social Union Framework Agreement. Gregory Marchildon and Brent Cotter observed:

> While rejecting federal unilateralism, the report also eschewed extreme decentralization. In deciding which order of government should be responsible and accountable for any given social program, constitutional jurisdiction was only one of eight questions that needed to be answered. The remaining seven questions were more instrumental or pragmatic in nature: How much personal contact is required to effectively provide the service or benefit? Is there a need to ensure flexibility in service design to meet local circumstances? Is there a national concern or national interest that needs to be addressed? Does one order of government already have an efficient delivery system in place? Is one order of government already involved in delivering services to a client group? Are related programs required to effectively manage the service? Can delivery by one government produce more effective outcomes? (2001: 367–80)

The approach to considering which order of government should have primary responsibility for particular programs or services and other considerations identified in the Ministerial Council Report were certainly consistent with the federal government's Program Review and Efficiency of the Federation initiatives. Thus, it is not surprising that the Council report resonated strongly with federal officials.

The report advocated federal-provincial agreement in principle that social policy reform be accompanied by a redesign of Canada's system of fiscal arrangements to ensure that provincial expenditure responsibilities and revenue capacities would be balanced, that government accountability would be improved and that governments would be able to provide social programs that were reasonably comparable across Canada. Such discussions remain crucial to the overall conduct of intergovernmental relations today. Other important recommendations included the development of proposals for social policy renewal and the delineation of roles and responsibilities by sector councils of ministers; the possible consolidation of income support for children into a single national program; the possible consolidation of income support for individuals with long-term and significant disabilities into a single national program; and federal-provincial negotiation of the financial arrangements required to support new directions in social policy design and delivery.

The report was unacceptable to the Quebec government because it contemplated "power-sharing," which is contrary to Quebec's position that social security policies fall within exclusive jurisdiction of the provinces; promoted the notion that standards, principles and objectives should be applied uniformly across Canada; and advocated national principles and national standards in social programming that left "no room for the uniqueness of Quebec culture and society" (Quebec, 1996). However, Quebec officials participated in the meetings of officials and the Ministerial Council as observers and contributed their experience, knowledge and analysis to the discussions. Their familiarity with the Ministerial Council's discussions may have eased the way for Quebec's eventual participation in the provincial/territorial consensus on the Social Union Framework Agreement negotiations, in 1998. As well, opinion was divided within Quebec, with the Quebec Liberal Party characterizing progress on the report's recommendations as an example of the benefits to Quebecers of remaining in the federation.

The Ministerial Council report, which was received positively by federal ministers, had substantially raised the profile of national social policy reform in Ottawa. There was also some critical comment. For example, a *Globe and Mail* editorial on February 8, 1996, referred to the report as "a swaggering proposal to fracture national social policy and the common quality of Canadian citizenship." An article in the *Toronto Star* reported the warnings of critics that the plan outlined in the Report could "drive down wages, destroy Medicare and destabilize the political union" (Toughill, 1996).

In an open letter to the Ontario Premier, the chair of the Ontario Social Safety Network expressed concerns that few Canadians had heard of the Ministerial Council and that Canadian social policy was being rewritten in secret. The letter referred to the process as "social policy by fax" because the Premiers had not met to discuss the report but had indicated their approval by fax. Another open letter to the Ontario Premier, dated February 1, 1996, from several public advocacy organizations, including the Child Poverty Action Group, Ontario Social Safety Network, Ontario Federation of Labour the Ontario Social Development Council, expressed similar concerns and called for public consultations. Such comments reflected the challenges the provinces and territories would have in securing legitimacy for a leadership role in social policy renewal.

Public concern about the social policy renewal process was also expressed in an open letter to the Prime Minister, dated September 6, 1996. The letter was signed by a coalition of social advocacy and other interested organizations, including the Canadian Labour Congress, Campaign 2000, Child Poverty Action Group, National Action Committee on the Status of Women, Canadian Council on Social Development, Catholic Health Association of Canada, Canadian Health Coalition, Child Care Advocacy Association of Canada, Citizens for Public Justice, National Anti-Poverty Organization, Canadian Association of Social Workers and Canadian Association of Family Resource Programs. The letter called for the government of Canada to sponsor a public debate on the Canadian social union and the responsibilities of the federal, provincial and territorial governments.

A 1996 Caledon Institute review of the Ministerial Council Report noted that in Ottawa there was "a good deal of simple astonishment that provinces and territories were able to agree on anything at all, let alone a substantive document with some real policy proposals." The Institute predicted that the report could have a "significant and lasting impact on the shape of security in Canada" and that, "as one of the only substantive documents on social policy ever agreed to by all provinces (except Quebec), it could be a touchstone for reform over the next several years." The Caledon Institute review concluded that the report offered "some positive and significant proposals for social policy reform," was "not simply a self-serving grab for more provincial powers" and "demonstrated provincial openness to new ideas... fresh approaches [that] could be the basis for meaningful discussions between Ottawa and the provinces and give renewed life to the social security reform process" (Mendelson, 1996: 1–2).

In June 1996, at a Caledon Institute-hosted roundtable of national organizations to discuss the Ministerial Council report, the participants agreed that the federal government should "use the Ministerial Report as the basis for renewing cooperative federalism to rebuild the social union" (Caledon Institute, 1996: 1).

The Premiers' initiative on social policy reform established an unanticipated and unprecedented consensus among the provinces and territories. It was cautiously interpreted as a development that could revive the national discussion on social policy reform. The report of the Ministerial Council provided a framework for change along with recommendations that addressed a wide range of social policy issues. Through the Council, the Premiers had successfully set an ambitious agenda for national social policy reform that would dominate federal-provincial discussion and collaboration for the next several years. The agreement of the federal government to work with the provinces on specific priorities, the creation of a mechanism to facilitate federal-provincial cooperation and early progress on a priority issue were essential to advancing the reform initiative throughout 1996 and 1997.

The creation of the Ministerial Council on Social Policy Reform and Renewal, and the subsequent creation of a federal-provincial-territorial Ministerial Council on Social Policy Renewal, also set the stage for a new way of managing intergovernmental relations in Canada that at least some provinces hoped would be more acceptable to Quebecers, thereby blunting the Quebec sovereigntists' critique of the ineffectiveness of the Canadian federation. Further, it forced the First Ministers to meet and act together in the national interest, something Prime Minister Chrétien had avoided throughout the first three years of his mandate. Thus, the Ministerial Council held the promise not only of substantive social policy improvements but also of improvements to the processes of intergovernmental affairs in Canada.

Reflections

Francie Harle

Francie Harle was the executive officer, social and fiscal policy of Alberta Federal and Intergovernmental Affairs from 1995 to 1997. She is currently a member of the Region 6 (Edmonton and Area) Child and Family Services Board.

The 1995 federal budget was clearly a pivotal one and no less so for those working in the arena of intergovernmental affairs. The enormity of the changes, not just in funding but for the fundamental structure that formed the basis of our social policy approach, created a period of uncertainty and challenge for those who worked within the many intricate relationships that had developed over the years to enhance how the federation functioned in the best interests of its citizens. There was certainly a new game in town and no one had a rule book.

The 1995 Annual Premiers Conference allowed Premiers to discuss the import of the changes and come to agreement on the need to work collaboratively on moving forward in the social policy field. The role of the federal government in these largely provincial areas of responsibility was changing dramatically, and there was a need to rethink how governments should work together in an increasingly complex world, where few functions of government were neutral in their impact on other government functions. The establishment of the Ministerial Council on Social Policy Reform and Renewal was a milestone, and those assigned to carry out its work were very cognizant of the fact that there were no rules for this game either. This was new territory in terms of scope, scale and responsibility and there was very little time to get it right.

Nevertheless, provinces assigned the resources that they could and all involved were extremely committed to the task and to ensuring that no province felt left out or not listened to in the process, even though they could not have representatives at every meeting. Fortunately, technology at the time was such that e-mail, fax machines and conference calls allowed officials to share thinking and get feedback very quickly. (Quebec chose not to participate at all even though officials were prepared to keep them "in the loop" as work proceeded. Quebec did, as I recall, eventually send observers to the Council meetings, and there was always an open door in terms of a willingness to discuss issues with Quebec.)

The make-up of the Council was very interesting. Each Premier assigned a minister and there was an array of areas represented at the table. Two provinces, Alberta and Ontario, assigned their Ministers of Intergovernmental Affairs, while the other representatives had specific portfolios in one of the social policy fields under review. There were Ministers of Social Services, Education and Health to name a few.

At first glance, one wondered how this mixture of portfolio responsibilities would function effectively given the different perspectives that each brought to the table. This turned out to be a source of strength since it allowed Ministers to focus on the overarching, common challenges that they all faced rather on programs or service issues pertinent to specific portfolios. Following the first Council meeting, officials were asked to do a re-write of the report to Premiers, and I believe that was a reaction to Ministers reviewing the individual portfolio analysis and concluding that there were common problems in all areas — basically too much entanglement between federal and provincial activities — and that their work needed to address this broad, complex issue in a manner that would lead to greater clarity and balance of responsibility and resources across all sectors. This brought a sharp focus for officials to the task at hand. We needed to look closely at the structures and systems for delivering social policy and programming, rather than focus on the programs themselves, if we were to come up with workable recommendations for change that would be relevant across the broad social policy spectrum.

Prior to the 1995 federal budget and APC, intergovernmental officials in a couple of provinces had been directed to do some work on thinking about how better to realign the activities of both orders of government so the federation functioned more effectively in meeting the service needs of Canadians *in keeping with the existing Constitutional allocation of responsibilities*. Called "rebalancing" or "disentanglement," officials supporting the Ministerial Council were able to draw upon this prior, substantive work on potential adjustments to the multitude of federal-provincial arrangements for consideration by Ministers. The existence of this work and the willingness to share and consider each others' thoughts and ideas were enormous pluses in the ability of officials to meet the timelines set by Premiers after their 1995 APC and the initial meeting of the Ministerial Council.

Another strength found in the mixture of representatives to the Council came from the participation and contributions from the so-called "line" ministries. Most intergovernmental tables of Ministers had one member who was also a member of the Ministerial Council. This was extremely helpful in getting both the line expertise required and support for the work of the Council. Officials supporting the work of the Council usually had some sort of internal coordinating group of line department officials in their home province both to draw upon specific program/service knowledge and to keep line departments in the loop as the Council work unfolded. Because

Ministers of Health, Social Services, Education, etc. were discussing the Council and its work at their meetings, the interdepartmental coordination was much smoother than it might otherwise have been. Feedback was timely and constructive. This was a critical aspect to meeting the tight timelines as well as securing broad support around the respective Cabinets for the Ministerial Report.

One other aspect of the early days that remains memorable was the relatively quick convergence around the principles that were developed. That is not to say that there were no in-depth discussions and intensive word-smithing to get the right words down, but the debate was often on how the thought should be stated rather than a major philosophical divergence around the intent behind the principles. A first draft of these principles was developed through a very intense work session by officials from Saskatchewan and Alberta. Some joked that if those two provinces could agree then there must be merit in them! In reality, once one put the so-called partisan differences between provinces aside and focused on the issues surrounding the functioning of the federation there was a good deal of commonality. I believe that the very tight timelines and the ability to focus on and work from where there was commonality rather than difference of thinking allowed us to get the task completed and produce a report that met with broad support.

A final thought about some of the challenges relates to the fact that what was being discussed was not what one would consider to be of great interest to the general public. While the public does get concerned over poor services, there are few people who spend a lot of time thinking about how the federation works. Given the complexity of most federal-provincial arrangements, take the equalization program for example, it is not surprising that the nuts-and-bolts discussion of how these arrangements work are of less interest than the result — how much money is there, what kind of service does one get and how does one access it. The Council was concerned with the principles and the overall structure for federal-provincial relationships and arrangements rather than the specific outcome for a particular service or program. While Council certainly felt that outcomes were important and needed to be articulated, it would be line Ministries that would determine what they ought to be. The media coverage of the work of the Council was meagre because the issues being dealt with by the Council did not lend themselves well to good sound bites or concise news stories.

The above is only a brief offering of some reflections that stick in my mind from the early days of the work of the Council. There is no doubt that the social policy renewal process gave me a wonderful opportunity to work with many creative, dedicated and talented people throughout the country in what remains one of the highlights of my intergovernmental career. While the task was enormous, the timelines and necessary coordination nearly impossible and the travel, meetings and conference calls exhausting, the outcome, I believe, was a Report to Premiers that in some small way at least contributed to providing a focus on how to strengthen the social union at a time when fiscal realities were a huge threat to the social fabric of the country.

Doug Smith

Doug Smith was a senior policy analyst with Newfoundland-Labrador Intergovernmental Affairs from 1995 to 1998. He is currently assistant deputy minister with Newfoundland-Labrador Intergovernmental Affairs.

In this chapter, Mr. Warriner has captured the genesis of and progression of the work by provinces and territories to redefine the Canadian social union. He has asked several of us who were involved in that work to provide some personal observations in an endeavour to capture the gestalt of the time. The caveat on these recollections must be that it is difficult to look back more than ten years and assess the work that was done then without having one's recollections coloured, perhaps even clouded, by the events and changes that occurred since.

The work began in part as a reaction to federal unilateral changes and cuts to funding for social programs by changing the Established Financing Program (in support of health and postsecondary education) and the CAP (in support of social welfare) to the CHST. But there was also an impetus provided by a nascent view, not formulated but present, that our society and the way governments worked within and for it was changing, and that this would change the Canadian intergovernmental dynamic.

Those of us charged with the task of conceiving a new model for the social union began our work with a common view that provinces and territories are co-equal governments in the Canadian federation, and we took a dim view of what we perceived as a federal stance that the Government of Canada was the "senior" level of government. This informed our work and helped us overcome differing views to achieve consensus that the social union and a social union framework agreement should be based on principles not on rules.

Hammering out the original set of principles was no easy task. The people around the officials' table represented a broad a spectrum of political and social thought and worked for governments that had divergent views of how the Canadian federation ought to work. We had no guidelines other than the view of Premiers that there was a need to redefine the intergovernmental dynamic and their determination that provinces and territories had to speak with a common voice when dealing with the federal government.

Although our country is, purportedly, one of the most decentralized federations in the world, there were those espousing a greater degree of decentralization and federal-provincial disentanglement. There were also those who held the competing view in favour of a strong central government. That said, those of us who favoured the strong central government approach were very aware that the federal government had missed that mark. What we were dealing with, and still are, is a federal government with a strong centralist orientation rather than a strong central government.

Federal unilateralism was, in our view, an underlying problem that could not be overcome simply by trying to change the rules. In its 1995 budget, the federal government had demonstrated that it was quite prepared to change the rules unilaterally, and it had its spending power to back up those changes. Further, we were aware that few people make a distinction between orders of government and that few had any patience with what they perceived as interjurisdictional squabbling over which order of government delivered and/or funded programs. Canadians wanted, and continue to want, need and deserve, high quality social programs. By way of example, this "popular view" continues to be evidenced today with a low tolerance for intergovernmental disagreement over health-care funding.

We were faced with an environment in which the federal government was moving to solve its deficit problem by offloading its costs to provinces and territories through a disproportionate reduction in transfers to provinces and territories (when compared to the cuts it was imposing on its own departments and agencies). While the federal government was characterizing the changes in its transfer programs as a redesign that would give provinces and territories more flexibility to meet social needs with fewer conditions, it was also severely impeding those jurisdictions, especially the smaller and less wealthy, by severely constraining cash transfers. It was further spinning its own tale by including in the CHST the tax points which it had some time before ceded to the provinces, neglecting to mention that this same "tax room" had been ceded to it by provinces as a temporary measure thirty odd years previously to aid in financing World War II.

Despite the unease we all felt about the direction we perceived the federal government to be taking, we worked from the premise that clearly articulated principles that upheld common values, provided reasonable flexibility and assured that social programs were affordable and reasonably comparable across the country could form the basis through which provinces and territories could arrive at a mutually respectful working arrangement with the federal government. Two important precepts of this renewed relationship would be the means to curtail the unilateral use of the federal spending power and the propensity of the federal government to act as the sole arbiter of how social programs, most notably health care, should be delivered.

The experiment continues to evolve. While there has been progress made on redefining the Canadian social union, it has been slower than we had hoped. It took some years after our initial report and the subsequent creation of the Ministerial Council on Social Policy Renewal for the Social Union Framework Agreement to be completed and yet more time to reach the dispute settlement mechanism to address disagreements over the interpretation of the *Canada Health Act.*

The economy has improved. The federal government, enjoying a long run of what many be characterized as excessive surpluses, has conceded additional health-care funding to provinces and territories and it is moving to redefine the equalization program. Yet much remains to be done in redefining our social union and in developing the collaborative federalism that will assure that Canada and each of its regions, provinces and territories will continue to be able to develop the right social policy and deliver effective social programs that support our commonwealth.

Chapter Four

Process and Structure
for Social Policy Renewal

The Government will work with the provinces and Canadians to develop by mutual consent the values, principles and objectives that should underlie, first, the Canada Health and Social Transfer and, building on this, the social union more generally. (Canada, 1996)

The Quebec Sovereignty Referendum

The course of social policy renewal was profoundly affected by events unrelated to social policy. On October 31, 1995, after a campaign in which the future of the Canadian federation was seriously brought into question, the Quebec government's referendum on sovereignty was defeated 50.6 percent to 49.4 percent. In the closing days of the referendum campaign, as well as immediately afterward, the federal government recognized the critical need for action that would convince Quebecers that sovereignty held less promise than a reformed federation. However, in the aftermath of the damaging failure of the Meech Lake and Charlottetown accords to secure constitutional amendments that would have brought Quebec into the constitution, conventional wisdom was that constitutional renewal would end in grief and was thus to be avoided. This led to a two-pronged strategy: "Plan A" involved non-constitutional renewal of the federation in a way that would be more acceptable to "soft nationalist" Quebecers, and "Plan B" involved highlighting the difficulties and costs of the sovereigntist option. Along with such federal actions as a resolution to recognize Quebec's distinctiveness and legislation to effectively "lend" the federal government's veto over future constitutional amendments to provincial governments (acting within five regional blocs), social policy renewal through intergovernmental collective action (managed by the Ministerial Council) became part of the "Plan A" strategy of several provinces and the federal government.

The 1996 Federal Throne Speech and Budget

The 1996 federal throne speech and budget indicated an increased willingness to engage provinces in a comprehensive discussion on social policy reform. These and other federal statements on social policy appeared to be generally consistent with proposals contained in the Ministerial Council report, which was after all, generally in line with federal objectives, in particular, developing a common agenda to renew the federation and delineating federal and provincial roles and responsibilities. Also, federal officials generally supported increased federal-provincial consultation and cooperation on values, principles and objectives for social policy and the health-care system. In any event, there appeared to be an opening for further discussions.

The throne speech linked the modernization of social policy with national unity. It noted Canadians' concern about economic uncertainty, the sustainability of social programs and the unity of the country. The speech indicated that the solution to social policy challenges would require cooperation "at the level of values" and identified the need for federal-provincial cooperation to ensure the sustainability of the social safety net.

The throne speech stated that a strong economy creates the ability to realize the values of "equality of opportunity, compassion for the underprivileged and protection of the vulnerable." Many social policy commentators saw this language as reflecting a regressive, marginal, welfare orientation rather than an inclusive, social insurance approach. Clearly, the federal position was further indication of a more general shift away from universal programming toward a more targeted approach. This position was a pragmatic response to fiscal restraints, it was in line with the international trend, and it was consistent with the direction being taken by provincial and territorial governments, but it did not reflect public opinion on Canadian values as reflected by a prominent study by the Canadian Policy Research Network (Peters, 1995).

The speech expressed a federal commitment to "ensuring opportunity through a sustainable social safety net" and to "secure Canada's social union," and it expressed the federal government's commitment to "work with provinces and Canadians to develop agreed-upon values and principles to underlie the social union and to explore new approaches to decision-making in social policy." In this regard, the speech announced federal intentions for a First Ministers' Conference to discuss job creation, securing the social safety net and setting a common agenda for renewal.

Perhaps the most important announcement was that the federal government would not use its spending power to create new shared-cost programs in areas of exclusive provincial jurisdiction without the consent of a majority of the provinces and that any new programs would be designed so that non-participating provinces would be compensated, provided they established equivalent or comparable initiatives. While a "knee-jerk" reaction to the near-victory of the sovereigntist option in the Quebec referendum and insufficient to satisfy the Quebec government of the day, this commitment would be cited often in interprovincial and federal-provincial discussions related to negotiations on Canada's social union.

The 1996 budget reflected the emerging federal recognition of the im-

portance of social policy reform and successful federal-provincial cooperation on Canada's social union. However, that recognition had not yet been
reflected in terms of budget allocation. While the federal government was
prepared to engage the provinces in a more comprehensive discussion on
social policy reform, it continued to focus on fiscal restraint measures. This
agenda continued to raise concerns regarding the fundamental principles
and objectives of Canadian social policy.

The budget established a five-year funding arrangement for the CHST,
which included a minimum "floor" for the cash portion of the transfer. The
level of CHST funding (including Quebec abatement) would decrease from
$18.8 billion in 1994–95 to $11.8 billion in 1998–99. The budget also announced a doubling of the Working Income Supplement portion of the Child
Tax Benefit to $1000 annually by July 1998 and changed the tax treatment
related to child support payments such that custodial parents would no longer
pay tax on child support payments. The budget established a new seniors
benefit that would replace the existing Old Age Security, the Guaranteed
Income Supplement and age and pension tax credits, beginning in 2001.
It also replaced UI with a new Employment Insurance (EI) system, which
would redesign income benefits, establish measures to assist re-employment
and create a fund to encourage employment creation in high unemployment
areas. The new system involved a reduction in expenditures by a minimum
of 10 percent, about $700 million, in 1996–97.

Saskatchewan View of the National Agenda

In a presentation at the Federal-Provincial-Municipal Summit in Montreal on
May 14, 1996, entitled "The Inequality Crisis: The Need for a New Agenda
of Progressive Change," Saskatchewan Premier Romanow set out a vision
of a new national agenda that would include stronger social programs; a
national debt management plan; a national strategy for investing in "human
capital"; a comprehensive review of the taxation system; harmonization of
labour standards and tax policies towards those that are most beneficial for
workers; and recognition of Quebec's distinctive linguistic and cultural identity. Notably, the Premier's speech referred to Judith Maxwell's paper "Social
Dimensions of Economic Growth" and observed that "the economic and
the social are interdependent... social capital is the foundation of economic
success" (Romanow, 1996d).

In a presentation to the Canadian Council on Social Development in
Montreal on May 24, 1996, entitled "Renewing Federalism: Why Social
Reform is Necessary," Premier Romanow reiterated his proposal for a national agenda and identified initial goals for social policy reform, including
acceptance of the *Ministerial Council on Social Policy Reform and Renewal: Report
to Premiers* (P/T Council on Social Policy Reform and Renewal, 1995) as the

general framework for a major administrative overhaul of the federation; a statement of principles for social policy reform; a commitment from the federal government for stable and predictable funding for social programs; agreement that social policy reform must be accompanied by a redesign of Canada's system of fiscal arrangements; and a proposal for a National Child Benefit that would coordinate federal and provincial resources, reduce welfare dependency, support labour market involvement by parents, and increase transfers to the working poor.

Saskatchewan supported an approach to intergovernmental discussions on social policy initiatives that was generally consistent with the provincial/territorial consensus and included achieving federal-provincial agreement on the following:

- principles and recommendations outlined in the Ministerial Council Report as the general framework and agenda for federal-provincial negotiations on social policy reform;
- a comprehensive national undertaking on income security and social service reform, with specific attention to the reduction of child poverty and development of a National Child Benefit program, integration of seniors' benefits and consideration of a national approach to disabilities benefits;
- a process to develop a federal-provincial mechanism to strengthen government commitment to the national health-care system through joint consultation on the clarification, refinement and interpretation of the *Canada Health Act*;
- a process to improve access to postsecondary education and enhance student mobility through the development of national strategies to finance their education, harmonization of the student loan programs and expansion of credit transfer arrangements;
- a process for redefining the roles and responsibilities of the federal and provincial governments, and encouraging innovation in labour force development programming including apprenticeship, institutional training, adjustment programs, adult basic education, literacy, vocational rehabilitation, employment enhancement, and labour market services (Saskatchewan, 1996a; Saskatchewan Intergovernmental Affairs, 1997).

1996 Western Premiers' Conference

As in previous years, the Western Premiers' Conference facilitated the further development and strengthening of a western consensus on social policy initiatives. At the June 1996 Western Premiers' Conference, Premiers strongly endorsed the Ministerial Council Report and expressed their intention to seek agreement by First Ministers on specific measures to advance the report's recommendations. In particular, the Premiers agreed to consider a national strategy to reduce child poverty through the development of a National Child Benefit program.

The Western Premiers advocated federal-provincial agreement on a statement of principles, a negotiation process and timelines for social policy reform which would establish a federal/provincial/territorial council of ministers to manage and coordinate the reform and renewal process; a commitment to negotiate the delineation of federal and provincial roles and responsibilities, and to develop mechanisms for settling differences and monitoring social policy initiatives; and a commitment to the principle that social policy reform must be accompanied by a redesign of Canada's system of fiscal arrangements in order to ensure that provincial and territorial expenditure responsibilities and revenue capacities would be balanced, government accountability would be improved and governments could provide reasonably comparable social programs across Canada. It is worth noting that, shortly after the Western Premiers' Conference, the Prime Minister expressed his interest in addressing the issue of child poverty at the forthcoming First Ministers' Meeting. The federal social policy review and the work of the Caledon institute, Campaign 2000 and the attention of the media had contributed to growing public awareness of the degree and persistence of child poverty. It would not have been politically acceptable for the Prime Minister or for any of the Premiers to be seen as less than fully supportive of such a proposal.

1996 First Ministers' Conference

The First Ministers' Conference in June 1996 presented an opportunity to advance the framework for social policy reform outlined by the Ministerial Council Report and to develop the national unity dimensions of social policy reform through the concept of "Canada's social union." The Prime Minister expressed federal support for the principles and general approach outlined in the Ministerial Council Report, with the exception of statements ascribing federal responsibility for services to Aboriginal peoples. The Premiers and Prime Minister agreed to establish the federal/provincial/territorial Council on Social Policy Renewal to further pursue the issues raised in the report, to coordinate the social policy reform and to address their priority objectives. The Prime Minister designated the Minister of Human Resources Development (Young) as the federal chair of the proposed council, assisted by the Minister of Health (Dingwall). The First Ministers called for the development of a National Child Benefit as a priority.

Social programs are widely regarded a fundamental feature of the Canadian identity. First Ministers were aware of the connection between social policy reform and national unity objectives. Cooperation between governments in addressing social security concerns was seen as a progressive and popular approach to demonstrate that "the federation works." Measures that would enhance social and economic security would address the basic aspirations of Canadians, including those in Quebec. In the longer term, action on social policy that reaffirmed the national commitment to collective welfare could undermine much of the separatist argument that Canada could not modernize its economy or reform its social policies in a way that would address the needs of Quebec. Under this scenario, time would be on the side of the federalists.

The government of Quebec refused to participate in the social policy renewal process, though Quebec officials did attend meetings as observers. This was consistent with Quebec's long-standing claim that social policy was within the exclusive jurisdictional of provinces. The Premier of Quebec criticized the initiatives for reform of the federation, including the social policy reform objectives, as either insufficient to address Quebec's concerns with the federation or as centralizing power in the hands of the federal government. Quebec sovereignty was regarded as the precondition for the *Projet de Société*. The Parti Québécois argument for sovereignty was that Canada's ability to respond effectively to the rapidly changing economic and social environment was restricted by jurisdictional disputes and related inefficiencies. Accordingly, Quebec argued that it would be better able to advance its economic, social and cultural objectives as a separate (possibly associated) state with exclusive domain over revenue and expenditure structures.

1996 Annual Premiers' Conference

The August 1996 Annual Premiers' Conference had a dramatic element to it. Premiers gathered in Edmonton and were then transported by a special train, complete with helicopter escort, to Jasper. The Premiers were immediately confronted with an aggravating issue in that Ontario had just days earlier released a report on the future of Canadian federalism by economist Thomas Courchene (1996). The paper proposed a major decentralization of responsibility for social policy. Following a clarification of Ontario's intentions, the issue was resolved in a manner that has been referred to as one where "Courchene was tossed from the train." Perhaps the train and the mountain air, the hospitality and the resolution of the misunderstanding about the Ontario report, created a camaraderie; the Premiers were able to reach consensus on a program for national social policy renewal. They discussed key economic, social and intergovernmental issues including jobs and economic growth, social policy reform, the national infrastructure program, international and internal trade, research and development and youth employment. A particularly important part of the conference concerned the Premiers' review of the decisions taken at the First Ministers' Meeting and their consideration of measures to facilitate interprovincial and federal-provincial cooperation.

To maintain the momentum on social policy reform the Premiers expressed their expectations regarding the establishment of a process for federal-provincial negotiation and provided direction on priority items through a discussion paper entitled *Issues Paper on Social Policy Reform and Renewal: Next Steps* (APC, 1996a). The paper identified the following priorities: National Child Benefit; integrated income support for persons with disabilities; proposals for reform of the health system; financial arrangements; negotiations on labour market matters; federal offloading of costs for services to Aboriginal people; and options for intergovernmental mechanisms to develop and promote adherence to national principles and standards. In accordance with proposals outlined in this discussion paper, the Premiers established the provincial/territorial (P/T) Council on Social Policy Renewal to coordinate the provincial/territorial perspective in deliberations that would be undertaken through the federal/provincial/territorial (F/P/T) Council on Social Policy Renewal. As lead for the Premiers' Conference, Alberta Premier Klein designated the Alberta Minister of Family and Social Services, Stockwell Day, as chair of the provincial/territorial council and co-chair of the federal/provincial/territorial council.

The P/T Council was also responsible for monitoring and reporting on the progress of social policy initiatives that Premiers assigned to sector ministers. It was agreed that, in January 1997, the council would provide a progress report to Premiers. The council also provided annual reports that were reviewed and addressed by Premiers at their annual conferences. These reports are available through the Canadian Intergovernmental Conferences Secretariat.

Premiers further advanced the idea of a National Child Benefit program by directing provincial Social Services Ministers to work with the federal Ministers of Human Resource Development and Finance to develop a proposal that could be implemented within existing fiscal frameworks. It was specified that an integrated National Child Benefit system should help to prevent and reduce child poverty; be designed in accordance with the principles for social policy reform outlined in the Ministerial Council Report; reduce overlap and duplication; and promote attachment to the work force, resulting in fewer families having to rely on social assistance.

Premiers directed the P/T Council to "design options for mechanisms and processes to develop and promote adherence to national principles and standards, for review by Premiers within six months." Accordingly, Intergovernmental Affairs officials drafted an options paper entitled *New Approaches to Canada's Social Union* (P/T Council on Social Policy Reform and Renewal, 1997b), which provided alternatives for federal/provincial/territorial and provincial/territorial commitments to strengthen the social union and guide future use of the federal spending power in the social policy area; new mechanisms to develop and promote the adherence to national principles and standards; and options for implementing intergovernmental commitments.

Premiers recommended that the council work with Ministers of Health, Finance, Aboriginal Affairs, Social Services and Labour Market on a strategy to advance the agenda agreed to in the Ministerial Council Report. The council subsequently established a working group to coordinate the development of possible strategies for advancing the provincial/territorial position.

Premiers supported the recommendation that "Ministers of Health obtain a consensus with the federal government, if possible, on a vision document for Canada's evolving health system which would include goals and principles, clarification of roles and responsibilities, financing arrangements, and a joint administrative mechanism for interpreting the *Canada Health Act*." However, despite efforts, no federal-provincial consensus was forthcoming on a joint vision. Nor was agreement reached about funding requirements or alternate ways to address *Canada Health Act* interpretation disputes. Only limited federal-provincial agreement was reached to work more cooperatively on strengthening national health surveillance capabilities, national health education programs and written health promotion materials. Nevertheless, provincial Health Ministers agreed to continue collaboration with Health Canada to integrate federal and provincial initiatives.

Premiers reiterated support for the First Ministers' initiative for development of a proposal on a national approach for the provision of income support for persons with disabilities. The Premiers endorsed a recommendation that Social Services and Finance Ministers work with their federal counterparts, in consultation with other ministries, to review existing programs and services provided to persons with disabilities; identify gaps and overlaps; develop a proposal for integration of income support for persons with disabilities; and develop a progress report with a work plan and time frames by January 31, 1997. Ultimately, this initiative stalled and was dropped as a national priority.

It is worth noting that, at the September 1996 meeting of Social Services Ministers and the Minister of Human Resources Development Canada, the Ministers created a special working group of social services officials to pursue, as a priority, the Premiers' direction regarding an integrated income support program for persons with disabilities. The Social Services Working Group on Disabilities Issues met in October and subsequently prepared a preliminary report that was reviewed by Social Services Deputies in December. The report of the working group reflected a cautious, incremental approach, rejecting the concept of a single integrated benefit. The report proposed a series of reforms focused almost exclusively on administrative improvement and harmonization of program delivery. The report noted that income support programs for disabled persons have different objectives, different financing models, different benefit designs and are delivered by different orders of government. The report was restricted by the adoption of several assumptions, including that any change must be fiscally neutral, should not affect the role of the private sector in disability insurance, rehabilitation or other services, and, most importantly, should remove disincentives to work.

Provincial/Territorial Council on Social Policy Renewal

The provincial/territorial Council on Social Policy Renewal held its first meeting on October 2, 1996, in Calgary. As directed by Premiers, the council planned to coordinate implementation of the Social Policy Reform agenda outlined in the Ministerial Council Report and to address the priorities identified in the *Issues Paper on Social Policy Reform*. Accordingly, the council agreed to write to the ministerial sector councils and request status reports and work plans.

The council considered the Premiers' directive that Social Services Ministers work with HRDC and provincial and federal Ministers of Finance to develop a proposal for an integrated National Child Benefit. The council reviewed a status report by Social Service Ministers and noted that the National Child Benefit would require reallocation of federal and provincial funding. The Council agreed that the issue of funding should be addressed within the context of comprehensive reform, including the potential for reallocation and reconciliation of responsibilities and resources across sectors and between governments. The council agreed to advance a recommendation on a National Child Benefit for First Ministers' consideration in January 1997.

The council also discussed the Premiers' directives regarding intergovernmental mechanisms to develop and promote adherence to national standards. In addition, the Council agreed to the following "ground rules" as a basis for the federal/provincial/territorial partnership for advancing Social Policy Reform initiatives:

- equal partners — each government comes to the negotiations as an equal partner;
- discretion — each designate is authorized by respective Cabinets to speak for his or her government;
- whole of government perspective — each designate should take a broad perspective to address issues that cut across sectors;
- cooperation — begin a process of effective and respectful cooperation, with major decisions in areas of shared jurisdiction or that impact on

both orders of government, made through agreement by both orders of government;

- transparency — any offer or agreement made available to one province or territory from the federal government should be communicated and made available to all provinces and territories.

Federal/Provincial/Territorial Council on Social Policy Renewal

We are entering a new phase of strengthening the social union by modernizing the social safety net, and by clarifying the roles and responsibilities of the two orders of government. (Pettigrew, 1996)

The federal/provincial/territorial Council on Social Policy Renewal held its first meeting in Toronto on November 27, 1996. The meeting provided an opportunity to review the background, themes and objectives of the Social Policy Reform initiative and reiterate commitment to cooperation and partnership. In particular, the meeting provided a forum for the new Minister of Human Resources Development Canada, Pierre Pettigrew, to express support for the process.

The meeting marked the beginning of a new federal-provincial partnership for the reform and renewal of Canadian social policy. The F/P/T Council acknowledged that the social policy renewal initiative was defined by the principles, recommendations and general approach outlined in the Ministerial Council Report; the priority issues identified by First Ministers at their June meeting; and the priority issues discussed in the *Issues Paper on Social Policy Reform and Renewal: Next Steps*, which was endorsed at the 1996 Premiers' Conference.

Council members expressed their commitment to work together in a spirit of trust, openness, and mutual respect, and to ensure more effective cooperation among governments in the design and delivery of social programs. The council discussed priorities such as the National Child Benefit and income support and services for persons with disabilities. The council also discussed reports on issues related to health, financial arrangements, labour market matters and mechanisms to develop and promote adherence to national principles and standards.

The council met again on January 29, 1997, and confirmed its consensus on the general approach to the development of a National Child Benefit. At this meeting, the Council also discussed plans for the development of a National Children's Agenda and options for an integrated approach to income support for persons with disabilities. The F/P/T Council did not meet again in 1997. However, federal and provincial/territorial Ministers and officials responsible for Intergovernmental Relations, Social Services and Finance met numerous times to facilitate work on the social policy renewal agenda. In particular, discussions proceeded on the National Child Benefit, National Children's Agenda, and New Approaches to Canada's Social Union. The development of these initiatives is elaborated in the following chapters.

1997 Annual Premiers' Conference

At the 1997 Annual Premiers' Conference, Premiers discussed the relationship between federal deficit reduction and cuts to federal transfers to provinces. The Premiers agreed that provinces should have a role in determining the allocation of any emerging federal fiscal surplus, and they identified reinvestment in the health-care system as a key priority. Premiers expressed support for the principle of "equalization" and directed Finance Ministers to reduce disparities in the equalization formula. Premiers also directed Finance Ministers to consult with Intergovernmental Affairs Ministers to prepare guidelines for fiscal compensation resulting from rebalancing roles and responsibilities and to develop a strategy for advancing these guidelines with the federal government. Premiers endorsed the work of the P/T Council on Social Policy Renewal and approved the continuation of their work, based on the priorities identified in the Council's *Progress Report to Premiers*. The Premiers also directed Social Services Ministers to complete work on the National Child Benefit as soon as possible (APC 1997).

First Ministers' Meeting on the Social Union, December 1997

> *Our basic goal is to show that Canada works, and can work better, for individual Canadians. That is the best possible way to build the unity of this country.* (Romanow, 1997a)

The Prime Minister and the Premiers met on December 11–12, 1997. The purpose of the meeting, publicly communicated as a First Ministers' summit on social policy, was to review the status of social policy renewal and give direction to the next phase of federal-provincial discussions. The meeting also had significance for national unity objectives. The Premiers, at their September meeting, had identified the importance of practical, non-constitutional approaches, including cooperation on social policy renewal, as part of an overall strategy to reform, strengthen and improve national unity (Premiers' Communiqué, September 14, 1997). The First Ministers meeting provided an opportunity to reaffirm their commitment to the social policy renewal project and to demonstrate the ability of federal-provincial relations to act as an effective instrument of reform. Social policy renewal had come to represent the non-constitutional reform dimension of the national unity strategy, characterized by some as an 80/20 strategy, with non-constitutional renewal of the federation forming the 80 percent.

The main objective of the meeting for the federal government was to highlight progress on social policy initiatives, especially youth employment, a National Children's Benefit and National Children's Agenda, benefits and services for persons with disabilities, and a protocol on interpretation of *Canada Health Act* principles. It was believed that focusing on the progress of these sector initiatives would reinforce the federal government's public message that Canada's social union was working well and that national social programs could be maintained and strengthened in the post-deficit era (Saskatchewan and New Brunswick, 1997; Saskatchewan, 1997g).

The primary provincial/territorial objective for the meeting was to obtain federal agreement to negotiate a framework agreement on managing Canada's social union, based on the provincial/territorial paper, *New Approaches to Canada's Social Union* (Saskatchewan and New Brunswick, 1997; Saskatchewan, 1997g). However, during preparations for the meeting, federal officials resisted such a commitment. In a December 4 meeting, a federal representative identified the following criteria as the federal "bottom line" for negotiating a framework agreement: the principle of mobility in social programs must be addressed, both orders of government must acknowledge responsibility for Aboriginal peoples, the federal government must retain final decision-making authority in enforcing national standards, and there would be no elaboration of the spending power (Saskatchewan, 1997g). Notwithstanding the reluctance of the federal officials, the decision to proceed with negotiations was made by the Prime Minister.

First Ministers reviewed the *Progress Report on the National Child Benefit* and reconfirmed their commitment to launch the National Child Benefit system by July 1, 1998. They agreed to develop a plan for the second federal contribution of $850 million and for provincial reinvestment strategies. In addition, they also reviewed the *Status Report on Work Toward a National Children's Agenda*, reaffirmed their commitment to new cooperative approaches to ensure child wellbeing and agreed to fast-track work on the agenda through the F/P/T Council (FMM, 1997a).

In addition, the First Ministers (except the Premier of Quebec) agreed to mandate designated ministers, under the auspices of the F/P/T Council on Social Policy Renewal, to negotiate a framework agreement for Canada's social union by July 1998. The objectives for these negotiations included principles for social policy; collaborative approaches to the use of the federal spending power; a mechanism for settling disputes between governments; ground rules for intergovernmental cooperation; and processes for clarifying roles and responsibilities within various social policy sectors (FMM, 1997a).

Chapter Five

National Child Benefit

As a society, we have a deep and abiding interest in the well-being of our children. Investing in children expresses our profound optimism and confidence that Canada will continue to grow and flourish. (Chrétien, 1997: 1)

Program Details

The National Child Benefit (NCB) was a joint initiative of the federal and provincial/territorial governments and First Nations communities to improve income support and other services to low-income families with children. It was established to help prevent and reduce the depth of child poverty, to promote attachment to the labour force and to reduce overlap and duplication through harmonization of program objectives and benefits and simplified administration (F/P/T Ministers Responsible for Social Services, 1997a). The new program involved the restructuring of federal, provincial, territorial and First Nations income and support programs for children to create a single, integrated system. By increasing child tax benefits, the federal government provided an additional federal income supplement for low-income families with employment incomes as well as those receiving social assistance and other benefits. Corresponding with the increase in federal child benefits, provinces, territories and First Nations decreased their social assistance payments on behalf of children and redirected the savings toward complementary programs and services to decrease child poverty, enhance child development and/or increase employment opportunities and incentives for low-income families with children.

In 1997, the federal government converted the Child Tax Benefit to the Canada Child Tax Benefit (CCTB) by restructuring the existing $5.1 billion benefit and its Working Income Supplement; redirecting $250 million that was previously committed to increase the Working Income Supplement and adding $600 million in new money. This was referred to as the "crucial first step" toward the National Child Benefit (Canada, 1997). The Canada Child Tax Benefit has a two-tier structure. The foundation provides a basic, income-related benefit for all low-income and middle-income families with children. When it was introduced, the program provided benefits to over 80 percent of Canadian families with children. The second tier of the CCTB is the National Child Benefit (NCB) Supplement, which delivers additional benefits to low-income families with children.

Beginning in July 1998, the CCTB provided a maximum annual benefit of $1,625 for the first child ($1,020 from the base CCTB and $605 from the NCB Supplement), and $1,425 for each additional child (for the second child, $1,020 in base CCTB and $405 from the NCB Supplement; for the third and each additional child, $1,020 in base CCTB, $330 from the NCB Supplement and an additional $75). The supplement paid its maximum amount to families with net annual incomes up to $20,921, depending on the number of children, and above that income threshold supplement payments declined to end at $25,921 in net family income. This resulted in an increase in Government of Canada benefits for about 1.4 million Canadian families with 2.5 million children.

Ottawa subsequently boosted its investment in the NCB through phased increases in the CCTB. By July 2004, the maximum payment had been increased (through incremental enhancements to the NCB Supplement) to a total of $2,719 annually for the first child, $2,503 for the second child and $2,507 for each additional child. The maximum supplement was provided for families with net annual incomes below $22,615. Families with somewhat higher incomes qualified for partial payments. Eligibility ends once net annual family income exceeds $35,000 for families with between one and three children. The federal government has committed to increase spending on the CCTB through 2007, when the maximum payment will reach a projected $3,243 for the first child, $3,016 for the second child and $3,020 for each additional child.

The new CCTB provides benefits to families in relation to the number of children and income level, *regardless of the source of income*. Consequently, families in receipt of provincial social assistance qualified for the federal benefits. However, since provincial social assistance is determined by need, the increase of federal benefits resulted in a decrease of provincial social assistance benefits for children. This is an intended feature of the NCB system and central to its purpose, which is to replace needs-tested provincial and First Nations welfare benefits for children with income-tested child benefits delivered by the federal government.

The federal-provincial "understanding" on the NCB initiative was that provinces would reallocate the savings in their social assistance budgets toward programs and services to benefit children and facilitate employment for low-income families. Some provinces provided more funding for child and employment related initiatives than was required by their NCB re-investment commitments (F/P/T Ministers Responsible for Social Services, 1997a). While seeming to be a simple understanding, this agreement constituted a radical departure in how federal-provincial relationships in social policy were managed. A similar situation existed with respect to federal social assistance provided to First Nations families through the Department of Indian and

Northern Affairs Canada — First Nations communities would re-direct any savings from social assistance adjustments toward programs and services that were consistent with the objectives of the NCB.

NCB re-investment initiatives included provincial, income-tested child benefits; earned income supplements; additional child-care spaces; child-care subsidies for low-income working families; early childhood intervention programs such as nutrition, prenatal-screening, recreation and youth/community programs; supplemental health benefits for children in low-income working families, including coverage of prescription drugs, dental and optical care; and employment and training programs (F/P/T Ministers Responsible for Social Services, 1999, 2000, 2001). First Nations investments go beyond these to also include community enrichment activities intended to increase self-awareness, self-esteem and cultural pride. By the end of the 1998 to 1999 fiscal year, provincial, territorial and First Nations investments under the NCB were an estimated $305 million. The amount of these investments were expected to increase as the federal government increased NCB Supplement benefits (P/T Council on Social Policy Reform and Renewal, 1999).

Consistent with its aim to maintain control of income support programs, the Quebec government did not participate in the NCB. However, that the Quebec family policy was consistent with the orientation of the NCB (P/T Council on Social Policy Reform and Renewal, 1997a).

Development of the Child Benefit Concept

The concept of child benefits followed from the recognition that wage rates are not determined by, or related to, the needs of families and that low wages are insufficient to provide for the needs of families with children (Kitchen, 1987). This issue was recognized as early as 1918, when the Government of Canada introduced the Child Tax Exemption, Canada's first child benefit and one of its first social programs. This measure provided income tax savings that varied with taxable income and number of children. However, the poorest families did not benefit from the program because they had no taxable income and did not pay any tax.

In 1943, the Marsh report, *Social Security for Canada*, observed that family size and the inflexibility of wages were the main factors affecting the ability of families to provide for adequate maintenance and health. The report indicated that if a family's income was moderate or adequate the situation could be allayed through federally administered Family Allowances (Marsh, 1975). In reviewing the introduction of the Family Allowance, Brigitte Kitchen concluded "The particular social and economic significance of Family Allowances in 1945, as well as today, rests on the impossibility of providing for the needs of children through a wage and a social security system that fails to take into account the varying sizes of family units" (Kitchen, 1987: 239).

In addition to the positive effect of Family Allowances for maintaining the wellbeing of children and families, there were other economic arguments that supported the general concept of family income support. Scholars observed that "Government interest in the concept and principle of family allowances was raised because of its commitment to its anti-inflationary price and wage stabilization policy" (Kitchen, 1987: 234), and "to deflect trade union pressure to lift wartime wage controls and allow wage increases for low-paid workers" (Moscovitch and Drover, 1987: 28). Federal finance department files from 1943 noted that "children's allowances are the most direct and economic method of meeting the current strong demand for relaxation of wage control in respect of the lower wage rates" and "are likely to protect Canada's ability to compete with other countries in world markets. In the long run minimum wages and average wages are likely to be pushed higher in the absence of family allowances" (Finance Central Files 101-53-114, quoted in Ursel, 1992: 193).

The same type of economic forces and interests have influenced current economic and social policy. It provides a striking demonstration that concern for global trade and international competition, the pressure to increase labour productivity by suppressing wages and the role of Family Allowances in ameliorating and/or enabling low wage rates are features that support the implementation of family related benefits.

In 1944, the government of Canada, aware of the Marsh proposal and other economic considerations and certainly influenced by Keynesian fiscal policy as a means to maintain employment and increase purchasing power, introduced the universal Family Allowance program to assist families in the support of their children. Kitchen observed that support for the Family Allowance legislation was focused on economic arguments, and, in particular, "prominence and emphasis was given to Keynesian economic principles which considered Family Allowances as a sure and valuable economic primer which would stimulate the economy through increasing the spending capacity of those Canadians with the highest 'propensity' for consumption" (Kitchen, 1987: 236).

The Social Security Review of the early 1970s revisited the issue of inadequate incomes and considered the need for public measures to assist families. The following key reports addressed income security matters, including child poverty: *Income Security for Canadians* (1970); *Poverty in Canada: The Report of the Special Senate Committee on Poverty* (1971); *Working Paper on Social Security in Canada* (1973); and the *Federal-Provincial Social Security Review Background Paper on Income Support and Supplementation* (1975). Notably, the 1973 report proposed a model social security system that included family income supplementation for those working at or near the minimum wage and whose incomes were inadequate by reason of family size. The report suggested that this family income supplementation could take the form of a universal Family Allowance or targeted, income-related supplement. In 1975, a federal-provincial report advanced specific proposals to address child poverty that included increased Family Allowances, an income-tested child allowance and a refundable child tax credit.

Federal income tax provisions were revised during this period to increase benefits to families. In 1973, the Family Allowance was tripled, indexed to the cost of living and made subject to income taxation. In 1978, the government introduced the Refundable Child Tax Credit, which, for the first time, used the personal income tax system to deliver benefits to families based on income and family size. The use of the tax system in this way to deliver social assistance benefits provided the administrative precedent for subsequent initiatives, including the NCB.

In 1985, the *Report of the Royal Commission on the Economic Union and Development Prospects for Canada* (MacDonald Commission) advocated a universal income security program that would pay a basic income supplement to all Canadians. It was proposed to fund this program through the elimination of Family Allowances, Child Tax Credits, Married Exemptions, Child Exemptions, Federal Social Housing Programs and Federal Contributions to the CAP. The report argued that the program would provide a wage subsidy for low-wage workers and, therefore, it would become less important, in dealing with poverty, to maintain high minimum wages. Here again there is the connection between wage rates and, by implication, productivity and competitiveness, and the particular policy mechanism of income supplementation.

The Conservative government of the time was inclined to reduce or redirect social security expenditures and introduce "proactive " labour force adjustment measures, rather than consider universal income security. In 1985 federal child benefit programs were partially de-indexed, and in 1989 the federal government began to tax back Family Allowances from families with higher incomes. The government was sharply criticized for these and other cutbacks in social programs and was accused of "social policy by stealth" (Battle, 1990) for the means by which program reductions were imposed.

In 1991, the report of the Standing Senate Committee on Social Affairs, Science and Technology, *Children in Poverty: Toward a Better Future,* recommended alleviating child poverty through either a National Child Benefit (consisting of the Family Allowance and an enhanced Refundable Child Tax Credit) or an enhanced Refundable Child Tax Credit. The Senate report contained the first ever costed options for a National Child Benefit and, significantly, both options would be financed partly through the elimination of provincial welfare-delivered child benefits. Also in 1991, the report of the Standing Committee on Health and Welfare, Social Affairs, Seniors and the

Status of Women, *Canada's Children: Investing in Our Future*, outlined a plan to eliminate child poverty by the year 2000.

In 1993, the federal government introduced the Child Tax Benefit, which replaced Family Allowances, the Refundable Child Tax Credit and the Non-Refundable Child Tax Credit. This benefit was paid monthly but, like the programs it replaced, was only partially indexed (to the amount of inflation over 3 percent). The Child Tax Benefit included a Working Income Supplement that paid up to $500 per family for lower-income families with employment earnings above $3,750. The refinement of this approach to coordinate the federal tax system and the provincial social security systems provided the infrastructural basis for the National Child Benefit.

In 1994 the federal Social Security Review discussion paper, *Improving Social Security in Canada*, proposed options for the reform of child benefits, including an integrated federal-provincial child benefit (the basic structure of what would later become known as the National Child Benefit). The supplementary paper, *Income Security for Children*, argued that the primary means of addressing child poverty should be to strengthen the capacity of parents to earn income and that measures to enhance the employability of low-income parents and reduce barriers to work would reduce the incidence of poverty among children. The paper identified three possible approaches: 1) enhanced and re-targeted Child Tax Benefit; 2) integrated federal-provincial child benefit; and 3) enhanced Working Income Supplement.

The follow-up 1995 report of the Standing Committee on Human Resources Development Canada, *Security, Opportunities and Fairness*, identified the following three broad priorities: 1) the increasing pressures on Canadian families and the unacceptably high number of Canadian children living in poverty; 2) the challenges facing Canadian youth and the need for more effective support, particularly in making the transition from school to work; and 3) the needs of unemployed and underemployed adults, especially those coping with major shifts in the economy. The committee concluded that social security must include, as a fundamental priority, a comprehensive and unwavering commitment to reducing child poverty and improving the quality of life for Canadian children. It recommended that the federal government enhance the Working Income Supplement and work with the provinces and territories to create a new integrated benefit for children of low-income families.

It is worth noting that, in the late 1980s and early 1990s, around the time of the federal Social Security Review, several provincial governments conducted policy development work and, in some cases, introduced measures to assist low-income families. Such provincial initiatives included both income supplementation and support programs and services. In 1988, the Ontario Social Assistance Review Committee proposed that the federal and provincial governments integrate their income support and social assistance benefits for families with children and create a new program, outside the welfare system, to provide benefits for children in low-income families (SARC, 1988). This was an influential proposal that informed subsequent work toward an Ontario Child Income Program and provided important conceptual support for a national approach to family income support.

In 1993, the Ontario Ministry of Community and Social Services released a policy paper entitled *Turning Point: New Support Programs for People with Low Incomes*. This document asserted that social assistance was not an effective means of addressing child poverty and proposed an Ontario Child Income Program, to remove children from the welfare system and replace social assistance with a new child benefit. Under the proposed program, all low-income families would be eligible for benefits, dependent on level of income and the number of children. Never implemented, due mainly to cost constraints, it affirmed the concept of providing children's benefits outside the welfare system.

In 1988, the Quebec government introduced the Parental Wage Assistance program, which facilitated employment of families with children by providing employment income supplements and subsidized child care. In 1994, New Brunswick introduced a monthly Income Supplement Benefit for income assistance families with children who were not in subsidized housing. Also in 1994, the Newfoundland Economic Recovery Commission proposed an income supplementation program that would encourage employment by providing wage supplements for low-income individuals and families

The Manitoba Child Related Income Support Program, available to families that received the CCTB, provided monthly supplements to low-income families raising children. Manitoba also developed an extensive array of child and family services to complement income security systems. A similar program in British Columbia, the B.C. Family Bonus, provided income benefits to low- and modest-income families with children. The program was specifically intended to assist families with children to leave welfare by providing benefits in respect of children outside the welfare system.

The Saskatchewan Family Income Plan provided income-tested benefits based on family size. Separate from social assistance, the plan provided income supplements to assist low-income families with children to meet the costs of food, shelter and other necessities. In 1992, a discussion paper entitled *Creating a New Child Benefit Program for Saskatchewan* proposed an income and asset tested child benefit that would supplement the federal Child Tax Benefit. In addition, Saskatchewan initiated discussions with HRDC to determine if the federal government would be prepared to participate in an integrated child benefit initiative. The proposal was part of a broader, interdepartmental "Action Plan for Children" that was intended to protect the most vulnerable families while offering supports and incentives to help families increase their independence and financial wellbeing. Work toward a Saskatchewan child benefit was superseded by the National Child Benefit initiative.

Development of the National Child Benefit

Our first task is to complete the job of implementing the National Child Benefit and its companion provincial/territorial programs. This will be the first new national social program in 30 years. (Romanow, 1997a)

In 1989, just under 15 percent of Canadian children lived in families with incomes below the Statistics Canada low-income cut-offs. The issue of child poverty appeared to be manageable and, in a unanimous gesture of optimism and good intentions, the Canadian Parliament adopted a resolution to "seek to achieve the goal of eliminating poverty among children by the year 2000." By 1993 the extent of children living in poverty in Canada had increased substantially, to 21 percent. Government policy analysts have identified several contributing factors, including changing economic conditions, the increased number of single-parent families, declining employment and earnings among low-income families and increased reliance on government transfers by low-income families (F/P/T Ministers Responsible for Social Services, 1999).

Low-wage employment was obviously insufficient to maintain families with children, with families on social assistance often better off economically than those relying on low wages. The former received child benefits (welfare benefits directed towards children) that were not available to low-income families not on social assistance. Welfare families typically received about double the amount of child benefits — both provincial/territorial welfare child benefits and federal child benefits — whereas the working poor got only federal child benefits.

Families on social assistance also received tax-exempt benefits like shelter and health allowances. Low-wage families had their earnings reduced by income taxes and payroll tax deductions; had to pay work-related expenses such as clothing, transportation and child care; and did not qualify for health and other in-kind benefits often available to welfare families. Where welfare benefits exceeded wages levels, there were compelling reasons to choose welfare over employment. Consequently, low wages and the negative wage impact of economic restructuring for low skilled workers have contributed to increased demand for social assistance (August, 2003: 2–4). This impediment to employment experienced by families on social assistance is referred to as the "welfare wall" (Battle and Muszynski, 1995).

Social welfare and child advocacy organizations, community groups, unions, business organizations, policy institutes and the general public called for government action to reduce the high level of child poverty. Key organizations included the Canadian Council on Social Development, Child Poverty Action Group, Child Care Advocacy Association, Child Welfare League, National Anti-Poverty Organization, Family Service Canada, Canadian Teachers' Federation, Canadian Child Care Federation, Canadian Association of Social Workers, Canadian Council of Churches and many other others, which came together under the umbrella organization, Campaign 2000.

The Caledon Institute of Social Policy was a prominent contributor to the discussion on child poverty and proposed options for a national approach to addressing the issue. Caledon had been directly involved in the development of the integrated federal-provincial child benefit option that had been presented in the 1994 Social Security Review discussion paper *Income Security for Children*. In an influential 1995 Caledon paper, *One Way to Fight Child Poverty*, Ken Battle and Leon Muszynski provided an elaboration on the Social Security Review proposal for an integrated child benefit. The Caledon paper outlined a detailed, costed design for a federal-provincial child benefit system with a single integrated benefit to all low-income families with children, *regardless of their source of income*. The proposed child benefit would assist parents on welfare to take up employment because they would receive a significant low-income supplement. This was the basic design for the subsequent NCB.

The Caledon proposal advocated replacing the federal Child Tax Benefit, provincial welfare payments on behalf of children and other federal and provincial child-related benefits with an integrated child benefit for low-income families. The unique aspect of this approach was that it could remove children from the welfare system by providing benefits to all low-income families, regardless of income source. Families receiving social assistance would receive benefits in respect of their children through the child benefit program rather than through welfare payments. This would provide an incentive for working parents to remain in the labour force and would enable parents on welfare to enter the work force (Battle and Muszynski, 1995).

This approach was endorsed and further developed through subsequent discussions by federal and provincial/territorial ministers and officials. Ken Battle and Michael Muszynski concluded that an integrated National Child Benefit "progressed from a concept to a political reality largely due to the efforts of provincial and territorial governments in the landmark *Report of the Provincial/Territorial Council on Social Policy Reform and Renewal* of 1995" (1997: 2). The report recommended that the "consolidation of income support for children into a single national program, jointly manage by both orders of government" should be included in an agenda for discussions with the federal government. The Caledon Institute identified this recommendation as the first of four good proposals for reform at the heart of the report (Mendelson, 1996).

Provincial Social Service Ministers met in April 1996 to review the progress on follow-up to the Ministerial Council Report. The Ministers instructed their Deputies to meet with the federal Deputy of HRDC to explore federal interest in redefining roles and responsibilities and to prepare for a meeting of federal and provincial Ministers in September. Federal and provincial Deputy Ministers held follow-up meetings in May and June.

In May 1996, Saskatchewan Premier Romanow referred to the concept of an integrated National Child Benefit in his speech at the annual meeting of the Canadian Council on Social Development. He indicated that a National Child Benefit would allow federal and provincial governments to coordinate resources to assist low income families; reduce welfare dependency and move family income security away from the welfare approach and toward a more advanced and efficient approach; and support labour market involvement by parents, while increasing transfers to the working poor (Romanow, 1996b).

At the June 3–5 Western Premiers' Conference, Premiers agreed that "development of a National Child Benefit proposal that would integrate and improve the various federal, provincial and territorial programs supporting low-income families with children should be raised at the First Ministers' Meeting in June" (APC, 1996a: 6).

At the First Ministers' Meeting on June 21, 1996, the Premiers and the Prime Minister called for the development of a proposal for a National Child Benefit program, to be a priority. The Prime Minister named the Minister of HRDC, assisted by the Minister of Health Canada, to work with their provincial counterparts in implementing the proposals set out in the report of the Ministerial Council, including that for an integrated National Child Benefit.

Premiers further advanced the NCB initiative at the 1996 Annual Premiers' Conference by endorsing the recommendations of the *Issues Paper on Social Policy Reform and Renewal*. The recommendation required Social Services Ministers to work with provincial Ministers of Finance and federal Ministers of Human Resources Development and Finance to develop a program that could be implemented within existing fiscal frameworks. The recommendation specified that the proposed child benefit system should help ensure an effective response to preventing and reducing child poverty; be designed in accordance with the "Principles to Guide Social Policy Reform and Renewal"; reduce overlap and duplication; and promote attachment to the work force, resulting in fewer families having to rely on social assistance. The Premiers also requested that the Ministers prepare an interim report for First Ministers by January 31, 1997, and a final report by June 1997 (APC, 1996a; APC, 1996b).

At the September 17, 1996, meeting of provincial Social Services Ministers and the Minister of HRDC, the Ministers approved development of a proposal for a National Child Benefit. As prescribed by the Premiers, the Ministers agreed that such a program should help ensure an effective response to preventing and reducing child poverty; promote attachment to the work force, resulting in fewer families having to rely on social assistance; and reduce overlap and duplication. The Ministers also agreed that the national program should not result in any reduction in benefits to families receiving social assistance.

At the meeting, the HRDC Minister, Doug Young, expressed the federal interest in "fast tracking" work on the NCB to meet the federal budget and legislative agenda and indicated a December 15 target date for completion. The provincial Social Services Ministers were disturbed by the imposition of federal timelines, and they concluded that they would follow the timelines set out by Premiers, while also working as expeditiously as possible. The Ministers directed their officials to immediately establish the NCB Working Group to develop an interim proposal for Premiers that addressed costs, flexible approaches for different regions, impact on social assistance clients/rates and related family benefits, research and definition issues, and alternative options. Notably, with respect to timelines and the sense of immediacy expressed by the federal Minister, the provincial ministers asked that the Working Group give "best efforts" to advance the process.

The NCB Working Group included officials from provincial/territorial departments responsible for Social Services and Finance, and officials from the federal departments of Human Resources Development, Finance, Revenue and Health. The working group met and held conference calls throughout October and November of 1996 and formed five task groups to lead work on data collection, analysis and rationale, model design, administration and delivery, and implementation and governance (F/P/T Social Services Officials, 1997a). The officials addressed issues such as the interface between the federal Child Tax Benefit and provincial social assistance, the provincial reinvestment framework, legislative changes, accountability and governance, and public consultation and communications. They estimated that a Child Tax Benefit sufficient to take children off welfare would cost about $2.5 billion annually in addition to current expenditures and noted that this would allow provincial reinvestment of approximately $1.25 billion for programs for children and families (Saskatchewan 1996a, 1997a).

At their meeting on October 8, 1996, the Working Group reviewed the main design issues and planned to present options for consideration at the November meeting of the F/P/T Council on Social Policy Renewal. Federal officials demonstrated a willingness to consider various design possibilities and to contribute positively to the development of a multi-lateral proposal.

The productive collaboration between government officials and across departments bode well for an accelerated time frame; their intention was to develop a proposal for consideration by First Ministers in early January.

Federal and provincial/territorial officials of Social Services and Finance departments met again on October 29, 1996, in Regina and November 21–22, 1996, in Toronto. They determined that potentially feasible design options would require the federal government to reallocate $5 billion used for the Child Tax Benefit and Working Income Supplement. The federal and provincial/territorial governments would also need to come up with an additional $600 million to $2.2 billion. Depending on the specific design and eligibility parameters, the NCB would partially or substantially replace provincial/territorial social assistance for children, allowing provinces and territories to reallocate social assistance funds toward NCB funding and/or supplemental services.

Federal officials indicated that initial federal funding would likely to be limited to somewhere between $300 million and $600 million. They also suggested that the initiative should develop incrementally, beginning with the harmonization of a moderate federal base benefit with provincial/territorial supplementation, and moving toward benefit enhancement and integration. Federal officials were particularly interested in maintaining or increasing the level of provincial funding for services for children following any increased federal commitment.

The P/T Council on Social Policy Renewal reviewed progress on the initiative at their meetings on October 2 and November 26. The NCB was discussed with the federal Minister, Pierre Pettigrew, at the first meeting of the F/T/P Council on Social Policy Renewal on November 27, 1996. On the same day as the council meeting, Saskatchewan Premier Romanow was also in Toronto as the keynote speaker at the Canada's Children, Canada's Future Conference, where he said: "Today's news reports indicate that expectations should be lowered at today's meeting of Ministers in Toronto. I say to those officials — elevate those expectations. Because, if we succeed, we provide children with basic benefits based on their family's income" (Romanow, 1996c).

Social Services Ministers and the Minister of HRDC met on January 13, 1997, and reviewed an options paper on the NCB. They approved the program's objectives: to help prevent and reduce the depth of child poverty; to promote attachment to the work force; and to reduce overlap and duplication. They also approved the following operating principles to guide development and implementation of the NCB system:

The National Child Benefit:

- is a partnership between federal and provincial/territorial governments;

- requires a significant, incremental and permanent investment, as well as appropriate and complementary provincial/territorial investments benefiting children in low-income families;
- will be developed in a staged approach, with the initial investment representing a starting point to a more significant investment in the future — an investment which is sufficient to remove benefits for children from the welfare system;
- involves provincial and territorial governments reinvesting social assistance funds made available by the federal government's investment in low-income families with children in a manner consistent with the NCB objectives;
- will see provinces/territories exploring whether incremental funds can be devoted to the provincial/territorial component of the NCB, fiscal resources permitting;
- will not result in the reduction of the overall level of income support for families in receipt of social assistance;
- will simplify administration and delivery of children's benefits by governments, and simplify receipt of benefits for families with children; and
- is one of a number of measures needed to combat child poverty (F/P/T Ministers Responsible for Social Services, 1997).

The ministers agreed to seek confirmation from their respective Cabinets on approval for the development of the NCB; approval for development of a framework for "re-investment" of social assistance funds freed up by the increase in the federal Child Tax Credit; and priorization on optional approaches for the NCB. They also agreed that an effective program would require a significant, incremental and permanent federal investment, as well as appropriate and complementary provincial investments benefiting children in low-income families. The HRDC Minister indicated federal plans to announce the NCB in its 1997 budget (Saskatchewan, 1997b; F/P/T Ministers Responsible for Social Services, 1997c; F/P/T Social Services Officials, 1997b).

These ministers met again on January 28, 1997 to review and finalize their interim report. The *Report on the National Child Benefit* was provided to the F/P Council on Social Policy Renewal at its January 29 meeting and also forwarded to First Ministers (Saskatchewan, 1997c; F/P/T Council on Social Policy Renewal, 1997).

The ministers' report proposed that the NCB be composed of a basic federal income support benefit and a provincial component that could be made up of either income support benefits or services to support the overall initiative. It was a fundamental principal of the design that provinces and territories would redirect saved social assistance funds to other programs targeted at children in low-income families. It was also understood that the federal government would not prescribe, approve or regulate the specific application of provincial contributions (Saskatchewan, 1997c; F/P/T Ministers Responsible for Social Services, 1997d). Provinces and territories would report on their cost savings and "reinvestments" to the F/P/T Ministerial Council on Social Policy Renewal, not the federal government.

Essentially, the Social Services Ministers' report outlined an agreement between the federal and provincial/territorial governments that the joint approach to implementing the NCB would involve three simultaneous elements: 1) the federal government would increase benefits to low-income families with children through the CCTB; 2) provincial and territorial governments would make corresponding decreases in their social assistance payments for families with children; and 3) provincial and territorial governments would reinvest these newly available funds in complementary programs targeted at low-income families with children. In addition, the federal government would reinvest "reallocated federal social assistance funds for Aboriginal children living on reserve" into programs and services that were consistent with the general objectives of the NCB initiative (P/T Council on Social Policy Reform and Renewal, 1997a). These design features constituted a new model for federal-provincial shared-cost programs. Several provinces hoped this model would be more acceptable to Quebec — an important consideration given the uncertainty about national unity in the aftermath of the 1995 referendum — while still providing the foundation of a national program and ensuring that there was a net increase in funding to address child poverty across the country. The model was also focused on transparency and accountability to the public, through the requirement that provinces and territories report to the Ministerial Council, rather than the accountability to the federal government that came with conditional transfers to the provinces. While not utilized again since the establishment of the NCB, this model remains available as a means by which the federal, provincial, and territorial governments could cooperatively establish new national social programs.

The P/T Council on Social Policy Renewal met on January 29, 1997. Important objectives of the meeting included sustaining a positive and cooperative environment in developing the National Child Benefit and advancing the joint work of Health and Social Services Ministers in developing a National Children's Agenda. The provincial chair of the Social Services Ministers, Newfoundland Minister Joan Marie Aylward, presented the Social Services Ministers' Interim Report on the National Child Benefit (Saskatchewan, 1997c; F/P/T Council on Social Policy Renewal, 1997).

On February 17, 1997 the co-chairs of the F/P/T Council on Social Policy Renewal sent a letter to the Prime Minister and Premiers reporting on the status of their work. The letter noted that addressing child poverty would require a combination of income support measures and complementary services. The letter referred to the Social Services Ministers' *Report on the National Child Benefit* and noted that all participating governments endorse, in principle, the development of a NCB system. The letter also observed that "a National Child Benefit should remove a major barrier to employment because families would keep their child benefits when they move from social assistance to low and modest income jobs." In addition, the letter reported that Social Service Ministers would develop a mutually agreed federal/provincial/territorial framework to guide reinvestment under the program, whereby savings resulting from federal funding of the National Child Benefit would be reinvested for children in low-income families, recognizing the need for appropriate flexibility" (Pettigrew and Day, 1997).

The 1997 throne speech identified investing in children as a key objective and the budget provided increased funding to replace the Child Tax Benefit and Working Income Supplement with a new Canada Child Tax Benefit and its National Child Benefit Supplement. The design of the Canada Child Tax Benefit and National Child Benefit Supplement would enable provinces to redirect savings resulting from increased federal spending and thereby increase provincial spending on initiatives that would have the general objective of reducing child poverty. Although the Liberal election platform had promised to at least double the $850 million additional funding for the CCTB as resources became available, the budget did not indicate the total federal funding commitment, nor did it propose an implementation schedule. The replacement of the Working Income Supplement with the NCB Supplement was a major policy departure for the federal government, which, to that point, had been committed to encouraging labour force attachment through the supplementation of wages. The CCTB and the NCB Supplement were different in that they would provide equal benefits in relation to family income, regardless of employment status or source of income.

The day after the federal budget announcement, the federal/provincial/territorial Ministers Responsible for Social Services issued a press release indicating that the initiative was a "critical building block" toward a National Child Benefit that would enable provinces to "identify initiatives that build on the federal contribution by providing better supports to low-income families" (F/P/T Ministers Responsible for Social Services, 1997e). In an interview shortly after the budget, the federal Minister of Human Resources Development noted the positive aspects of the NCB as a model for federalism, observing that "This kind of approach shows that federalism works" (Tibbetts, 1997). Saskatchewan Premier Romanow considered that the federal Budget commitment of $600 million for the National Child Benefit was "a good start," but that it should have been accompanied by a "road map" that specified a schedule for increasing funding for the program to $2 billion annually within five years (Wyatt, 1997).

Provincial Social Services Deputy Ministers met with the Deputy Minister of HRDC on April 7, 1997. Given the high profile of work on the NCB, the meeting was also attended by Intergovernmental Affairs officials from several provinces. Although the federal government had taken a first step toward the NCB with the introduction of the CCTB and its NCB Supplement, there were many elements of the child benefit design that were yet to be completed, and commitments between governments remained somewhat fragile (Saskatchewan, 1997c). There was agreement that provinces and territories would reinvest social assistance savings, but there was disagreement on the criteria that would be used for deciding the range of acceptable programs. Many provinces considered the federal expectations for reinvestment to be unreasonable given the limited financial commitment it had made in the budget. The federal government clearly wanted investment focused on areas that supported re-entry to the labour market, while some provinces wanted more flexibility. Several provinces, notably Manitoba, Ontario and the Atlantic provinces, were only just beginning to consider reinvestment plans (Saskatchewan, 1997d).

Although Quebec disagreed with the national approach to social policy, it did support the basic objectives of the child benefit initiative and had plans to develop a Quebec integrated child benefit. The issue of how Quebec would handle participation with other provinces and the federal government in what was clearly a national undertaking had yet to be resolved. Quebec representatives attended meetings of the Council on Social Policy Renewal and those of Social Services and Health ministers, but it became the practice for Quebec to note its opposition in public communications and reports related to those meetings. A typical Quebec exemption note would say the following: "Quebec agrees with the basic principles of the National Child Benefit, which aims to increase resources available for poor children and promote employment retention and the return to work. The family policy implemented by Quebec is consistent with this orientation. However the Government of Quebec has not taken part in the development of the National Child Benefit because it wishes to assume control of income support for the children of Quebec. Consequently, any reference to joint federal, provincial and territorial positions in this text does not include Quebec" (F/P/T Ministers Responsible for Social Services, 1998b).

Public consultations were planned for the summer of 1997. Federal government officials indicated a particular need to communicate with national organizations, and federal and provincial Social Services deputies agreed that there was a need to jointly manage the flow of information to ensure that accurate information was provided. Technical work was initiated to ensure an adequate interface between federal and provincial income-support programs and to ensure that no one would be worse off following the elimination of the federal Working Income Supplement. The federal government had begun consultations on the NCB with national Aboriginal organizations, but regional consultations had not yet been undertaken (Saskatchewan, 1997d).

Substantial progress had been achieved on the first phase of developing the NCB, but officials needed to complete work on the details of the program, particularly the provincial reinvestment framework. It was also important to expand the discussion on child poverty and focus attention on the need for a fully developed national program that involved substantially more federal funding and corresponding provincial commitments.

Provincial Social Services ministers met together and with the HRDC Minister in April, September and October of 1997 to review progress on the NCB. At the April meeting, they affirmed their commitment to the three objectives of the NCB and also agreed that the reinvestment framework would provide provinces with the flexibility to design or enhance programs that recognized the special needs and priorities of each province or territory. The ministers committed to implementing the NCB by July 1998 (F/P/T Ministers Responsible for Social Services, 1997f).

At the 1997 Western Premiers' Conference, the Premiers reaffirmed their commitment to the social policy renewal initiative. They agreed that "fighting child poverty is of the highest priority" and called for "a full federal government investment in the National Child Benefit of at least $2.5 billion by the year 2000." The Premiers emphasized the importance of federal/provincial cooperation and maintaining flexibility for provincial reinvestment in programs for low-income families with children (WPC, 1997).

In July 1997, provincial and territorial Social Service ministers submitted their *Status Report on the National Child Benefit* to Premiers. The report indicated that provinces and territories would soon confirm the social assistance funds that would be available for reinvestment and identify the children's programs and services to which these funds could be reallocated. The report also indicated that federal and provincial/territorial ministers responsible for Social Services would undertake the legislative and administrative changes, systems development and staff training necessary to implement the NCB (P/T Ministers Responsible for Social Services, 1997).

At the 1997 Annual Premiers' Conference, Premiers noted substantial progress toward the NCB and directed Social Services Ministers to complete work for implementation as soon as possible. Premiers also called for the federal government to provide the investment necessary — about $2.5 billion annually — for the program to fully meet its objectives by the year 2000 (APC, 1997). At their December 1997 meeting, First Ministers reconfirmed their commitment to the NCB and agreed to develop a plan for the second federal contribution and complete provincial reinvestment strategies as soon as possible.

The February 1998 federal budget committed additional federal contributions of $425 million in 1999 and $425 million in 2000. This second federal instalment of $850 million over two years did not meet the expectations expressed by Premiers for full funding by the year 2000, but it did reflect progress and suggest that, eventually, the target program would be met.

As the NCB program became more established and as benefits increased and design details were addressed, the issue of benefit indexation became more important. There was some discussion about the relative merits of pushing for indexation immediately or waiting until target benefit levels had been achieved. Should additional funding be used to increase base benefits or provide indexation at current levels? Eventually, both increased benefits and indexation would be achieved.

At their meeting of March 12 1998, federal and provincial Social Services Ministers released their *Governance and Accountability Framework*, which committed the federal and provincial/territorial governments to the objectives and operating principles of the NCB. Essentially, this was the intergovernmental agreement for the operation of the program. According to the framework, Ministers Responsible for Social Services would "constitute the principal mechanism for governance of the National Child Benefit." The ministers would provide overall strategic policy directions for the program at the national level; monitor and assess all aspects of implementation; identify areas of potential concern and seek solutions; and adjudicate and resolve disputes where required. Social Service Deputy Ministers were delegated responsibility for general management, implementation and operation of the program (F/P/T Ministers Responsible for Social Services, 1998a, 1998b). The ministers also released a paper, *Approaches to Measuring and Reporting on Results*, and committed to reporting annually on the NCB performance, with the first report to be released by the end of 1998. Through regular public reporting, governments would provide information on complementary investments and would develop ways to measure the impact of the NCB on reducing child poverty and increasing labour force attachment (F/P/T Ministers Responsible for Social Services, 1998b).

On June 18, 1998, federal and provincial Ministers Responsible for Social Services, in a coordinated communications strategy, announced the launch of the new National Child Benefit as a collective initiative to help reduce the depth of child poverty and promote employment for all lower income families (Canada, Press Release, June 18, 1998; Brennan, 1998). Considerable emphasis was placed on both the poverty reduction and employment enhancement aspects of the program. For example, a *Globe and Mail* commentary entitled *Tearing down Canada's "welfare wall"* noted that the goals of the new initiative were to "increase the money available for children in poor families and break down the welfare wall that stops many parents from accepting jobs because they would lose benefits for their children" (Greenspon, 1998). Special note was also taken of the high degree of federal-provincial cooperation involved in developing the program (Brennan, 1998).

Once the design of the NCB became public, substantial concern was expressed about the benefit structure. In particular, the reduction in provincial social assistance that resulted from increased federal benefits was sharply criticized by child advocacy organizations, anti-poverty groups and other community organizations. It was argued that, as a result of the "provincial claw-back" of benefits, social assistance recipients would not benefit from the new program. Advocates of the NCB responded that these critics did not understand the concept of the "welfare wall" and would not accept that low-income families could have less access to resources than families on welfare. Advocates also argued that income-tested child benefits are more likely than needs-tested welfare to improve the well being of children and families. They noted that, for most welfare families, social assistance was a temporary situation providing short-term relief, and that, over any significant period of time, virtually all low-income families with children would benefit from the increased federal and provincial/territorial benefits available through the NCB program (Battle and Mendelson, 1999).

In June and November 1998, HRDC hosted meetings of the National Child Benefit Reference Group, whose members included prominent representatives of the Caledon Institute, Campaign 2000, Canadian Council on Social Development, Child Poverty Action Group, National Anti-Poverty Action Group and National Council of Welfare. At the second meeting the group discussed plans for "Phase 2" of NCB implementation, including issues such as benefit structure, indexation, welfare reductions, poverty measures and communications (HRDC, 1998).

At the July 2–4, 1998, Western Premiers' Conference, Premiers called for full implementation of the National Child Benefit by the year 2000 and proposed additional federal investments of $850 million in 1999 and 2000 and additional provincial re-investments of $500 million these years (WPC, 1998). At the August 5–7, 1998, Annual Premiers' Conference, Premiers reiterated their agreement to cooperate in planning the NCB second phase contributions and ensuring that related federal, provincial and territorial programs would be complementary and effective. They expressed their support for full implementation of the program and noted that "future commitment to the National Child Benefit will be required to fully accomplish its major objectives and support families with children outside the welfare system" (APC, 1998a).

The momentum for full implementation of the NCB was growing.

Premiers had proposed a strategy for fully implementing the program and increasing benefits to a level that would remove children from welfare. The federal government was committed to periodic increases in the CCTB and in the 1998 budget had announced $850 million for implementing the second phase of the program. Once committed, federal officials sought to build on public support for government initiatives to address child poverty. Notably, in an address to a Liberal fundraising event in November 1998, Finance Minister Martin was quoted as saying that child poverty in Canada was "a national disgrace" and that "We should essentially establish the elimination of child poverty as a great national objective" (Stewart, 1998). The popularity of the NCB had become apparent and governments were interested in acknowledging their involvement.

The National Child Benefit was a remarkable achievement and its contribution to the Canadian social policy fabric is widely acknowledged. Perhaps the essential elements of the National Child Benefit are succinctly reflected in the following observation:

> The Canada Child Tax Benefit is a policy masterstroke: it makes a huge dent into child poverty; it encourages labour force attachment because it converts the children's component of welfare into a negative income tax; it respects the provinces since they are free to re-allocate equivalent welfare monies into priorities relating to children in working poor families; and it streamlines policy roles since Ottawa now looks after the kids and the elderly, leaving the provinces to design integrated programs for dealing with adults. (Courchene, 2004: 34).

Reflections

Rick August

Rick August has been a Saskatchewan representative to the National Child Benefit develop-ment and management process since 1996, and co-chairs the NCB sub-committee on policy and program analysis. He is currently executive director of strategic policy for Saskatchewan's Department of Community Resources and Employment.

Canada is a country where peoples' economic and social values are gener-ally both liberal and compassionate. Citizens expect the state to provide them with a high degree of social protection, but without unduly distorting or restricting the functions of a market economy. This is one of the basic challenges of this country's social policy development.

The National Child Benefit has to do with family Income Security Reform, an area where my province, Saskatchewan, had maintained a de-gree of interest over the years based on program reform experience of the 1970s. The province's experiments with employment-friendly child benefits lost steam over time because the expected national consensus for reform did not materialize. As time passed, however, the problems that motivated change in the 1970s became more pressing. By the early 1990s there was renewed interest, in Saskatchewan and elsewhere, in revisiting structural reform of family benefits.

I was assigned to work on the family income security file in 1992 by our deputy minister at the time, Con Hnatiuk. In the period that followed, while the Axworthy social security review came and went, Saskatchewan made several unsuccessful attempts to create room in the existing federal/provincial cost-sharing relationship for a new income-tested child benefit that would replace children's basic welfare.

Probably for good reason, the federal government was unwilling to embrace a bilateral approach, in the absence of any real consensus on a countrywide direction. Given the effectively divided constitutional jurisdic-tion over social policy, it is difficult for the country to change direction in a meaningful way without this consensus. The consensus that would facilitate the NCB reforms was in fact created, however, and under curious circum-stances, since the initiative came so close on the heels of major government spending cuts in the first half of the 1990s. Reflecting on it now, however, the chain of events makes some sense.

When the country began experiencing economic disruptions in the early 1970s these were interpreted as cyclical events, rather than stages in a longer-term restructuring trend towards globalization. Canadian governments responded with counter-cyclical spending strategies in the 1970s and 1980s, but as the cycles became a trend, they found themselves in untenable debt and deficit positions by the early 1990s. Both provincial and federal governments made deep spending cuts, culminating in the federal budget of 1995. That budget, among other things, buried the last symbol of the old income security order, the Canada Assistance Plan. It also left a vacuum in federal/provincial relations, in a political environment where the public had lost tolerance for intergovernmental squabbling. Circumstance, in this rare instance, favoured a new and more cooperative approach.

While the need for change is easily recognized, accomplishing it is another matter. All status quo situations create vested interests whose opposition to change, being very focused, often overwhelms the more diffuse forces in favour of change. It seems to take some unusual event, circumstance or crisis to provide a motive for change strong enough to overcome resistance and obstacles.

Looking back on the history of Canadian social policy, the Great Depression of the 1930s was one of the critical periods. The Depression led to recognition of social risks from forces beyond the control of the individual. World War II raised consciousness about social justice issues and produced our first major national social security programs, Unemployment Insurance and Family Allowance.

The reforms of the late 1960s and early 1970s, on the other hand, were built on a "crisis of prosperity." After two decades of growth, a social security system was developed that assumed a healthy economy, full employment and stable, traditional social relations. None of these assumptions would stand up for long, since two large forces were at work, one social and the other economic. On the one hand, from the late 1960s forward, the status of women was changing at an unprecedented pace, displacing traditional family norms in ways that we are still struggling to comprehend and absorb in public policy. On the economic side, the international oil crises of the 1970s were the first indicators that a change process was underway that would make the borders of national economies more permeable and would substantially modify Canadian labour markets and the way citizens relate to them.

The Social Security Review of the 1970s, had it been more successful, might have helped social policy to change along with economic and social trends. The review's income security proposals of that era were clearly based on structural thinking about the relationship between income security and work. These proposals disappeared, however, into the relative intergovernmental chaos of the late 1970s, and social policy debate descended into two decades of extremely unconstructive struggles over welfare policy — should its benefits be higher or lower, harder or easier to get, etc.

Fiddling while Rome burned, as it were. Canadian social security was notionally built on a "never again" perspective on the Depression, a time when advanced countries allowed their citizens to suffer from events far beyond their control. Policy neglect of labour market and family trends in the last quarter of the twentieth century was reproducing the extent, if not the degree, of marginalization of the 1930s. The background papers for the Rowell-Sirois Commission provide sufficient data to construct a "relief" dependency ratio roughly comparable to modern welfare dependency concepts. Comparing 1994 and 1935, dependency rates were identical at 11 percent of the population, even without adjusting for modern pensions, Medicare, etc.

While the public debate in the first half of the 1990s was about the growth and persistence of child poverty, in fact children were "collateral damage" in the economic marginalization of their parents. Worse, as economic indicators began to improve towards the mid-1990s, welfare numbers did not drop. The evidence was strong of a structural shift in the relationship of lower-skilled adults to the labour force. The impacts were more extreme for adults with dependents, and most extreme for single parents, who represented the majority of the new welfare poor. The policy challenge that was taken up in the NCB initiative can be set in fairly simple terms. For parents with relatively low employment skill levels, market earnings potential was declining relative to *de facto* subsistence standards, as represented by social assistance rates. The results included rising welfare utilization, high dependency costs to the public, ongoing family poverty and poor human resource utilization.

The tension between needs and market wages has been understood for a long time, as a quick reference to Beveridge or Marsh will indicate. This problem is not easily resolved by direct policy levers like minimum wage, since forcing minimum wages up to accommodate family needs may suppress employment and certainly provides the childless with an undeserved windfall. At any rate, such direct intervention by government in micro-economic relations is less acceptable as an approach to problem-solving than it used to be. The employment contract is basically about productivity, and there are significant economic risks to trying to solve broad social problems at the enterprise level. Governments still certainly do have the consent of the public, however, to make equity adjustments at the societal level. I would view the NCB, both in respect of benefits and services, to be such an equity adjustment.

The NCB uses benefits and services to support work, which I would argue is more important than its more direct or immediate impacts. The federal benefit supports children's needs, regardless of parents' labour force status. This equalizes living standards per unit wage between parents and others and removes the draw towards welfare to access child benefits. The provincial and territorial NCB reinvestments have improved services that support employment as a potential path out of poverty. The success of this strategy needs to be established empirically, and it is far too early to do that with certainty. Beyond anti-poverty effects, however, the NCB is an example of a coherent structural approach to a problem of family income, as well as an approach that takes into account the energies and resources of people in the process of improving economic and social outcomes for citizens.

In policy and governance circles, people still muse upon why the NCB came about and why it has been so difficult to reproduce. Unfortunately, it's still rare to find circumstances where governments have strategic agreement on both the nature of a problem and approaches to solutions. With the NCB, for a brief period of time and under very specific circumstances, most of the people with the power and capacity to make the initiative happen thought it should be done.

Some of the criticisms of the NCB have served to obscure the scale of its achievement. Decades ago, Canada set out to eradicate seniors' poverty using a variety of policy levers, including very large transfer programs. Without belittling the reform process, governments attempting to address seniors' poverty can deploy relatively straightforward measures like generous income guarantees, since seniors, by broad social consensus, are considered outside the work force. The reforms launched in the 1960s in Canada for seniors worked. There are now few poor seniors and fewer still in deep (welfare-level) poverty.

Poor children, however, live with poor parents, and the history of even meagre welfare guarantees demonstrates the risk of this approach relative to work effort of adult members of families. The national benefit system constructed within the NCB and many of the related provincial/territorial reinvestment programs are a means to place resources in the hands of working-age parents for their children's needs, in a manner that is neutral to modestly positive with respect to parents' economic behaviour. This is no small matter, because it means that when the NCB benefit system is notionally mature, Canada will have a "children's guaranteed annual income" program.

Having secured the economic interests of children independent of their parents' behaviour, it becomes more feasible to reconsider, at a fundamental level, the workings of income security systems for adults in Canada. The present jurisdictional divide, for example, between Unemployment Insurance and social assistance makes less sense in a world where the federal benefit is less and less related to premiums paid and as both federal and provincial/territorial service systems focus more specifically on employment outcomes. It has been observed that there is only one taxpayer, not a separate one for federal and provincial governments. Compartmentalizing benefits and services to citizens between governments makes no more sense than pretending federal and provincial tax revenues come from different pockets.

There were also lessons for me in the *process* of doing the NCB. An atmosphere of bitterness and mistrust prevailed in federal/provincial relations of the early 1990s, and social policy development was largely isolated within provincial jurisdictions. Over the course of about a year's interaction in NCB contexts, that began to change, at least around the children's file. Levels of horizontal structure were created across governments that reached from mid-level officials to ministers, each with a mandate and commitment to make the initiative take shape and produce results for families.

For the most part, it worked remarkably well, particularly in the formative years of the initiative. The consensus model imposed a kind of moral discipline I have not seen elsewhere in government processes. Instead of the usual self-contained policy process within governments, analysis was conducted jointly and positions tested against many other perspectives. Not too surprisingly, better public policy resulted. Relationships were occasionally tested by politics, but the officials within the group almost uniformly defended the integrity of the process.

This is not to say that the process was neat, but consensus does not have to be neat to be effective. Despite its lack of symmetry, the NCB has a core national program and a degree of overall consistency in its employment-based approach to child and family poverty. Evaluation of this type of complex initiative is difficult, but I hope the effort continues to build the evidence base around NCB and related programs. Social policy is a young behavioural science that could certainly benefit from less reliance on ideology and anecdotalism.

Will the NCB phenomenon happen again? Signals so far are that the NCB and the Social Union Framework Agreement — an attempt to institutionalize the NCB relationship — have not entrenched the idea of strategic partnership among governments. True collaboration and partnership means joint definition of problems and strategic agreement on proposed solutions. We've seen no parallels since the NCB of major issues coming forward from multilateral bodies for joint analysis and action, but have since experienced several social policy initiatives defined and directed by the federal government, generally to the detriment of good policy outcomes.

This is unfortunate to say the least. Most citizens do not really appreciate the "zero-sum" aspects of social policy development — the extent to which a decision to follow expedient or ideological courses, by committing public resources to questionable actions, effectively precludes implementation of better policy, at least for many years to come. For me, the NCB proved the value of honest, open collaboration in development of social policy that is more coherent, outcomes-based and sustainable than what we have now. Let's hope it does not take another fiscal crisis or other inescapable threat to the *status quo* to reproduce the NCB approach to policy development.

John Stapleton

John Stapleton was manager of Operational Policy and manager of Special Projects in the Social Assistance Programs Branch in Ontario's Ministry of Community and Social Services from 1994 to 1999. John was a member of the National Child Benefit Working Group (and several related subgroups) from 1997 to 2002. He is currently the director of research for a project to modernize income security, undertaken by the Toronto City Summit Alliance and St. Christopher House in Toronto.

In the early summer of 1986, the Social Assistance Review Committee had its first working meeting. The chair, George Thomson, asked committee members to voice their principal concern with the social assistance system as it then existed in Ontario. When it came to her turn, Alderman Ruth Wildgen from Ottawa said something to the effect that although she could see why the welfare system took away a lone parent's part of the benefit once s(he) started to realize non-welfare income, she believed it to be most unfair that the welfare system also took away the children's portion of the allowance. Going around the table, other committee members stressed other issues like the importance of making the welfare system smaller.

With the problems voiced in this way, our research team set out to see how we could respond to these seemingly unconnected concerns. We realized quickly that in order to solve the first issue, we would have to devise different rules for the children's portion of a social assistance benefit but if we designed a benefit that kept the benefit part of the welfare system, the size of the social assistance system would undoubtedly grow. However, if we took the child benefit "out of welfare," the overall social assistance system would become smaller.

From these beginnings, the vision incorporated into *Transitions: Report of the Social Assistance Review* called for a National Child Benefit that would be retained while a welfare recipient earned their way off the system and would be equally available to low income workers with children who were not in the welfare system. We knew if a National Child Benefit came into being that was sufficiently high to supplant social assistance, it would follow that at some point in time, a reduction in social assistance would have to take place.

In July 1998, almost ten years after *Transitions* was published, the National Child Benefit Supplement (NCBS) was implemented consistent with the "recovery reinvestment" model agreed to by provincial, territorial and federal authorities. At that time, most if not all members of the NCB Working Group believed that the "recovery reinvestment" model was a temporary measure that awaited completion of federal contributions to the NCBS and broad-range welfare restructuring exercises to be conducted by provinces and territories.

In the meantime in Ontario, we had quickly realized that the only way to implement the (temporary) social assistance offset was to treat the NCBS as an unearned income charge. Facing Y2K concerns and separate computer systems in Toronto and the rest of the province, we did not have time to deliver a responsiveness effort on behalf of those recipients with higher previous year income. This would have been especially problematic had we implemented a rate decrease to satisfy the general agreement to offset social assistance. This approach of treating the NCBS as an unearned income charge became known as the "NCBS clawback" and remains in place in several jurisdictions.

Turning to the situation we have today, the acid test for completion of the NCB initiative remains simple. The federal government should be able to consolidate the CCTB into one child benefit for all Canadian families with children, and this change ought to have no effect on (restructured) social assistance systems in provinces and territories. Reinvestments should be also stabilized and properly funded in order to make the claim of completion of the NCB initiative.

Yet it is now 2005 and we continue to await the completion of the NCB initiative and the end to the clawback. Although Newfoundland and Nova Scotia would have no trouble, all other jurisdictions would have various levels of difficulty if the federal government announced an intent to move to a unitary child benefit. I suspect that it would be comparatively easy to resolve in Quebec, Saskatchewan and British Columbia but much more difficult in Ontario.

One of the key reasons for the delay in completion is that in February 2003, the previous federal Finance Minister John Manley asked provinces and territories to "pass on" all of the scheduled benefits to the NCBS through to 2007 to recipients of social assistance. Pressured by members of his own caucus and others, Manley chose to call for the eradication and the growth of the welfare wall at the same time and got away with it. In effect, he asked provinces to fund their own restructuring exercises and cap their reinvestments in favour of all future increases going to all poor families with children, with no distinction to be made between social assistance families and others. With the temporary recovery-reinvestment approach already long in the tooth and under attack, it is not surprising that all provinces (by 2004) complied with the Manley request. Mr. Goodale, in the intervening period, has made no adjustments to Mr. Manley's policies on the NCB.

However, the result is that we now have two National Child Benefit Supplements — the one to be clawed back and the one to be left alone — and one CTB — in effect, a three-part child benefit that few understand. This three part structure has almost certainly slowed the progress required to complete the National Child Benefit initiative at the federal level and to implement restructured welfare systems in all provincial and territorial jurisdictions.

Given both the real and symbolic importance of the NCB initiative as a true example of cooperative federalism in an area where it has been noticeably absent, it is important for provinces and territories to meet with the federal government to break the logjam to complete the job they started in 1998. With the will to succeed and modest funding, provinces, territories, and the federal governments could once again meet the high standards set through the cooperative implementation of the NCB in 1998 and provide the NCB initiative with the unambiguously excellent reputation that it deserves.

Barbra Senchuk

Barbara Senchuk was the director of operations in federal-provincial relations with HRDC from 1996 to 2000. She is currently senior advisor with the Aboriginal Affairs Secretariat, Privy Council Office, Government of Canada.

I was taking graduate courses in political science in 1996–97 when the agreement on the National Child Benefit was reached between federal and provincial/territorial governments. It seemed an obvious choice to write a paper on the NCB and speculate on the reasons for its success. In it I described seven or eight winning attributes, listing everything from the fiscal and political realities at that time to the lead federal minister's considerable charm. Many of these attributes have since been studied in detail and documented as "best practices" in federal/provincial/territorial relations. Eight years later, two stand out in my memory: the commitment and creativity of officials in pushing the envelope in an important policy area and the determination of all governments to see success in the federal-provincial/territorial arena.

I was director of operations in federal/provincial relations in HRDC when work started on the NCB. Mine was not the hands-on involvement of Margaret Biggs or Marta Morgan on the NCB Working Group; my role was intelligence gathering and occasionally trouble shooting as well as coordinating federal/provincial/territorial deputy ministers' and ministers' meetings, of which there were many in the fall and winter of 1996–97. We were a small, closely knit, interdependent team in daily contact with an equally dedicated group of officials in provincial and territorial governments.

I remember well our first meeting with provincial/territorial officials. It was September 1996. We met in a small boardroom at Queen's Park. First Ministers had agreed in June that the two orders of government should work together to develop a child benefit, and a meeting of ministers had been held earlier in September to mark its launch and task officials to develop a national initiative.

Our Assistant Deputy Minister, Jim Lahey, was the lead HRDC official at the September meeting, and British Columbia official Ken Armour led for the provinces and territories. It was as I recall a remarkably convivial and productive discussion. The tone was set by the two lead officials. Both had an easy manner and an inclination to candour. Throughout the day's discussion, I was struck not by the differences between the two orders of government, which I had expected to see, but the commonality of objectives and purpose and the apparent ease with which officials on both sides reached preliminary agreement on a joint process to take forward to deputy ministers. Prior to this meeting, and before the June First Ministers Meeting, there had been considerable work done on a children's benefit both federally, as part of the Social Security Review, and among provincial and territorial governments. This early work was important in the relatively rapid development of the NCB. But the mutually respectful working relationship among officials set at this opening meeting, and sustained by Margaret Biggs and Ken Armour and other lead provincial/territorial officials in the NCB Working Group, played a hugely significant role in moving this work forward.

I remember the deliberate way in which officials set about defining objectives and principles and agreeing on a work plan. Establishing common objectives and obtaining early agreement on them before moving ahead seemed obvious at the time. Yet I have seen many federal-provincial/territorial initiatives stall or flounder because this step was skipped, or agreement on basic objectives could not be reached, or one order of government decided to act on its own.

The second chief attribute that distinguished this process in my view was the determination of those involved to show that governments *could* work together to develop a successful national program. The NCB happened following a particularly fractious period in federal-provincial/territorial relations and a close call in the first Quebec referendum. Officials and politicians dug deep to make the NCB work. Provincial and territorial governments banded together in a move that initially troubled the federal side but proved to help maintain focus and unity at the federal-provincial/territorial table. That the lead federal minister was a Quebecer and naturally disposed to be respectful of provincial/territorial sensitivities helped. Pierre Pettigrew was the right minister to strike a federal-provincial/territorial deal and achieve ministerial consensus in the hectic run up to the 1997 federal budget and the first announcement of funding for the NCB.

For these reasons and others, the NCB earned the distinction of being a model federal-provincial/territorial process. It is true that the NCB was blessed in that there was federal money to invest. It also had an objective that everyone could get behind and no one could fault — helping to bring children out of poverty. But what stands out in my memory is that it was supported by a group of officials and ministers who brought to the process an unprecedented combination of pragmatism, determination and leadership.

The NCB was my first experience of a federal-provincial/territorial initiative. There have been many others since then but none approaching the success of the NCB process. In most cases I have known, progress is glacial, with the two orders of government battling over jurisdiction and bogged down in disagreement over roles and responsibilities. This despite ongoing public polling that shows Canadians are fed up with governments' inability to work together.

These experiences notwithstanding, I continue to believe — because the NCB proved it's possible — that two orders of government can work together to their mutual benefit and the benefit of all Canadians.

Ken Battle

Ken Battle is the president of the Caledon Institute of Social Policy, which he founded in 1992.

No social policy reform as complex and significant as the National Child Benefit could have been achieved without the combined efforts of numerous dedicated people — many of them unnamed federal and provincial/territorial officials whose contributions typically go uncredited. Nor could the initiative have emerged without the support and commitment of key "political champions," notably the federal Minister of Finance (Paul Martin), the Minister of Human Resources Development (Doug Young and his successor Pierre Pettigrew) and their provincial/territorial counterparts, among whom then Saskatchewan Premier Roy Romanow was a leading proponent. The Caledon Institute of Social Policy played a key and unique role as an independent think tank working on the NCB both inside and outside government, as documented in a paper for the Policy Research Institute's journal *Horizons* (Battle, 2003a).

The NCB was launched by the federal and provincial/territorial governments over a relatively short period — albeit its implementation took longer than one ideally would have liked, frustrating anti-poverty groups and contributing to their widespread misunderstanding/rejection of its purposes and impact. But the reform — touted as the most important advance in Canadian social policy since Medicare — in fact was developed over many years through many changes to child benefits. Also important to the NCB's gestation were ideas that were not implemented but nonetheless advanced thinking on reform. A notable example is the Ontario proposal for an integrated child benefit, put forward in the 1988 *Transitions* report on welfare and subsequently designed into the Ontario Child Income Plan, which that the NDP government of Bob Rae was forced to shelve because of financial constraint (due in part to cuts to federal social transfers). So the NCB had several "architects" and "builders" working at different times over the years. Indeed, one can go at least as far back as Leonard Marsh's landmark 1943 report, which sketched architecture for a modern social security system for Canada — only part of which was built — with a prominent place for what we today would call an integrated child benefit, the essential design of the NCB.

The NCB's remarkable and rare achievement goes beyond establishing the platform on which to build a strong system of child benefits. It also offers some useful and, hopefully, applicable lessons and insights for other public policy reforms. Elsewhere I discuss some of these lessons as well as the future of the NCB, which we at Caledon regard as a crucial but temporary stage in constructing an adequate child benefit. Bill Warriner asked me to reflect briefly here upon my roles and experience in the National Child Benefit: I'll mention some of my main contributions in policy conceptualization and "selling" the reform.

I am fortunate to have been one of the chief architects of the NCB and its longest-serving proponent, having worked on both its policy and political development since the early 1980s, when I was director of the National Council of Welfare, a citizens' advisory body to the Minister of National Health and Welfare (now Social Development). To my knowledge I was the first person in the NGO social policy community to break from universalist orthodoxy and advocate integrating the child benefit programs of the day into a single, fully indexed, refundable credit in which the amount of benefits would be geared to family income but coverage of benefits would be broad-based, serving the low- and middle-income majority of Canadian families. In 1993, that vision was realized when the federal government integrated Family Allowances, the Refundable Child Tax Credit and the nonrefundable Child Tax Credit into the Child Tax Benefit.

I designed and costed the first ever proposal for a national, integrated child benefit in a 1991 senate report on child poverty (Battle, 1991). Using the "welfare wall" imagery (of which more below), which later was adopted by governments for the National Child Benefit reform, I proposed a costed design for a National Child Benefit in a 1995 Caledon report co-authored with Leon Muszynski (Battle and Muszynski, 1995). With Sherri Torjman, vice-president of Caledon, I wrote a think piece on social policy reform for the incoming (and first) Minister of Human Resources Development Canada, Lloyd Axworthy, that proposed a framework for comprehensive social security reform with an integrated child benefit as a key element (Battle and Torjman, 1993). Later I succeeded in putting child benefit reform (including an integrated benefit) full-square on the policy table when I served as a member of Minister Axworthy's Task Force on Social Security Reform and also worked on its final report (the so-called Green Paper) and supporting paper on child benefit reform (HRDC, 1994a, 1995).

My most influential role came as policy advisor to the federal Minister of Human Resources Development in 1996 and 1997. I wrote the internal report making the case for the National Child Benefit (*Do the Right Thing: The Case for a National Child Benefit*) and defended the paper in a spirited one-on-one discussion one Sunday morning with Finance Minister Martin — who, characteristically, had read and absorbed the entire document. With Human Resources Development Minister Pettigrew and Deputy Minister Mel Cappe, I presented the NCB proposal to a Cabinet committee on social development; helped HRDC officials make the case with Finance for a sufficient "down payment" on the NCB announced in the 1997 Budget; and wrote the initial draft of the budget document launching the NCB (Department of Finance Canada, 1997). I also served as a member of the NCB Working Group of federal/provincial/territorial officials in its early months. The working group was crucial to the reform because it had the tough task of translating the budget proposals into action. Its federal and provincial co-chairs (originally Margaret Biggs from Canada and Ken Armour from B.C.), and its other members, deserve enormous credit for their commitment, tenacity, expertise and hard work.

What I would characterize as "informal policy coalitions" were crucial to the creation and implementation of the NCB. These were informal and morphing groups — mainly federal and provincial/territorial politicians, political aides and government officials, with the odd outsider like me brought temporarily "inside the tent" — that worked in various ways at different stages to advance the cause of child benefit reform. The informal policy coalition in which I participated in Ottawa during my time as policy advisor to the Minister of HRDC included Ministers Young and Pettigrew, senior officials Mel Cappe, Jim Lahey and Margaret Biggs (among others) from HRDC, Alex Himelfarb from the Privy Council Office, and political aides Terri O'Leary and Ruth Thorkelson from Finance and on occasion Eddie Goldenberg from the Prime Minister's Office.

I was especially fortunate to be one of the outside experts that Finance Minister Martin "reached out to" for advice. I had first established credibility with Martin when I advised him and his officials on the proposed seniors benefit — an idea that I had proposed in a 1993 Caledon piece, *Thinking the Unthinkable: A Targeted, Not Universal, Old Age Pension*. Sadly, the seniors benefit ended up in the dustbin of Canadian public policy history, with lower-income seniors the losers — but that is a story for another place (see Battle, 2003b for one account). I think my *Do the Right Thing* report and subsequent communications with Martin helped garner his support for the NCB — without which the initiative never would have seen the light of day.

Initially Martin was understandably leery about embarking on a reform that would require working hand in glove with the provinces, but the NCB succeeded in embodying a welcome and major advance in a new style of federalism. The NCB is probably the most successful social policy application to date of the emerging philosophy of "collaborative federalism" (aka "handshake" or "framework" or "SUFA" federalism) in which the federal and provincial/territorial governments work closely together as equals to pursue policy objectives that neither can achieve alone (Torjman, 1997).

Framework federalism requires a clear and sound policy rationale that can garner broad consensus across the political spectrum. The NCB is one of the rare reforms in the history of Canadian public policy that sold itself to governments of all political stripes and hues by virtue of the logic of its substantive policy rationale — which is one, to break down the welfare wall that looms in front of families moving from welfare to work; two, to provide a secure, fully indexed, portable and non-stigmatizing benefit that treats all low-income families equally and includes them in a social program that serves the vast majority of families with children, poor and non-poor alike; and three, to help reduce the depth of child poverty

At the heart of the policy rationale for the National Child Benefit is the concept of "welfare wall," coined by Caledon and adopted by the federal and provincial/territorial governments. Under the old system, families on welfare received child benefits from two sources — provincial/territorial welfare payments on behalf of their children, and the federal Child Tax Benefit — while other low-income families (e.g., the working poor and those on EI) got federal child benefits only. As a result, welfare families on average received about double the amount of child benefits as other poor families with children. Families that managed to move from welfare into the work force encountered the "welfare wall": They lost thousands of dollars in provincial/territorial child benefits and, often, in-kind benefits (e.g., supplementary health care) at the very time that they saw their (typically low) earnings reduced by income and payroll taxes and stretched by work-related expenses such as child care, clothing and transportation. By equalizing child benefits among all low-income families and disembedding child benefits from social assistance, the NCB sought to remove a major part of the welfare wall. Thus the change from the Child Tax Benefit to the Canada Child Tax Benefit involved not only boosting maximum benefits but also delivering equal payments to all low-income families, regardless of their other source(s) of income.

But that process of equalizing child benefits among all low-income families generated the reform's chief criticism, which came from anti-poverty and social advocacy groups, the NDP and the left generally. Social assistance families in most jurisdictions did not receive an increase in their net child benefits while the NCB was being implemented; rather they saw an increase only in the proportion coming from the federal CCTB and provincial/territorial income-tested child benefits, with a concomitant decline in the share from child benefits embedded in provincial/territorial social assistance. Only the working poor, EI poor and other low-income families not on social assistance enjoyed an increase in their child benefits — to bring them *up to* the child benefits level of families on welfare. But the welfare wall rationale, with its criticisms of the two-tier child benefits system under the *status quo* (i.e., welfare families got double the child benefits of other low-income families) was ignored by social advocacy groups and not grasped by most politicians and journalists. To add fuel to the critics' fire, the NCB — touted by its supporters as a key advance in anti-poverty strategy — arrived after years of overt and/or covert cuts to social assistance benefits that had shrunk families' income and amidst increasing efforts on the part of most provinces to require recipients to enter the work force (e.g., workfare and tightening eligibility rules in many provinces).

A key issue here is strategy: If Ottawa had gone with a big-bang approach (as proposed in the 1995 Caledon report, *One Way to Fight Child Poverty*) rather than an incremental, multi-year phased-in approach, and put enough money on the table at the outset, it could not only have displaced social assistance-delivered child benefits almost immediately but also could have raised the level of the new CCTB high enough to exceed the previous amount of combined federal and provincial/territorial child benefits payable to families on welfare. While welfare families still would have seen a smaller net increase in child benefits than the working poor, at least the former would have been better off financially than before. As well, the idea that one type of benefit was simply replacing another would have been apparent and easily explained. The incremental strategy adopted instead has been a contributing factor to the never-ending criticism of the NCB from social advocates.

True "architectural" reform in public policy takes a lot of time, effort and commitment in the face of often-formidable obstacles and controversy. It is typically undertaken through a lengthy and not always linear process of "relentless incrementalism" (Battle, 2001). A relevant personal example nicely illustrates this point. I was thirty-one years old when I started working on what eventually became the NCB and fifty when it was announced in 1997.

At the age of fifty-seven, I am still working on the NCB (with my Caledon colleague Michael Mendelson) to advance it from its stage as an *integrated* child benefit, which has been largely achieved, to an *adequate* child benefit, which would meet the cost of raising children in low-income families (see Mendelson, 2005) and also improve financial support to modest and middle-income families with children.

Looking back on my three decades-long career, it seems miraculous that the NCB reform was achieved. Such "deep structural" change in public policy is incredibly difficult to make, requiring advances in both political and policy architecture — especially a reform whose scope and substance is national, not just federal, nor just provincial/territorial. When as his newly named policy advisor I first pitched the idea of the NCB to HRDC Minister Young, I told him that "the stars were in alignment." Incredibly, that turned out to be the case.

Note

1. For a full explanation, see Stapleton, 2004.

Chapter Six

National Children's Agenda

The federal, provincial and territorial governments agreed to work together to establish the National Children's Agenda — a long-term strategy with the objective of ensuring that all children have the resources and capacities they need to be ready to learn when they begin school, and to ensure that children have every opportunity to live happy and satisfying lives. (Chrétien, 1997: 1)

Development of the National Children's Agenda

The National Children's Agenda was not part of the initial Social Policy Renewal initiative. It was not identified as a specific recommendation in the 1995 Report on Social Policy Reform and Renewal, nor was it identified as an objective in the 1996 paper, *Next Steps*. Nevertheless, there had been significant discussions about the need for a comprehensive and integrated approach to child welfare that would complement child benefits with services such as early childhood development, child care and supplemental health services. The National Children's Agenda emerged as a pan-Canadian initiative to improve and coordinate programs and services to enhance childhood development.

A notable influence was the widely-known and promoted work of Dr. Fraser Mustard on population health and early intervention and prevention. On September 22, 1995, Dr. Mustard made a presentation at a meeting of provincial/territorial Ministers of Social Services that presentation stressed the importance of early childhood development in respect of both physio-neurological and socio-economic benefits. The Ministers were supportive of the principle advanced by Dr. Mustard, that "a nation's children should have first call on the nation's resources, in good times and in bad" (Saskatchewan Report on the meeting of Social Services Ministers, September 30, 1995). They agreed that "social services programs must give priority to the well-being of children and families" and that they would "explore a more holistic approach to the wellbeing of children and families including health, education and social needs" (Social Service Ministers' Communiqué, September 22, 1995).

Research and experience indicated that a public policy approach to addressing the complex process of improving the health and well being of children and their families would require a broad-based, multisectoral strategy. Social Services and Health officials concluded that a comprehensive and integrated approach to child welfare that provided services, such as child care and supplemental health services, would be a useful complement to the income support provided by the NCB. In April 1996, Social Services Ministers requested that welfare officials identify "shared priority issues" that could be addressed through joint action. In June 1996, the *Report on Child Welfare* identified priorities for collaborative action by federal and provincial governments. In particular, the report recommended that Social Services Ministers "propose the development of a national children's agenda which would incorporate key initiatives from the Social Services sector and reach out to other sectors (Health, Education, Culture, Recreation, Housing, Income Security and Justice) to incorporate their initiatives and strategies, and would involve the federal government and community groups and agencies." The report also suggested that a National Children's Agenda could provide a framework for government and community actions to improve the well being of Canada's children; provide a basis for coordinated and integrated efforts and partnerships among the sectors that share responsibility for services to children; increase the profile of social services issues in other sectors and facilitate movement towards intersectoral approaches for these issues; and provide a communications focus on actions for children (Senior Provincial/Territorial Child Welfare Officials, 1996).

At their meeting of September 9–11, 1996, Ministers of Health released the *Report on the Health of Canadians*, which identified income, education and employment as key factors affecting health and noted that particular and urgent attention is required to address the problem of families and children living in poverty, particularly families headed by single women. The report concluded that Canada should put a high priority on implementing successful initiatives to address child poverty and that the promotion of health improvement and health equity would require a collaborative effort across sectors. The report stressed that fostering healthy child development was "one of the major challenges facing Canada and should be a major area for government action" (F/P/T Advisory Committee on Population Health, 1996).

At the September 16–17, meeting of Social Services Ministers, they called for development of a National Children's Agenda that would provide a policy framework to promote an integrated, intersectoral approach to policies and programs targeted to children. The Social Services Ministers forwarded the proposal to the P/T Council on Social Policy Renewal for further consideration. They also noted the conclusions of the Health Ministers' report and discussed the need for coordinated action (P/T Ministers Responsible for Social Services, 1996a; Aylward, 1996).

The federal government had also indicated its interest in maintaining and developing services for children that would complement the NCB. In particular, the federal Health Minister was an advocate for federal and provincial initiatives in support of services to children and had expressed the view that income support through such measures as the National Child Benefit was insufficient and must be supplemented by services to improve the health and well being of children. In November 1996, he wrote to provincial Ministers of Health to propose collaborative work on children's issues and to suggest that this matter be discussed at their next meeting. The letter referred to federal work being undertaken by the federal/provincial Advisory Committee on Population Health on a "National Strategy on Healthy Child Development" (F/P/T Social Services Officials, 1997c). There was already some degree of federal-provincial program coordination for children in that Health Canada funded program delivery and collaborated with provincial Health and Social Services Ministries in the administration of the Canada Action Plan for Children and the Canadian Prenatal Nutrition Program. In addition, officials from HRDC were particularly interested in maintaining or increasing the level of provincial services for children following any increase in the federal commitment toward the National Child Benefit (Saskatchewan, 1996b).

The P/T Council on Social Policy Renewal also developed a position in support of a national initiative to increase services for children. At the November 26, 1996, Council meeting, during a discussion on the NCB, the Ontario Minister expressed the view that services for children and families might be more appropriate than income supplementation. Other ministers responded that it would be useful to establish programs and services that would complement the NCB. The issue was further discussed the following day at the first meeting of the F/P/T Council on Social Policy Renewal. The Ministers noted that "tackling child poverty requires an approach involving both income support and child development services" (F/P/T Council on Social Policy Renewal, 1996).

At the December 17, 1996, meeting of federal and provincial Social Services Deputies, federal and provincial co-chairs agreed to begin discussions aimed at collaboration on the concept of a National Children's Agenda. It was proposed that these discussions initially involve Health and Social Services sectors and later be expanded to include other sectors such as education and justice (Record of Decisions, Meeting of Social Services Deputy Ministers, December, 1996).

By early 1997, Ministers of both Health and Social Services had observed the need to coordinate policies and services relating to the healthy development of children. At the January 28, 1997, meeting of provincial/territorial Ministers of Social Services, the Ministers directed their deputies to arrange a joint meeting of federal and provincial Ministers of Health and Social Services to explore the potential for a coordinated effort in the development of the National Children's Agenda (Saskatchewan, 1997b).

At the January 29, 1997, meeting of the F/P/T Council on Social Policy Renewal, the Ministers discussed plans to coordinate the work of Social Services and Health Ministries towards the development of a National Children's Agenda. The Council also received a presentation of the Health Ministers' document, *A Renewed Vision for Canada's Health System* (P/T Ministers of Health, 1997), and the federal Health Minister provided information on health reform issues, especially those related to services to children (F/P/T Council on Social Policy Renewal, 1997).

In February 1997, the federal/provincial/territorial National Children's Agenda Steering Committee of Health and Social Services Deputy Ministers and officials was established to develop a framework for a National Children's Agenda. The National Children's Agenda Steering Committee, sometimes referred to as the National Children's Agenda Working Group, was a unique structure that was both intergovernmental and cross-sectoral. The Steering Committee was co-chaired by the Assistant Deputy of Health Canada and the Saskatchewan Deputy Minister of Social Services. The committee structure and process was referred to as the "four-cornered approach" because it involved representation from federal and provincial departments of Social Services and Health (Saskatchewan Briefing Notes, 1997; P/T Ministers Responsible for Social Services, 1997; NCA Steering Committee, 1998a).

In April 1997, the federal and provincial Social Services Ministers reviewed preliminary work on a comprehensive National Children's Agenda, which would be developed in conjunction with Health Ministers (Social Services Ministers Communiqué, April 18, 1997). The proposed National Children's Agenda would provide a national policy framework to promote an intergovernmental and intersectoral approach to policies and programs targeted to children.

At the Western Premiers Conference in May of 1997, Saskatchewan reported on the status of the National Children's Agenda initiative and stressed the importance of early childhood care and development for social and economic well being. Premiers agreed that the National Children's Agenda provided an excellent opportunity for national collaboration on a comprehensive framework of initiatives to improve the health and well being of Canada's children. The Premiers also agreed that the National Children's Agenda would be a western priority at the 1997 Annual Premiers Conference (WPC, 1997).

The Liberal platform document for the June 1997 federal election referred positively to the federal-provincial collaboration on the National Children's Agenda and stated that a new Liberal government would be "committed to working in partnership with Canada's provincial and territorial governments to develop a National Children's Agenda" (Liberal Party of Canada, 996: 58–60).

The National Children's Agenda Steering Committee met on June 4, 1997, to discuss development of a policy framework and to consider principles and objectives for the National Children's Agenda. Representatives of the education and justice sectors also attended the meeting (P/T Ministers Responsible for Social Services, 1997).

In June 1997, the final report of the National Health Forum was released. The report noted that the period from birth to the age of six is critical and that "healthy development affects health and the capacity to participate fully as a citizen and be a productive member of society in later life." The Health Forum report recommended that "governments give priority to ensuring that families have access to such services [as high quality care and development] in early childhood" and that "different levels of government should work together to negotiate mutually agreeable solutions" (National Forum on Health, 1997).

On July 31, 1997, the chair of the P/T Social Service Ministers wrote to Premier Klein, as chair of the 1996 Premiers' Conference, to submit status reports on the National Child Benefit and National Children's Agenda. In the cover letter, the National Children's Agenda is referred to as "a cooperative initiative of both the social services and health sectors, federally and provincially, and responds to policy issues in both sectors that point to the need for a coordinated approach and an overarching strategic policy direction" (Bettney, 1997). The status report on the National Children's Agenda indicated that "a National Children's Agenda would focus on the development of a national policy framework for children's issues" and that it could "emphasize the development of a long term plan for achieving positive outcomes for Canadian children, establish common (F/P/T) priorities for action, provide a basis for coordinated and integrated efforts and partnerships among the sectors which share responsibility for services to children" (P/T Ministers Responsible for Social Services, 1997).

In August 1997 the National Children's Agenda Steering Committee completed several reports on the proposed agenda. These reports included *National Children's Agenda Framework* and *National Children's Agenda: Vision, Values and Principles*, which together developed the concept of the National Children's Agenda, identified areas of common interest and proposed a process for proceeding. The committee also prepared a report entitled *Beyond Governments*, which proposed a public dialogue to engage citizens in the process of developing the National Children's Agenda. The Steering Committee reports confirmed that improved early childhood care and development would require assessment, rationalization and stabilization of existing programs and services to serve as a base for development of a coordinated national strategy.

At the August 1997 Annual Premiers' Conference, Premiers expressed their support for the development of a National Children's Agenda as a priority initiative of the Social Policy Renewal agenda and as a complement to the NCB (APC, 1997).

The September 3, 1997, meeting of the National Children's Agenda Steering Committee saw general agreement around policy objectives for the National Children's Agenda, across jurisdictions and sectors. The Committee identified the following policy directions: enhanced early childhood development, intervening early for vulnerable children, supporting parents and families, strengthening income security for children, providing early and continuous learning experiences, supporting transition to adulthood and creating supportive, safe and violence-free communities (F/P/T Health Officials, 1997; F/P/T Social Services Officials, 1997c). The Committee also identified the following possible initiatives that could be included in a National Children's Agenda: optimizing early child development; family-friendly workplaces; partnerships for effective learning; healthy child development campaign; and an integrated justice system (F/P/T Health Officials, 1997).

On September 23, 1997, the federal throne speech expressed a commitment to work with the provincial governments in the development of a National Children's Agenda that would be a "comprehensive strategy to improve the well-being of Canada's children" (Speech from the Throne, 1997). Provincial Social Services Ministers and the Minister of HRDC reviewed progress on the National Children's Agenda at their meeting in October 6–7, 1997. Saskatchewan provided a report on the progress of the work of the National Children's Agenda Steering Committee. The Ministers agreed to prepare an up-dated status report for the F/P/T Council on Social Policy Renewal and the First Ministers (F/P/T Ministers Responsible for Social Services, 1997g).

At the First Ministers Meeting in December 1997, the Premiers and the Prime Minister reviewed the *Status Report on Work Toward a National Children's Agenda*, and agreed to "fast track work on the National Children's Agenda through the Ministerial Council on Social Policy Renewal" (FMM, 1997a).

At the January 19, 1998, meeting of the P/T Council on Social Policy Renewal, the provincial co-chair of the National Children's Agenda Steering Committee reported that the committee had completed or was continuing work on several documents, including an inventory of provincial and territorial programs for children in the health and social services sectors; a synthesis of selected Canadian research on children and families; a draft framework for the NCA; a proposal for engaging Canadians in the process of developing the NCA; and options for its governance (P/T Ministers Responsible for Social Services, 1998).

At the March 13, 1998, meeting of the F/P/T Council on Social Policy Renewal, the provincial co-chair of the National Children's Agenda Steering

Committee presented a draft framework for the NCA. The Ministers considered options for governing the process and agreed that the Council would provide direct oversight of the initiative (F/P/T Council on Social Policy Renewal, 1998a). The common briefing note for this meeting referred to the draft policy framework for the NCA, which proposed the following policy themes: enhancing early child development (Headstart, early learning programs, prenatal nutrition and infant stimulation); supporting parents and strengthening families (parental benefits, parenting programs, counselling); improving the standard of living for low-income families (NCB, health and dental benefits); providing early and continuous learning experiences (community schools, family resource centres, tutoring and mentoring); encouraging healthy adolescent development (affordable and accessible recreation and youth participation and volunteer programs); and, creating supportive and violence-free communities (child abuse awareness, positive community activities and enhanced public spaces). The proposed framework also identified the following principles for the development of the NCA: community participation; a focus on new and creative ideas; emphasis on holistic and multi-sectoral approaches; and commitment to monitoring outcomes and regular reporting (F/P/T Council on Social Policy Renewal, 1998b).

After considering the proposed approach for the National Children's Agenda, the Council Ministers requested that the framework be revised to include the following: a vision linked to measurable objectives; strategies, taking into account the roles and responsibilities of federal and provincial/territorial governments; resource considerations; and a commitment to evaluation and a processes for measuring outcomes (F/P/T Ministers Responsible for Social Services, 1998c; F/P/T Council on Social Policy Renewal, 1998c).

Also in March 1998, the F/P/T Advisory Committee on Population Health released *Building a National Strategy for Healthy Child Development.* The report provided a framework for a strategy to improve the health and well being of Canadians by fostering healthy child development. The report identified key determinants of healthy child development.

Premiers, ministers and officials involved in the Social Policy Renewal initiative were interested in facilitating and encouraging the involvement and participation of Aboriginal organizations in reform initiatives. Premiers had met with national Aboriginal leaders on November 18, 1997, to address several matters, including social issues related to Aboriginal people and a comprehensive process of social policy renewal. Following from this, the Council on Social Policy Renewal co-chairs met with Aboriginal leaders on March 13, 1998, to discuss social policy renewal initiatives. In addition, formal structures had been established to facilitate the participation of First Nations in the NCB "reinvestment" initiatives. On March 30–31, the National Children's Agenda Steering Committee hosted a meeting of federal and provincial officials with five national Aboriginal organizations to establish the Aboriginal Perspectives Task Group. The Aboriginal organizations included the Assembly of First Nations, Métis National Council, Native Woman's Association of Canada, Congress of Aboriginal Peoples and Inuit Tapirisat of Canada. The Task Group would participate in the NCA process and provide advice on Aboriginal issues to the National Children's Agenda Steering Committee.

On May 20, 1998, federal and provincial Aboriginal Affairs Ministers met with Aboriginal leaders and initiated work on the "comprehensive approach" to facilitating Aboriginal involvement in addressing social policy issues. The parties agreed that effective solutions require a comprehensive, cross-sectoral and coordinated approach, based on the premise that the federal/provincial/territorial governments, without prejudice to their respective policy positions, need to work with Aboriginal leaders to address the circumstances of Aboriginal peoples.

On June 18, 1998, the co-chairs of the National Children's Agenda Steering Committee made a major presentation to the F/T/P Council on Social Policy Renewal on the strategic considerations concerning the criteria, framework, and process for further development of the NCA. The Steering Committee proposed a "phased approach" to building support and commitment for that involved approval of the NCA concept and process; building the agenda through public dialogue; and agreement on the priorities and recommendations for ongoing action (NCA Steering Committee, 1998a; Saskatchewan, 1998). The Council also considered a draft discussion paper on the NCA that was intended to become a central feature of the proposed public consultations. The discussion paper defined the NCA initiative as a "comprehensive strategy to improve the health and well-being of all Canadian children" and included a vision and underlying values; discussion of developmental stages and environments; identification of measurable objectives; discussion of policy themes and directions; and an approach for measuring child outcomes and monitoring progress. The paper proposed an approach to the NCA that would build on the efforts of governments, community groups, academics, professionals, businesses, volunteers and families and would involve various sectors, including health, education, justice, social services, housing and recreation (NCA Steering Committee, 1998b).

The Council discussed the need to develop a "shared vision" on how to enhance the well being of Canadian children and affirmed that such a vision "must be developed through an inclusive approach that allows the participation of all segments of Canadian society." The Ministers agreed that the approach "should be integrated and recognize the importance of families, communities, and the volunteer and private sectors" (F/P/T Council on Social Policy Renewal, 1998d; P/T Council on Social Policy Reform and

Renewal, 1998a). This explicit promotion of a partnership and collective responsibility was, in part, motivated by an interest in managing public expectations and avoiding commitments that had not been approved by governments (Saskatchewan, 1998; WPC, 1998).

At the August 5–7 Annual Premiers Conference, Premiers re-affirmed their commitment to "fast-track" work on the NCA. The Premiers endorsed the work of the Council on Social Policy Renewal to strengthen public involvement through the development of a shared vision for the NCA and encouraged the council to finalize its discussion paper and develop options for engaging the public (APC, 1998a).

Following from the direction provided by the Council on Social Policy Renewal and the Premiers, the National Children's Agenda Steering Committee continued to develop plans. In September 1998, the steering committee submitted two documents to the co-chairs of the Council on Social Policy Renewal: *Beyond Governments* outlined options for public engagement; and *A National Children's Agenda: Developing a Shared Vision* was a revised "rolling draft" of the public discussion paper. The committee also provided status reports for the September 17–18, 1998, meeting of Health ministers and the October 27, 1998, meeting of Social Services ministers.

On May 7, 1999, the F/P/T Council on Social Policy Renewal met in Saskatoon to release public discussion papers on the NCA and launch the public dialogue process. The discussion papers included *A National Children's Agenda: Developing a Shared Vision* and *A National Children's Agenda: Measuring Child Well-Being and Monitoring Progress*. The vision document identified the following four goals for a National Children's Agenda: to ensure that Canadian children are healthy physically and emotionally; safe and secure; successful at learning; and socially engaged and responsible (F/P/T Council on Social Policy Renewal, 1999).

Over the following months HRDC and the provincial and territorial departments of Social Services conducted national roundtable discussions. In addition, the provinces and territories conducted regional consultations. The results of these consultations were released on June 21, 2000, in a public report on the dialogue process. The National Children's Agenda is an ongoing process that has contributed to several intergovernmental initiatives for children, including the intergovernmental agreements on early childhood development and the national child care program.

Reflections

Marta Morgan

Marta Morgan was director of children's policy with HRDC from 1997 to 2000. She is currently vice president, Trade and Competitiveness, with the Forest Products Association of Canada.

I had the privilege of playing a role in the development of both the National Children's Agenda and the National Child Benefit from 1997 to 2001 as director of children's policy at HRDC. These complementary initiatives shared the objective of improving the lives of children and families in Canada. They were the first demonstrations of how the Social Union Framework Agreement (SUFA) could be put into practice, with shared goals, objectives and principles, respect for federal and provincial roles, and agreement on accountability frameworks focused on outcomes.

These initiatives resulted in important new policies initiated by the government of Canada and by provinces and territories. The NCB substantially increased the income available to low income working poor families with children, while at the same time making it easier for low income families on welfare to accept paid employment without losing benefits for their children. Under the NCB, provincial and territorial governments expanded direct supports to working poor families, such as dental and health benefits, and increased services available to children at risk.

The NCA provided the umbrella for substantial funding for early childhood development programs across the country. It also led to direct federal contributions to early childhood development, in the form of an extension of parental benefits under EI from six months to one year, an expansion of the successful Head Start program for Aboriginal children and an expansion of the First Nations and Inuit child care program.

From the perspective of a policymaker, these initiatives were a success. Coming on the heels of an acrimonious period of federal-provincial relations in social policy, they were also a success from a federal-provincial perspective. The fruit of lengthy federal-provincial negotiations, both the NCA and the NCB provided concrete examples of shared values and priorities among Canadian governments of all jurisdictions and political stripes; they also provided examples of a practical approach to the development and implementation of new social initiatives in a post-CHST environment.

All in all, the period from 1996 to 2001 was a period of great progress and innovation for policies to improve the lives of Canada's children and families. Children were at the top of the national agenda, both federal and provincial governments were seeking innovative and practical ways to improve outcomes for Canada's youngest citizens, and children's policy was a testing ground for new approaches to Canadian federalism.

What made these initiatives successful? In my view there were three key factors: leadership, policy convergence and flexibility. The leadership of key players in both federal and provincial governments, at the political and public service levels was a critical element to the success of both the NCA and NCB. Key ministers early on developed a respectful working relationship and set the tone for federal-provincial-territorial discussion. Within the public service, leaders at various levels of their organizations worked together to move these issues forward. The working style that developed was intensely collaborative, with all meetings being co-chaired by a federal and a provincial representative and with documents and briefings being co-authored by at least two jurisdictions.

At the same time, the national non-government organizations with an interest in children and family policies also provided coordinated national leadership. Led by Al Hatton and Diane Bascombe, the National Children's Alliance brought together non-governmental organizations with diverse interests (such as anti-poverty, recreation, child welfare and child health) under one umbrella to advocate for the NCA and to provide input into its development. This leadership allowed for the development of a broad consensus and provided the political support for the initiative.

Paradoxically, one of the reasons that the two children's initiatives were successful is that they operated somewhat under the radar screen. Their strongest proponents at the provincial level were generally Ministers responsible for Social Services, who tend to be less at the political centre of events than, for example, Health or Education Ministers. These ministers tend to struggle for increased funding and to be acutely aware of the need for better preventative social services, such as the NCA advocated. At the same time, the intense focus on health care at the federal-provincial table also allowed the sectoral departments to work together relatively independently of their interdepartmental ministries, with their focus on jurisdictional issues.

During this period there was a convergence of ideas that cut across the typical dividing lines of sectors and bridged the understanding of researchers and practitioners. Research into population health was increasingly demonstrating that a society's health outcomes are influenced more by societal factors such as the degree of income inequality than by the institutional health system. A key element in population health is early childhood experience; safe, nurturing and stimulating environments for children turn out to be a great predictor of childhood and adult health outcomes. In the social services and education sector, this research was supported by research into the efficacy of early interventions to prevent more difficult problems down the road. Fraser Mustard emerged as the champion for the research into early childhood development, captivating policymakers and political leaders with his credibility and force of argument. And his argument fell onto receptive ears, as it coincided with what policymakers and practitioners across the country increasingly believed.

During this period, a number of governments were exploring innovative new approaches to policies to support children and families. The B.C. Child Benefit, the Saskatchewan Action Plan for Children, Quebec's child care expansion, the federal Aboriginal Head Start program and many efforts to build a more integrated cross-sectoral approach to service delivery were underway. These initiatives provided examples of new policy and program directions to improve supports for Canadian children and families. Both the NCB and the NCA embodied an approach to federal provincial social policy that allowed for considerable flexibility in programs, combined with a focus on accountability for outcomes. This flexibility enabled provincial and territorial governments to build on their existing social program infrastructure in a way that was responsive to local needs and priorities. It enabled provincial governments with widely divergent ideological perspectives to coalesce around a common social goal — the well being of Canada's youngest citizens.

I have not been involved in the implementation of the accountability framework for the Federal-Provincial-Territorial Agreement on Early Childhood Development, which was one of the main priority initiatives to come out of the NCA. However, I believe that the accountability issues are ones that governments will continue to struggle with. It is clear that what matters to citizens is outcomes — e.g., how are our children doing? — not outputs — what did my government spend on early childhood programs last year? But the ability to actually link outcomes with specific actions is limited. A range of accountability mechanisms, from rigorous evaluation of programs; controlled research into the efficacy of different approaches; accountability for dollars spent to ensure that they actually go where it was agreed they would go; and monitoring and reporting of outcomes is required. The extent to which governments undertake these accountability measures, share their results and make them public will be an important factor in sustaining the credibility of this sort of approach to federal-provincial social policy development.

I hope that these comments have provided some insights into the NCA and NCB initiatives. I consider it a privilege to have worked on these issues and to have played a role in their success. I worked with many individuals in governments across Canada, public servants, political leaders and community leaders who were dedicated to improving the lives of Canadian children. I feel very lucky to have worked with them and to have seen our efforts rewarded with investments in Canada's future.

Reflections

Martha Friendly

Martha Friendly has been a senior research associate and co-ordinator of the Childcare Resource Unit at the University of Toronto since the early 1980s.

My perspective on social policy reform reflects the profound impact that the changes to social policymaking of the 1990s have had on my work on early learning and child-care policy. For me, social policy reform is part and parcel of a sequence of policy shifts that began with the Meech Lake Accord (or before) and prevail today in negotiations on a national early learning and child-care program. Doherty, Friendly and Oloman (1998) identified these shifts as "deficit reduction, devolution, downsizing and deregulation" and said that "roles and responsibilities between levels of government have shifted so dramatically that it is impossible to determine how a program of national significance like child care can emerge" (50). I have argued elsewhere (Friendly, 2002) that child-care policy is a good test case for assessing the efficacy of these changes to social policy and that Canadian children and families have been poorly served by these shifts.

To put this perspective in context, my involvement in child-care policy stretches back into the 1970s, when the Royal Commission on the Status of Women recommended a national "day-care act" as fundamental to women's equality, when the federal Canada Assistance Plan was the main financing arrangement for child care and when there was a National Day Care Advisor in a National Department of Health and Welfare. Then, in the 1980s, decade-long advocacy — much of it connected to the feminist movement — culminated in Mulroney's *National Child Care Act* (Bill C-144) in 1987.

The Mulroney legislation was criticized by most child-care advocates and experts as regressive and died on the order paper when the 1987 election was called (Friendly, 2002). Phillips described it as emblematic of the "Conservative view of a collaborative, decentralized federation" that "both anticipates and reflects the Meech Lake Accord because it deliberately and carefully avoided interfering with provincial jurisdiction… and represented a self-imposed restraint on the use of the federal spending power" (1989: 165).

The decentralizing Meech Lake Constitutional Accord, defeated in 1990, was followed by the equally decentralizing Charlottetown Accord in 1992. What is most pertinent about the Charlottetown Accord for this Reflection is that it was rejected by a majority of Canadians in national referenda. I, with the National Action Committee on the Status of Women, actively campaigned on the "no" side, criticizing both the behind-closed-door constitutional amending process and the devolution of social policy-making to provinces that had also been part of the Meech Lake Accord. This devolution — specifically, that a majority of provinces would be required to proceed with a national social program such as child care — would be recycled but de-constitutionalized in the Social Union Framework Agreement in 1999.

In the 1993 election, the Liberals promised to dramatically expand child care, recognizing that — as child care advocates and feminists had argued — it was a program for middle-income as well as low-income parents. Following their victory, work on both child care and a Social Security Review commenced. As Timpson describes (2001), while the Social Security Review may have been initially intended to review federal government services to "ensure the social security of Canadian citizens" (195), it came to an ignominious end as "the Department of Finance really stepped in" (196). It has been postulated that this takeover was motivated by the mounting tensions over Quebec separation, recognition that provincial social security programs too warranted review and — not least — increasing obsession with deficit and debt reduction. The theme of deficit reduction through program cutbacks was to be a key force driving social policy for at least the next five to seven years and would reemerge in the rationale for social policy reform (P/T Council on Social Policy Reform and Renewal, 1995). Thus, the Social Security Review ended among rumours of coming big changes in social policy-making (196).

And big changes did come. The 1995 federal budget radically restructured the Canadian welfare state with massive cuts to transfer payments to the provinces and replacement of the CAP and Established Programs Financing with the CHST, an unconditional block fund. This new scheme marked withdrawal of the spending power that had permitted an instrumental federal government role in shaping social programs over a thirty-year period. With the 1995 budget cuts and the CHST as a signal, the provinces took the initiative.

1995 was perhaps the low point of my work on child-care policy. For those of us working in the social policy area who were not "insiders," it was impossible to figure out what was going on as changes and rumours surged from day to day. Even though the usual pre- and post-budget hearings occurred, there was no expectation that citizens' and experts' views would be considered.

At the end of 1995, I was sent the *Report to Premiers* document written for the Ministerial Council on Social Policy Reform and Renewal (1995) that had been established at the previous annual Premiers' conference. It laid out the provinces' approach to national policies such as child care; indeed it said that *all* responsibility for social services including child care should belong to the provinces. This struck fear into the hearts of those of us who had been working for a national child-care policy and were well aware that this approach would not have produced Medicare had it prevailed at that time. This was especially true in Ontario, where the effects on child care of the Harris government's election the previous spring had become apparent by late 1995. A statement by a group of national organizations and social policy experts convened in the spring of 1996 by the Caledon Institute to respond to the *Report to Premiers* stated that "human services — especially investment in early childhood development — is fundamentally important, the federal government was urged to play a leadership role in setting directions for and supporting health and social services" (Mendelson, 1996).

It is important to remember what the climate for advocates for social policy was like at this time. Not only were cutbacks in women's shelters, child-care subsidies, child welfare, social housing, health care and social assistance eroding what many had believed to be Canadian fundamentals, but we who worked in these areas were denigrated as "stakeholders" and "special interest groups." While the transfer in focus from the welfare state, the collective and public services to the market, the individual and the private sector was not entirely new, its acceleration was abetted by the growing vacuum at the centre of governance and the embrace of right-wing ideology by governments across Canada.

Into this climate of diminished expectations came the NCB (1998); as the 1996 federal throne speech had suggested, this was a joint initiative with the provinces to consolidate support for children in poor families into a single program. As Boismenu and Jenson observed, "the difference between this initiative and previous social policy decisions is that the reform was co-coordinated *in advance*... thus [the provinces'] engagement to 'reinvest' the money they will save on social assistance" (1998: 63). While groups like Campaign 2000 (of which I am a national partner) had advocated for a National Child Benefit, these proposals had always supported a social policy package designed to alleviate Canada's persistent child poverty, including a generous child benefit, affordable housing and universal child care. However, the NCB became the *sole* anti–child poverty measure considered. As a federal Cabinet Minister observed in 1999: "We cannot implement a national child care program... this is not something we have the ability to initiate. In lieu of that, we came up with the child benefit" (McCarthy, 1999: A7).

Beginning in about 1996, behind-closed-doors work commenced on what emerged as the National Children's Agenda. I remember that there was quite a lot of jockeying about whether child care would or wouldn't be part of this conception. Although First Ministers agreed in 1997 to "fast-track" efforts to ensure the well-being of children, by 1999, my pre-budget brief to the federal Finance Committee (*Moving from Talk to Action*) observed that after four years, the National Children's Agenda was still in the talking stage

(1999). When there was finally a limited public consultation in 1999, many of us feared that "trying to institute major reforms for children is fraught with danger, given the provincial-territorial context and the drive for greater provincial autonomy" (Scott, 1999: 2).

The National Children's Agenda yielded a prosaic "shared vision on the well-being of children" with which it is hard to disagree. It — together with the Social Union Framework Agreement (also agreed upon in 1999) — became the frame for the social policymaking for children that has followed. In addition to commitments to transparency and accountability, SUFA featured the clause that had been opposed by the feminist movement in the Charlottetown Accord — that initiation of a new national social program in areas of provincial jurisdiction would now need consent of a majority of provinces. It is important to note, however, that negotiations on the children's agreements that followed (the Early Childhood Development Agreement, the Multilateral Framework on Early Learning and Child Care and the agreement on a national early learning and child-care program in 2005) have tended to seek agreement of *all* provinces, even if that means falling to a lowest common denominator.

As early learning and child care — the newest national social program — was being negotiated by federal and provincial governments in 2005, child care was still a good test case to determine whether the shifts in social policy that occurred in the 1990s under the rubric of social policy reform can deliver to meet the principles set out by Premiers in their 1995 report:

- social programs must be accessible and serve the basic needs of Canadians;
- social programs must reflect our individual and collective responsibility;
- social programs must be affordable, effective and accountable;
- social programs must be flexible, responsive and reasonable comparable across Canada. (P/T Council on Social Policy Reform and Renewal, 1995)

After many years of involvement in Canadian social policymaking, my question is still the one I posed (Friendly, 2002) as SUFA was about to be reviewed: "Is this as good as it gets"?

Chapter Seven

New Approaches
to Canada's Social Union

The Social Union is the web of rights and obligations between Canadian citizens and governments that give effect and meaning to our shared sense of social purpose and common citizenship. (Biggs, 1996: 1)

A Framework for the Social Union

The concept of the Social Union, which gained prominence during the constitutional discussions of the early 1990s, refers to the processes and mechanisms for intergovernmental cooperation in the development and delivery of social policies and programs. It includes the norms and expectations, structures and protocols, practices and procedures to facilitate intergovernmental collaboration in advancing social policy objectives. In the course of interprovincial and federal-provincial discussions on social policy renewal, the matter of defining and establishing a framework for intergovernmental collaboration became an increasingly important theme. From the perspective of the provincial/territorial social policy agenda, a new cooperative approach to intergovernmental relations was required in order to develop and protect social programs. Of particular importance was the establishment of a process to increase provincial/territorial involvement in the application of the federal spending power.

It is important to consider the development of the Social Union Framework Agreement (SUFA) in the context of the Social Policy Renewal initiative. The need to resolve certain social policy issues, such as increased levels of child poverty, encouraged or enabled or required the provinces and the federal government to consider measures to facilitate intergovernmental cooperation in the development and delivery of national social policy and program initiatives. The growing interest of the provincial and territorial governments in national social policy issues followed from the fiscal demands of social programming combined with a general opposition to federal unilateralism in dictating funding arrangements and setting and enforcing national principles and standards. The provincial/territorial dissatisfaction was further aggravated by the imposition of the CHST.

The other important context for the SUFA discussions was national unity. Provincial and territorial governments have long sought to constrain the federal government's ability to spend money in areas of provincial jurisdiction.

Conflicts over the federal government's use of its spending power to impose conditions on the provinces was a regular feature of post-war intergovernmental relations in Canada. In the 1990s, the federal government began to retreat from shared-cost programs without provincial concurrence, but still imposed conditions on what increasingly were provincially funded programs. On the other hand, such national standards were supported by social advocacy groups and many citizens as a way of ensuring that there was some consistency in the social programs that were available to all Canadians (see, for example, Battle and Torjman, 1995b). Thus, provinces and territories were in a difficult position in attacking the federal spending power without having an alternative proposal to develop and enforce consistent national standards for social programs.

In the decade prior to the commencement of discussions that led to SUFA, provincial/territorial governments had tried twice to constrain the federal spending power through constitutional amendment. The first attempt, in the 1987 Meech Lake Accord, was a brief clause that stated:

> 106A. (1) The Government of Canada shall provide reasonable compensation to the government of a province that chooses not to participate in a national shared-cost program that is established by the Government of Canada after the coming into force of this section in an area of provincial jurisdiction, if the province carries on a program or initiative that is compatible with the national objectives (Canada, 1987: 16–17)

Advocacy groups saw within this clause a weakening of the federal government's commitment to ensuring consistency in social programs across the country. Whether this interpretation was correct or overstated the importance of the relatively minimal federal conditions on transfers to the provinces at the time, this criticism was one of the factors in the Accord's eventual defeat.

The second attempt at constraining the federal spending power through constitutional amendment came in the Charlottetown Accord of 1992. In contrast to the Meech Lake Accord, the Charlottetown Accord proposal was anything but brief. The Accord would have added seven new provisions to the Constitution to address the whole range of issues that had become part of the intergovernmental and public discussion about social policy. While the wording of the Meech Lake Accord's section 106A was replicated, this was supplemented by lengthy sections on such issues as housing and labour market development and training that committed the federal government to negotiate agreements with provinces either to withdraw from an area of provincial jurisdiction, while providing compensation to the provinces, or to maintain its expenditures, depending on each province's preference (Canadian Intergovernmental Conference Secretariat, 1992: 17–20).

As well, the Accord proposed a mechanism to protect intergovernmental agreements from unilateral amendment through legislation. This provision was created largely at Ontario's initiative in response to the unilateral federal action in 1990 of capping Canada Assistance Plan payments, an action that particularly damaged Ontario's fiscal situation (Canadian Intergovernmental Conference Secretariat, 1992: 27–28).

The federal, provincial and territorial governments also committed to the principle of preserving and developing Canada's social and economic union. The social union described in this provision included a comprehensive, universal, portable, publicly administered and accessible health-care system across Canada; adequate social services to ensure that all residents have reasonable access to housing, food and other basic needs; high quality primary and secondary education and reasonable access to postsecondary education; workers' rights to organize and bargain collectively; and the integrity of the environment (Canadian Intergovernmental Conference Secretariat, 1992: 44–46). This provision had several sources. A "social charter" or "social covenant" had originally been proposed by the Ontario government of Bob Rae and the federal NDP in 1991. This idea was a way to assure socially progressive elements in Canadian society that the social safety net would remain secure in the future, thus countering concerns that had contributed to the downfall of the Meech Lake Accord.

A description of the social union that was almost exactly the same (with the exception of the provision on the environment) and that was linked to the economic union, as in the Charlottetown Accord, was included in the February 1992 Report of the Special Joint Committee of the Senate and the House of Commons on a Renewed Canada (the Beaudoin-Dobbie Committee). This came about after intensive negotiations between the key Progressive Conservative and NDP members of the committee late in the process (Special Joint Committee of the Senate and the House of Commons on a Renewed Canada, 1992: 122–23). The Beaudoin-Dobbie Committee also proposed that an intergovernmental agency be created to review, assess and report on the performance of governments in meeting the goals of the "social covenant" (Special Joint Committee of the Senate and the House of Commons on a Renewed Canada, 1992: 123).

The last important provision in the Charlottetown Accord was a constitutional "Framework for Certain Expenditures by the Government of Canada" (Canadian Intergovernmental Conference Secretariat, 1992: 47). The federal and provincial governments were to establish a framework to govern federal expenditures in areas of exclusive provincial jurisdiction to ensure that expenditures contributed to the pursuit of national objectives, reduced overlap and duplication between governments; respected and did not distort provincial priorities; and ensured equality of treatment of the provinces while recognizing their different needs and circumstances. It also committed the First Ministers to reviewing progress in achieving these objectives annually at First Ministers Conferences. These ideas on constraining federal spending power, common social policy objectives and principles of intergovernmental policymaking, and intergovernmental review and reporting on social policy influenced the thinking of a number of those who would be involved in negotiating SUFA four years later.

With the defeat of the Charlottetown Accord in the referendum of October 1992, governments accepted that their efforts at constitutional reform had come to an end for the foreseeable future. Concerns over national unity and the effective functioning of the federation, however, remained unsettled. This became a matter of particular concern in the months before and after the 1995 Quebec referendum on sovereignty. The interest in creating new approaches for intergovernmental cooperation was outlined in the 1995 *Report of the Provincial-Territorial Ministerial Council on Social Policy Reform and Renewal.* The report proposed the delineation of federal and provincial roles and responsibilities and restrictions on federal spending power. It also recommended the development of a mechanism for settling differences and monitoring progress on Social Policy Reform initiatives. These matters were central to the subsequent discussions on SUFA.

In particular, the Ministerial Council report identified the following criteria, which reflected the main provincial concerns that would be reiterated in intergovernmental discussions leading to SUFA:

- Federal activity in areas of sole provincial responsibility should occur only after federal-provincial/territorial consultation and agreement on how federal spending can be effectively applied.
- As responsibilities within the federation are clarified and realigned, commensurate resources should also be transferred.
- Minimize areas of joint federal-provincial/territorial responsibility where this would improve effectiveness.
- Federal spending power in areas of sole provincial/territorial or joint federal-provincial/territorial responsibility should not allow the federal government to unilaterally dictate program design.
- The federal government should accept full responsibility for all programming for Aboriginal people, both on and off reserve, with a gradual transfer of authority to Aboriginal communities.

The Ministerial Council report also identified the connection between federal spending power and the unilateral imposition of federal standards on social programs. In this regard the report noted that the federal government had "unilaterally imposed conditions on programs delivered by provinces in areas of provincial jurisdiction, as a requirement for receiving federal funding" (P/T Council on Social Policy Reform and Renewal, 1995). The federal government was aware of such concerns, as well as of the implications for national unity in a post-Quebec referendum environment of not addressing these concerns, and it appeared to be interested in pursuing intergovernmental discussions on issues identified in the Ministerial Council report. In the February 27, 1996, throne speech, the federal government agreed not to create new shared-cost programs in areas of exclusive provincial jurisdiction without the consent of a majority of provinces and for any new program, to compensate non-participating provinces provided they establish comparable initiatives. As well, the government indicated its intention to withdraw from several program areas, including labour market training, forestry, mining and recreation, and to reduce its involvement in other areas, such as food inspection, environmental management, social housing, tourism and freshwater fish habitat. The throne speech also committed the federal government to securing Canada's social union and to discussing with provinces the principles that should underlie the CHST, and the social union more generally. The government indicated its intention to "protect and promote unhampered social mobility between provinces and access to social and other benefits."

The March 6, 1996, federal budget announced measures to eliminate or reduce federal involvement in several program areas and provided a five-year funding commitment for the CHST. The government expressed its continuing opposition to residency requirements for social assistance benefits and reiterated its intention to uphold the principles of Medicare. The federal government's position seemed to indicate a willingness, within specific limits, to address provincial concerns regarding federal spending in areas of provincial interest and the need to maintain national standards in provincial social programming. These issues and the matter of how to administer programs and resolve disputes were central to intergovernmental discussions for developing an agreement on the social union. The throne speech and budget opened the possibility of federal-provincial collaborative approaches on the establishment of shared principles and objectives for social programs.

At the June 4, 1996 Western Premiers' Conference, Premiers strongly endorsed the Ministerial Council Report. The Premiers discussed issues related to clarifying federal and provincial roles and responsibilities, and called for a mechanism for settling differences (Saskatchewan Intergovernmental Affairs, 1997; APC, 1996a). In addition, the Premiers endorsed the Western Finance Ministers' Report, which recommended rebalancing federal-provincial financial arrangements in accordance with the concepts of the Ministerial Council report, so that provinces and territories could access the revenues necessary to carry out their responsibilities (Western Finance Ministers, 1996).

At the June 21, 1996, meeting of First Ministers, the Premiers and the

Prime Minister committed to work together to "put into practice" the plan outlined in the 1995 Ministerial Council Report. This would include consideration of the report's central theme of clarifying federal and provincial roles and responsibilities in accordance with the identified criteria. The First Ministers agreed that a committee of ministers should be established to further pursue the issues identified in the report; this committee would become the F/P/T Council of Social Policy Renewal.

The Ministerial Council Report renewed public interest in social policy reform, and some community organizations and social policy institutions increased their involvement in discussing the issues. For example, Margaret Biggs, who was at the time with the Canadian Policy Research Network, anticipated and discussed some of the most important challenges concerning intergovernmental relations with regard to social policy issues. In her research paper, *Building Blocks for Canada's New Social Union*, released in June of 1996, Biggs defined the Social Union as "the web of rights and obligations between Canadian citizens and governments that give effect and meaning to our shared sense of social purpose and common citizenship." This definition was widely accepted as a useful guide in the absence of any official definition. The paper identified ten essential elements for building the social union and outlined five broad approaches or general models that might be considered.

The provincial/territorial interest in a renewed approach to intergovernmental collaboration on social policy was further developed in the *Issues Paper on Social Policy Reform and Renewal: Next Steps* (APC, 1996a), which was prepared for the August 1996 Premiers' Conference. At the conference, Premiers endorsed the eight recommendations that were included in the issues paper. Accordingly, the Premiers directed the provincial/territorial designates to the Council on Social Policy Renewal to "design options for mechanisms and processes to develop and promote adherence to national principles and standards" (APC, 1996a). It was intended that this review would include approaches to ensure that the federal government could not continue to unilaterally use its fiscal means to impose conditions on social programs. It was understood that measures for reconciling differences and settling disputes would also be required (APC, 1996a).

The Premiers noted that restructuring federal and provincial roles and responsibilities would require a commensurate rebalancing of financial responsibilities and necessitate executive and cross-departmental decisions potentially affecting fiscal transfer arrangements. Premiers agreed that financial arrangements must be a priority to support social policy renewal in order to ensure that provincial and territorial expenditure responsibilities and revenue capacities were balanced, that government accountability was improved and that governments could provide social programs that are reasonably comparable across Canada. Accordingly, Premiers endorsed the recommendation that Finance Ministers work with their federal counterpart to ensure that an agenda for the redesign of financial arrangements proceeded and was coordinated with social policy renewal (APC, 1996b).

A related issue dealt with federal government offloading of costs for services to Aboriginal people. At the 1996 Premiers' Conference, Premiers reiterated the position outlined in the Ministerial Council Report that the federal government accept full responsibility for all programming for Aboriginal people, both on and off reserve, with a gradual transfer of authority to Aboriginal communities.[1] Premiers directed the provincial/territorial designates to the Council on Social Policy Renewal to coordinate and work with Ministers of Health, Finance, Aboriginal Affairs, Social Services and Labour Market on a strategy to move provincial concerns forward with their federal counterparts (APC, 1996b). In addition, Premiers indicated that input from Aboriginal leaders should be sought.

On October 28, 1996, Premiers Filmon, Romanow and Klein and territorial Leaders Morin and McDonald met with leaders of five national Aboriginal organizations. The meeting focused primarily on the issue of federal offloading of social service responsibilities onto the provinces, as well as the effect of this offloading on the ability of Aboriginal people to develop social policies to address their specific needs. Aboriginal participation in the process of social policy reform was also discussed. Attending Premiers proposed that "national Aboriginal leaders be involved in discussions of the Council [on Social Policy Renewal], as they pertain to, but not limited to, federal offloading of services to Aboriginal people" (Premiers and National Aboriginal Leaders, 1996). To accomplish this, the Premiers asked that the co-chairs of the Council on Social Policy Renewal involve the national Aboriginal leaders in the discussions of the council.

Stockwell Day, provincial co-chair of the council, sent a letter to the leaders of five national Aboriginal organizations on December 23, 1996, inviting them to meet with the co-chairs on January 13 or 14, 1997. These dates were rejected by some of the national Aboriginal leaders, who were then asked to suggest alternative dates. While meetings between the co-chairs of the council and the national Aboriginal leaders proved difficult to arrange, a meeting between federal officials and national Aboriginal leaders occurred early in the social policy renewal process, in December 1996. The Aboriginal Technical Committee on Social Policy Renewal was formed to comment and advise on the all aspects of the social policy reform process, including the National Child Benefit. This committee met several times. Organizations represented on the committee included the Assembly of First Nations, Inuit Taparisat of Canada, Metis National Congress, Congress of Aboriginal Peoples, Native Women's Association of Canada and the National

Association of Friendship Centres. Eventually, on December 16, 1999, members of the federal-provincial-territorial Ministerial Council, Aboriginal Affairs Ministers and national Aboriginal leaders met together to discuss the social policy renewal process. Once the Social Union Framework negotiations were launched and a separate ministerial committee was established to oversee the negotiations, national Aboriginal leaders also played a role in this process, meeting with the committee co-chairs on May 13, 1998.

At the first meeting of the P/T Council on Social Policy Renewal, on October 2, 1996, the Council Ministers, in accordance with the Premiers' directive, requested that officials prepare a report on options for mechanisms and processes to develop and promote adherence to national principles and standards. This work would include consideration of new approaches to the use of federal spending power. Officials were asked to provide a draft report for the council to review in January 1997 so that the final report could be forwarded to Premiers in February (Shillington, 1996; Department of Intergovernmental Affairs, Government of Saskatchewan, 1996).

In related activities concerning Premiers' Conference directives, Finance Ministers worked with the social policy ministries respecting the coordination and redesign of financial arrangements in facilitating social policy renewal. This was a natural extension of the work that had already been undertaken by federal and provincial Finance and Social Services officials on the development of the National Child Benefit and proposals for integrated income support for persons with disabilities.

By the autumn of 1996, the federal government was directing attention toward the social union initiatives that had been identified by the provinces. For example, in a speech to the Canadian Club of Ottawa, the federal Minister of Intergovernmental Affairs, outlined his views on the social union, observing that there was widespread agreement that the federal and provincial governments must cooperate to preserve the social safety net. He predicted that the two levels of government would "increasingly focus on the renewal of Canada's social union" (Privy Council Office, Government of Canada, 1996). The Minister also noted that a joint federal-provincial response to child poverty would indicate another trend in the evolution of the Canadian social union.

At the November 27, 1996, meeting of the F/P/T Council on Social Policy Renewal, ministers reviewed a status report on mechanisms and processes to develop and promote adherence to national principles or standards. HRDC Minister, Pierre Pettigrew, expressed interest in opening discussions on the throne speech commitments, but provincial ministers indicated that their work on national principles and standards and on the federal spending power issue would need to be completed prior to any discussions with the federal government. The ministers directed council officials to consult with federal and provincial finance officials and assist the Finance Ministers' initiative on coordinating the redesign of financial arrangements with social policy renewal initiatives (Saskatchewan, 1996c; 1997e).

Following from this work, Intergovernmental Affairs officials prepared a draft discussion paper, *New Approaches to Canada's Social Union*, which was reviewed at the January 29, 1997, meeting of the P/T Council on Social Policy Renewal. This paper provided suggestions to strengthen the social union and guide use of federal spending power in the social policy area. It also identified potential mechanisms to develop and promote the adherence to national principles and standards, and proposed options for implementing intergovernmental commitments. The council agreed to develop options to address the following: policy principles, ground rules for managing the social union, possible spending power formulations, roles for First Ministers and ministerial councils, mechanisms for dispute resolution, mechanisms for ensuring funding predictability and implementation approaches (Saskatchewan, 1997b). The council recognized that the scope and complexity of the issues amounted to a reconsideration of the management of Canada's social union. It was clear that direction from Premiers and further interprovincial discussions would be required to fully achieve the provincial/territorial consensus that was a prerequisite for federal-provincial negotiations (Saskatchewan, 1997e).

In January 1997, the Canadian Policy Research Networks initiated a series of roundtable discussions intended to develop concrete proposals for the social union. The participants included government officials, academics and representatives of public policy research organizations. The discussions addressed a broad range of topics, including definition of the social union; its purpose, values and principles; measuring outcomes; new institutions; and citizen engagement. In the roundtable discussion paper, *New Institutions for the Social Union*, Kathy O'Hara advocated the "collaborative federalism" approach to the social union that had been described by Margaret Biggs. This approach included joint management and decision-making on national framework and enforcement issues; the creation of intergovernmental processes; a federal/provincial/territorial statement on values and principles for the social union and a joint work plan; and jointly mandated monitoring agencies and expert bodies (O'Hara, 1997a). While it is unlikely that this paper had any particular influence with government officials, its elements of this approach were generally acknowledged as central to discussions about the Social Union.

At the May 1997 Western Premiers Conference, Premiers discussed the status of the Ministerial Council's work on social union issues. Premiers reiterated support for new cooperative mechanisms to replace federal unilateralism and expressed their opposition to the unilateral development and enforcement of national standards by the federal government. The Premiers encouraged the provincial/territorial Council on Social Policy Renewal to complete work on new approaches for intergovernmental cooperation on social policy renewal, and called for the development of a "broad framework agreement with the federal government on managing the social union, together with a parallel provincial/territorial agreement" (WPC, 1997).

At the June 10, 1997, meeting of the P/T Council on Social Policy Renewal, ministers reviewed and finalized the options paper, *New Approaches to Canada's Social Union*, which was forwarded to Premiers for consideration at the 1997 Annual Premiers' Conference. The paper outlined options for cooperative intergovernmental approaches to managing Canadian social policy that would address the following objectives:

- maintaining an effective and efficient system of social programs that support the needs of Canadians;
- maintaining comparability in social policy across the country, while supporting innovative and flexible approaches, which address the different needs of different provinces and territories;
- allowing for the joint creation of national social policy principles, standards or outcomes measures through cooperative intergovernmental processes;
- ensuring that these principles are applied and adhered to fairly and objectively, so that intergovernmental disputes are prevented or resolved in a way that promotes the social union;
- meeting the special needs of different social policy areas and coordinating activities between those areas;
- ensuring adequacy and continuity of funds, both for the government delivering the services and for the people receiving the services;
- ensuring the ability of all provinces and territories to provide reasonably comparable social programs at reasonably comparable levels of taxation; and
- achieving greater cooperation and coordination in the management of social programs through improved intergovernmental processes.

The paper discussed the following five elements of federal/provincial/territorial cooperation, which could form the basis of an intergovernmental partnership for strengthening the management of the social union: identifying shared principles, standards and outcome goals; establishing procedural ground rules; clarifying roles and responsibilities; preventing conflicts and reconciling disputes; and developing a new approach to the federal spending power. It also discussed options for an intergovernmental framework on social policy renewal as one possible approach to "strengthen and maintain the social union in Canada" (P/T Council on Social Policy Reform and Renewal, 1997b).

At the 1997 Premiers' Conference, the Premiers agreed that the P/T Council on Social Policy Renewal should engage the federal government in the negotiation of a "broad framework agreement on the social union" and endeavour to complete negotiations by August 1998. It is important to note that in directing this work, the Premiers specified that this framework agreement should "address cross-sectoral issues such as common principles, the use of federal spending power, and new ways to manage and resolve disagreements." The Premiers directed Finance Ministers to begin negotiations with the federal government on renewing federal/provincial fiscal arrangements. They agreed that a provincial/territorial framework agreement should be developed to guide national social policy renewal in areas of provincial/territorial responsibility such as mobility, portability, comparability, common principles, outcome goals and processes for resolving disagreements. They also agreed to develop specific agreements in priority sectors such as education and health (APC, 1997).

The Premiers met again on September 14, 1997, in Calgary to discuss the issue of national unity and consider measures to strengthen the federation. The Premiers issued a *Framework for Discussion on Canadian Unity*, which outlined seven unity principles. They also committed to conduct public discussions on national unity. The document stated that "Canadians want their governments to work together particularly in the delivery of social programs," and it committed provinces and territories to "work in partnership with the Government of Canada" (Premiers' Meeting News Release, September 14, 1997). During this meeting, the Premiers were in telephone contact with the Prime Minister, and the First Ministers agreed that they would meet to discuss social policy renewal and that they would work cooperatively in the areas of health care and youth unemployment (Premiers' Meeting News Release, September 14, 1997).

In October the Premier of New Brunswick, Frank McKenna resigned. As New Brunswick had hosted the 1997 Premiers Conference, Saskatchewan, as host for the forthcoming conference, took on the duties of lead province and Premier Romanow took on the responsibilities of lead Premier. This would mean that Saskatchewan and Premier Romanow would coordinate planning for the upcoming First Ministers' Meeting, the 1998 Premiers Conference and other interprovincial and federal-provincial collaborative initiatives, including the social union framework negotiations. During this critical period in the Social Policy Renewal initiative, Saskatchewan would be the lead province for almost two years, from October 1997 to August 1999.

The P/T Council on Social Policy Renewal met on October 6, 1997, to discuss a work plan to develop a federal/provincial/territorial "framework agreement on roles and responsibilities in social policy." The ministers expressed the view that the framework agreement would "result in a new partnership approach to managing the social union in Canada, including new cooperative approaches to the federal government's use of its spending power in areas of provincial/territorial responsibility, alternatives to managing and resolving disputes, and common principles to guide social policy renewal" (P/T Council on Social Policy Reform and Renewal, 1997c). Materials prepared for the discussion of federal spending power observed that an effective constraint on this power was the most critical step in eliminating federal unilateralism and renewing the federal-provincial partnership. The limitation on spending power announced in the 1996 throne speech was considered insufficient, and it was proposed that measures be established to address federally delivered programs in provincial jurisdiction (Saskatchewan, 1997f). This reiterated the provincial/territorial position, designed in part to be attractive to the Quebec government.

In November 1997, the Canadian Policy Research Networks released a report by Kathy O'Hara entitled *Securing the Social Union: Next Steps*. This report discussed governance issues related to the social union, including outcome measurement and accountability, collective action on social priorities, creating new institutions and citizen engagement. The report concluded that "New institutions for the social union are required to respond to the need for increased collaboration, pressure from provincial governments for joint management, and citizens' demands for transparency and accountability" (O'Hara, 1997b: 2). The main functions of these new institutions would include vertical management of the social union, collection of outcome data, public reporting and dispute settlement. The report advised First Ministers to expand the scope of social union discussions by involving additional sectors, agreeing on more national projects and addressing framework issues; build more structure for the discussions by having regular meetings of First Ministers, clarifying the mandate of the Council on Social Policy Renewal and arranging for the collection and publication of outcome data; and open up the discussions by increasing transparency, accountability and citizen engagement (O'Hara, 1997b).

Federal and provincial/territorial Intergovernmental Affairs officials had undertaken discussions in preparation for the December 12, 1997, First Ministers Meeting. In a December 4 officials meeting, the federal representative identified the federal government's requirements for negotiation of a social union framework agreement. Included in the federal "bottom line" were requirements that the principle of mobility in social programs be addressed, both orders of government acknowledge responsibility for Aboriginal people, the federal government retain final decision-making authority in enforcing national standards and there be no elaboration of the federal spending power (Saskatchewan, 1998a). This appeared to be a hardening of the federal government's position in the nearly two years since the Quebec referendum and the 1996 throne speech.

At the December 12 meeting of First Ministers, discussions centred on the Social Policy Renewal initiatives, especially the proposal for a Social Union Framework Agreement. The main objective of the Premiers was to get the Prime Minister to agree to enter into federal-provincial negotiations on this (Saskatchewan and New Brunswick, 1997). In a letter to Prime Minister Chrétien regarding the agenda for the First Ministers' Meeting, Premier Romanow, on behalf of all the Premiers, wrote that "a principal outcome of the social policy renewal discussion must be a commitment to negotiate a framework agreement for the social union" (Romanow, 1997b). The Premiers also gave the Prime Minister a two-page *Outline of a Federal/Provincial/Territorial Framework Agreement on Managing Canada's Social Union*, which set out the main elements of a proposed agreement (Romanow, 1997c).

The issue of a Social Union Framework Agreement had become so central to further intergovernmental collaboration that the federal government refusing to negotiate an agreement might mean the collapse of work on the other social policy renewal initiatives. There is reason to believe that among federal ministers and officials there were opposing views on the concept of a framework agreement. According to information from the Privy Council Office, the Prime Minister was receptive to the idea of a framework agreement but was "receiving conflicting advice from his Cabinet on this matter" (Saskatchewan and New Brunswick, 1997). Federal officials were pushing sector level initiatives as the priorities for the First Ministers while remaining intransigent on the priority for a framework agreement. It was believed that, in part, the reluctance of federal officials to engage in negotiations on a framework agreement resulted from their view that such negotiations would be difficult to manage and that the prospects for a successful or acceptable outcome were unclear (Saskatchewan and New Brunswick, 1997).

Following from their discussions, the First Ministers, with the exception of the Premier of Quebec, agreed to "mandate designated Ministers, under the auspices of the Ministerial Council for Social Policy Renewal, to commence negotiations on a framework agreement for Canada's social union" (FMM, 1997a). The objectives for these negotiations included the following: a set of principles for social policy; collaborative approaches to the use of the federal spending power; appropriate dispute settlement mechanisms between governments; clarification of ground rules for intergovernmental cooperation; and identification of processes for clarifying roles and responsibilities within social policy sectors. The First Ministers agreed that this initiative would be undertaken with a view to completion by July 1998 (FMM, 1997a).

The Quebec Premier was very critical of the agreement to negotiate a social union framework, calling the proposed approach contrary to the Canadian constitution. In a press conference following the First Ministers' Meeting, Quebec Premier Bouchard indicated, essentially, that Quebec could not engage in a process regarding the management of the federal spending power without a countervailing recognition of the unconditional right to opt-out with compensation. Premier Bouchard stated "For the first time in the history of this country, the whole provinces, Quebec excepted, and the federal government are on the eve of concluding an agreement according to which the federal government will be allowed to step in all the jurisdictions of the provinces in spite of the Constitution.... There is some kind of a revolution in the perception of what should be the relation between the federal [government] and the provinces.... There is now a move towards constituting a central, a very centralized government with the provinces having no power, no responsibilities, but to accept what the federal government will decide in terms of programs and funding" (FMM, 1997b).

In responding to the Quebec position, British Columbia Premier Clark expressed his disagreement, saying that the purpose of the framework agreement was "the opposite of what Mr. Bouchard has just enunciated.... The purpose of the framework agreement is to stop the federal government from unilateral action in areas of provincial jurisdiction, but in fact to work together to set national standards as opposed to federal standards" (FMM, 1997b). Premier Clark subsequently noted that Quebec had identified the following three conditions for participation in the framework discussions: a statement about the Quebec position; opting-out with compensation; and no federal initiatives in a range of areas while the framework was under discussion. Quebec was proposing that the social policy renewal initiatives be suspended until a framework agreement had been worked out. Premier Clark observed that a consequence of this condition was that "the $850 million second installment of the child poverty plan in July would not proceed" (FMM, 1997b). The Quebec conditions clearly had consequences the other Premiers could not accept. The Prime Minister also expressed the conclusion that the Quebec condition regarding the suspension of social policy initiatives was generally unacceptable. Referring to the Quebec Premier's position, the Prime Minister said that "he had other requests that we should stop everything, you know, a freeze on everything, so there was no taker for that" (FMM, 1997c).

The other significant issue that was raised in the press conferences after the First Ministers' Conference concerned the status of the *Canada Health Act* in any negotiations for a social union framework agreement. The question was whether or not negotiations on a framework would involve federal-provincial negotiations on the interpretation and enforcement of *Canada Health Act* principles. In other words, was the *Canada Health Act* subject to federal-provincial negotiation? The Prime Minister and the federal Health Minister said that the *Canada Health Act* was not up for negotiation, and the Premiers said that the issues of interpretation and enforcement would need to be addressed in framework discussions (FMM, 1997b; 1997c). It is interesting to note that the September meeting of federal and provincial Health Ministers had established working groups to consider key issues relating to the Canadian health system. The Working Group on Canada Health Act Interpretive Issues was "to consider and develop a protocol for federal, provincial and territorial governments to discuss issues of concern regarding the interpretation of the Canada Health Act" (F/P/T Health Ministers, 1997). In November 1997, the Alberta Health Minister wrote to the federal Health Minister requesting that the terms of reference for the Working Group on the Canada Health Act Interpretive Issues not be tabled at the First Ministers' Meeting because the discussions on the framework agreement could have a bearing on the proposed protocol on the *Canada Health Act* (F/P/T Health Ministers, 1998). Work on the protocol was deferred pending decisions on the relationship of the Health initiative to the framework agreement negotiations. Subsequently, the F/P/T Council on Social Policy Renewal determined that work on the *Canada Health Act* protocol should be suspended (F/P/T Health Ministers, 1998).

The P/T Council on Social Policy Renewal met on January 19, 1998. The Ministers agreed that the Saskatchewan Minister of Intergovernmental Affairs, Bernhard Wiens, would lead the provincial side in the Social Union framework negotiations with the federal government, and that the provincial/territorial Council Ministers would act as principles in the negotiations, representing their respective provinces and territories (P/T Council on Social Policy Reform and Renewal, 1998b). The Ministers also agreed that the Deputy Ministers of Intergovernmental Affairs, or designates, would act as chief negotiators at the officials' level. In late January, the federal Minister of Justice, Anne McLellan, was assigned responsibility for framework agreement negotiations.

On March 13, 1998, the F/P/T Council on Social Policy Renewal launched negotiations on the Social Union Framework Agreement, with federal Minister of Justice and the Saskatchewan Minister of Intergovernmental and Aboriginal Affairs co-chairing the discussions. The council directed that work begin to develop a framework agreement on Canada's social union that would "define a new partnership approach between governments in the planning and managing of Canada's social union, and focus on principles, collaborative approaches on the use of the federal spending power, ways to manage and resolve disputes, ground rules for cooperation and processes to clarify roles and responsibilities within and across various social policy sectors" (F/P/T Council on Social Policy Renewal, 1998e). At their April 17, 1998, meeting, federal/provincial/territorial ministers reviewed a draft set of principles for the framework agreement and agreed that the priorities for framework negotiations included clarifying federal and provincial roles and responsibilities and collaborative approaches to the use of the federal spending power. The Quebec Intergovernmental Affairs Minister informed the meeting that Quebec would participate in negotiations if the federal government would agree to "include in the framework agreement an unconditional right of provinces to opt-out, with full compensation, of every new federal initiative or new federal program, regardless of whether or not it is co-funded, in the social programs sectors which fall under provincial responsibility" (F/P/T Ministers Responsible for the Negotiation of a Social Union Framework Agreement, 1998). The Ministers indicated that this issue would be the subject of further discussion and encouraged the participation of Quebec.

The approach to intergovernmental negotiations on the NCB was regarded as a positive example that should be modeled in federal-provincial relations generally, and could be especially instructive for their discussions concerning federal spending power. The Ministers directed officials to "develop principles and processes for the use of the federal spending power in areas of provincial/territorial jurisdiction which reflect the development, planning and implementation processes for the National Child Benefit" (F/P/T Ministers Responsible for the Negotiation of a Social Union Framework Agreement, 1998). In response, provincial/territorial Intergovernmental Affairs officials drafted a *Provincial/Territorial Officials' Consensus Working Document on Collaborative Approaches to Federal Spending on Canada-Wide Social Programs*, which listed the following "useful precedents established by the National Child Benefit which could inform an approach to federal spending in areas of provincial jurisdiction" (P/T Consensus Document, April, 29, 1998):

- joint priority-setting on federal cash and tax expenditures on new or modified Canada-wide programs in areas of provincial jurisdiction;
- joint agreement on objectives and principles for new or modified Canada-wide programs;
- agreement to develop, measure and publicly report on outcomes of new and modified Canada-wide programs, consistent with each government's roles and responsibilities;
- any new or modified Canada-wide program in areas of provincial jurisdiction to require the support of a majority of provinces;
- full financial compensation to any provincial or territorial government that chooses not to participate in any new or modified Canada-wide program, providing it carries on a program or initiative that addresses

the priority areas of the new or modified Canada-wide program; and
- measures to ensure the adequacy and certainty of funding to be incorporated.

Following the provincial/territorial working document, Quebec officials indicated interest in joining the Social Union Framework negotiations and supporting the provincial/territorial approach. Given that both Liberal and Parti Québécois provincial governments had avoided participation in intergovernmental arrangements since the defeat of the Meech Lake Accord in 1990 (with the brief exception of the Bourassa government's participation in the final negotiations leading to the Charlottetown Accord in the summer of 1992) and the fact that the Parti Québécois was in government in 1998, Quebec's interest in being part of the provincial/territorial consensus represented a major breakthrough for the provincial and territorial ministers and officials.

The prospect of Quebec participation raised concerns with the federal negotiators, who indicated that if negotiations did not progress positively they would consider withdrawal (Saskatchewan Meeting Overview, May 1998). In addition, Quebec was nearing a provincial election and it was unclear how the dynamics of Quebec participation in the negotiations, or the possibility of a subsequent withdrawal of Quebec from negotiations, would affect the prospects for the success of the initiative.

It should be noted that Newfoundland did not support the provincial/territorial consensus because it was opposed to any consent rules that might restrict federal spending and it could not accept program opt-out provisions beyond those outlined in the 1996 federal throne speech. In addition, and also for reasons that supported existing federal influence over national social policy initiatives, Newfoundland withdrew its support for provincial/territorial demands for joint interpretation of the *Canada Health Act*.

The provincial/territorial Ministers met on May 22, 1998, to discuss the framework negotiation process and to begin discussions on the federal spending power, managing interdependencies and roles and responsibilities. By this time it had become clear that the success of the social union framework negotiations would depend on reaching agreement on collaborative approaches to the use of the federal spending power (Saskatchewan Meeting Overview, May 1998). This came as no surprise, given the long history of provincial efforts to constrain the federal government's ability to use its spending power. At their June 18 meeting, the ministers agreed that federal and provincial/territorial officials should work together to develop joint work on the issues. They noted that the intent of the social union framework negotiations was to make social programs work better, while respecting constitutional jurisdictions, by improving public accountability and ensuring that programs are efficient, effective and adequately and predictably funded (F/P/T Ministers Responsible for the Negotiation of a Social Union Framework Agreement, 1998).

In preparing for negotiations, provincial and territorial officials had continued to revise the *Provincial-Territorial Consensus on Collaborative Approaches to Canada's Social Union*. The June 12 version of the document outlined a two-step approach to federal spending on Canada-wide social programs, which involved the same elements as the April document but framed the items in terms of collaboration and flexibility. The articles dealing with collaboration included joint priority-setting on federal cash and tax expenditures on new or modified Canada-wide programs in areas of provincial jurisdictions; joint agreement on objectives and principles for new or modified Canada-wide programs; agreement to develop, measure and publicly report on outcomes of new and modified Canada-wide programs, consistent with each government's roles and responsibilities; and agreement that federal-provincial arrangements should incorporate measures to ensure the adequacy and certainty of funding.

The flexibility aspects of the approach involved consent and opt-out provisions that could be invoked in the event that collaboration did not achieve agreement. These articles provided that any new or modified Canada-wide program in areas of provincial jurisdiction required the consent of a majority of provinces, and that the federal government would "provide full financial compensation to any provincial or territorial government that chooses not to participate in any new or modified Canada-wide program, providing it caries on a program or initiative that addresses the priority areas of the new or modified Canada-wide program" (P/T Council on Social Policy Reform and Renewal, 1998c). Although this appears to be a subtle change from the April version of the Consensus, this draft facilitated Quebec's participation in the Social Union Framework negotiations.

At the July 2–4, 1998, Western Premiers' Conference, the Western Premiers reiterated their commitment to successfully conclude a Social Union Framework Agreement. The Premiers noted that an agreement to accomplish the objectives set out by First Ministers would foster cooperation between governments, enhance capacity to establish national social programs and provide for flexibility in the delivery of national programs. The Premiers also endorsed the Western Finance Ministers' report, which called for the federal government to restore funding for health care, education and other social program; increase funding through existing fiscal arrangements; and introduce an escalator to the Canada Health and Social Transfer (WPC, 1998).

On July 16, 1998, the federal co-chair of the social union negotiations forwarded a document entitled *Working Together for Canadians*, which outlined the federal position on the Social Union Framework, to the provincial/territorial co-chair. The federal position paper identified a set of goals and principles to guide the evolution of the social union and proposed measures for managing federal-provincial interdependence in several areas, including mobility, joint planning, reciprocal notice and consultation, public accountability and transparency, social transfers to provinces/territories and dispute avoidance. On the issue of mobility, particularly important to the federal government, the paper proposed that "Sector Ministers will ensure that there are no barriers to mobility in any new policies and programs and will eliminate barriers that may exist in current health, education, and social policies and programs, such as residency requirements, limits to portability or other measures that inhibit access to basic services" (Canada, *Working Together for Canadians*, July 1998). The issue of the federal spending power and federal transfers were of particular importance to provinces and territories. The federal position paper proposed that "The federal government will not use its spending power to create new Canada-wide shared-cost programs in areas of exclusive provincial jurisdiction without the consent of a majority of the provinces. Any new shared-cost program will be designed so that non-participating provinces will be compensated, provided they establish equivalent or comparable initiatives" (Canada, *Working Together for Canadians*, July 1998). It is worth noting that the federal position paper referred to the National Child Benefit as providing important lessons on the benefits of collaboration (Canada, 1998: 3).

At the 1998 Annual Premiers' Conference, the Premiers, noting the federal proposal regarding opting-out of federal shared-cost programs, expressed the view that "flexibility to provinces/territories through the ability to opt-out of any new or modified Canada wide social program in areas of provincial/territorial jurisdiction with full compensation, provided that the province/territory carries on a program or initiative that addresses the priority areas of the Canada wide program, is an essential dimension of the provincial/territorial consensus negotiating position" (APC, 1998b). On this basis, the Quebec government agreed to join the other provinces and territories in their negotiations with the federal government on a Social Union Framework Agreement.

The main differences between the federal and provincial/territorial positions on the federal spending power and opting-out provision were two-fold. First, the federal position referred only to *shared-cost programs* in areas of *exclusive* provincial jurisdiction, whereas the provincial/territorial position contemplated provincial involvement in respect of all forms of federal funding in areas of provincial jurisdiction. Second, the federal position was that compensation was due to provinces that established equivalent or comparable initiatives, while the provincial/territorial position was that compensation was due to provinces that established programs that addressed the priority areas of the new national program. According to the Quebec Minister of Intergovernmental Affairs, "Quebec's participation in these negotiations is linked to the interprovincial consensus on the right to opt-out with full financial compensation" (Facal, 1998). Claude Ryan noted that the Quebec government, in accepting the principle that the right to opt-out should be accompanied by a commitment to implement a program in the same area had made a significant concession (Ryan, 1999).

In response to the 1998 Premiers Conference, Prime Minister Chrétien reiterated the federal government's commitment to work with the provinces and territories to strengthen Canada's social union. He also expressed the federal the position that the objectives of the social union framework were to promote equality of opportunity for all Canadians and to ensure that governments work collaboratively and are publicly accountable (Chrétien, Letter, October 9, 1998).

The provincial/territorial ministers responsible for Social Union Framework negotiations met on September 8–9, 1998, and discussed the federal position paper and social union issues of dispute resolution, ground rules for negotiations and public communications. This was followed on October 2, 1998, by a meeting of the federal/provincial/territorial ministers to discuss all the elements of the framework negotiations. The ministers agreed to develop a draft agreement that provided for square-bracketed text on items where there was disagreement, a common convention in the negotiation of intergovernmental agreements. Federal and provincial/territorial officials met several times and held numerous conference calls between September 1998 and February 1999 in an effort to resolve what had become very complex and contentious issues. The most difficult issues concerned federal spending power, dispute resolution and mobility.

The increased interest in developing the Social Union Framework became so intense that it detracted from the work on the NCB, the NCA and other social policy initiatives. The dominance of these negotiations was particularly apparent between October 1998 and February 1999, when plans for the Council on Social Policy Renewal to discuss progress on social policy initiatives, especially the NCA, were postponed several times. In effect, intergovernmental attention and resources for developing national social policy and program initiatives were redirected into negotiations to establish the process and the rules for intergovernmental collaboration.

Although discussions on the Social Union were perhaps somewhat obscure, there was a significant interest in the public expression of the various points of view. In November 1998 the Institute for Research on Public Policy journal, *Policy Options*, published a special issue on the Social Union that featured articles by some premiers and federal and provincial ministers who were directly involved in the negotiations. The view of the federal government was expressed by Justice Minister, Anne McLellan: "The Government of Canada believes a new partnership should have three objectives: promoting equality of opportunity for Canadians, wherever they live or move within Canada; improving collaboration among governments to serve Canadians better; and enhancing accountability to Canadians for results achieved" (McLellan, 1998).

Saskatchewan Premier Roy Romanow stated that, "The framework negotiations will provide three opportunities to strengthen the social union. First, they can address the Canadian citizen's desire for greater transparency, accountability and effectiveness by establishing common goals, clarifying roles and responsibilities, and building in more objective outcome measures. Second, they can restore the confidence of Canadians that governments are working together to maintain the social safety net in the face of globalization. Third, the framework provides the possibility of a new, more collaborative and more respectful federalism" (Romanow, 1998).

New Brunswick Premier Camille Thériault observed: "The framework agreement negotiations are the culmination of three years of provincial/territorial leadership in shaping the national agenda for social policy renewal. In shaping this agenda, provinces and territories have been united in a common purpose aimed at achieving the following objectives: showing Canadians that governments can work together to address their social needs; making the federation more efficient and effective by clarifying governments' roles and responsibilities, reducing overlap and eliminating duplication; securing adequate and stable funding for social programs; and preventing federal unilateral action in areas of provincial jurisdiction through the use of its spending power" (Thériault, November, 1998).

The Ontario Minister of Intergovernmental Affairs, Dianne Cunningham, noted: "Ontario's objectives in the framework negotiations are to reduce overlap and duplication in order to make programs more efficient and effective, to increase accountability to the public, to strengthen Canada-wide standards, and to ensure adequate funding for programs that Canadians value" (Cunningham, 1998).

In December 1998, the negotiations became complicated by a federal proposal for a Health Accord that would include increased federal transfers and establish federal-provincial ground rules for the funding and delivery of health care (Marchildon and Cotter, 2001). The proposal emerged at the December 2–3 meeting of federal/provincial/territorial Deputy Ministers of Health, when the Health Canada Deputy, David Dodge, indicated that the federal government was contemplating an increase to the CHST and was seeking complementary provincial/territorial commitments for increased health funding. He indicated that the amount and form of the increase would be contingent on concluding a health accord in advance of the 1999 federal budget. The deputies discussed the possibility of an accord that would express a common vision and principles for the Canadian health-care system.

Provincial and territorial officials initiated work on a draft Health Accord, and on December 22, the federal Health Deputy faxed a federal draft Health Accord to provincial/territorial deputies. The federal draft proposed to enhance federal involvement in the health sector, with limited federal financial commitment, and required increased provincial/territorial commitments on the level and standards of health services and on performance measures and accountability. Naturally, this proposal was not acceptable to provinces and territories. The federal and provincial/territorial Health Deputies discussed Health Accord issues in a January 7 conference call and a meeting on January 12–13, 1998, but they were unable to reach a consensus.

The provincial-territorial social union ministers met on January 11, 1999, to prepare for the January 12 meeting of federal/provincial/territorial ministers. At the federal/provincial/territorial meeting, the federal minister reflected on the federal government's interpretation of the Parti Québécois victory in the 1998 Quebec election and noted an increased federal resistance to negotiate on federal spending power and dispute resolution. In addition, Quebec and Alberta were unwilling to develop alternatives to the established provincial/territorial consensus position. Lack of progress threatened continued negotiations.

The federal government wanted to conclude a health accord in exchange for any commitment to increase federal funding for health care. Premiers were opposed to signing such an accord but agreed to offer written assurance that additional federal funding through the CHST would be used for health care. On January 22, 1999, in a letter to the Prime Minister signed by all the Premiers, including the Premier of Quebec, the Premiers confirmed that "any additional funds made available from the Government of Canada for health care through existing CHST arrangements will be fully committed to core health services and programs in accordance with the health care priorities within our respective provinces and territories." They also agreed to make information about the health system available to Canadians. With regard to the social union framework negotiations, the Premiers expressed their continuing commitment to conclude an agreement and advised the Prime Minister that they had instructed their officials to intensify their work on a draft document (Premiers and Territorial Leaders, 1999).

In response to the Premiers' letter, the Prime Minister tied increased health funding to progress on federal objectives on accountability and mobility and on the successful negotiation of a health accord and social union framework agreement. In his letter, the Prime Minister indicated a willingness to increase health-care funding in the 1999 budget, and, referring to the Premiers' commitments on health-care spending, he expressed interest in achieving progress on the federal objectives of "enhancing accountability" and "protecting the mobility of Canadians." Making a connection between the Health Accord, the Social Union Framework Agreement and increased health funding, the Prime Minister noted that "collaborative work on a renewed health partnership and on a new social union partnership more generally, along with increased health funding, will reassure Canadians that governments are working together to address their health and other social needs." He also noted that "progress has been made on a health accord and towards the successful conclusion of a social union framework agreement" and that he was hopeful that "negotiators can achieve a successful conclusion in parallel on both files in the very near future" (Chrétien, 1999). In essence, the Premiers' letter and the Prime Minister's response was taken by the federal government as tantamount to a health accord (Marchildon and Cotter, 2001).

On January 27, 1999, the Premier of Quebec, Lucien Bouchard, issued a statement on the social union. The statement explained that Quebec was participating in the framework negotiations because the provincial/territorial consensus of the 1998 Premiers' Conference "allows provinces which, like Quebec, wish to retain their jurisdictions and autonomy, to exercise their right to opt-out with full compensation of and federal initiative in these fields". The statement commented on the dynamics of the negotiations and, with regard to the proposed health accord, Premier Bouchard noted that "the federal government decided to open a second front and attempt to force the provinces to sign a separate agreement on health, outside the framework agreed upon for the Social Union." He explained that the federal draft agreement would give the federal government a substantial role in health care and expressed the view that the provinces should opt-out of the arrangement. His statement also referred to the January 14 conference call of Premiers during which the Quebec Premier "drew attention to the danger that the opening of this second front on health represented for the cohesion of the provinces in the negotiations pertaining to the Social Union" (Bouchard, 1999).

Following numerous conference calls and intensive meetings of intergovernmental officials on January 20–21 and January 26–27, the federal/provincial/territorial ministers responsible for the social union framework negotiations met in Victoria on January 29–30, 1999, to discuss developments on the two inter-related initiatives: 1) finalization of the 1999 federal budget, involving an anticipated increase to the CHST; and 2) negotiation of a proposed federal/provincial/territorial health accord that would include a federal transfer to provinces for health related programming. Disappointingly, there was no significant progress on the central issues, including the use of the federal spending power, which had impeded agreement on the social union framework.

On February 2, 1999, Prime Minister Chrétien forwarded a proposed text for a social union framework agreement to the Premiers and invited them to meet and negotiate an agreement. On February 4, 1999, the Prime Minister and Premiers met and, except for Quebec, concluded the *Framework to Improve the Social Union for Canadians*. In addition, the First Ministers reached an informal understanding that the federal government would increase health-related transfers to the provinces and territories.

The Social Union Framework Agreement contained guiding principles for social policy; measures to ensure that social programs support the mobility of Canadians; commitments to strengthen public accountability and transparency; commitments to improve partnerships between governments through joint planning and collaboration, and reciprocal notice and consultation measures; a collaborative approach for the exercise of the federal spending power; a process for avoiding and resolving disputes between governments; and provision for a comprehensive review of the agreement and its implementation, and making appropriate adjustments.

In addressing the central and most contentious issue of federal spending power, the Agreement included provisions regarding new Canada-wide initiatives supported by transfers to provinces and territories and provisions regarding direct federal spending. On federal transfers to provinces and territories the agreement provides:

> With respect to any new Canada-wide initiatives in health care, postsecondary education, social assistance and social services that are funded through intergovernmental transfers, whether block-funded or cost-shared, the Government of Canada will:
>
> - Work collaboratively with all provincial and territorial governments to identify Canada-wide priorities and objectives
> - Not induce such new initiatives without the agreement of a majority of provincial governments.
>
> Each provincial and territorial government will determine the detailed program design and mix best suited to its own needs and circumstances to meet the agreed objectives.
>
> A provincial/territorial government which, because of its existing programming, does not require the total transfer to fulfill the agreed objectives would be able to reinvest any funds not required for those objectives in the same or a related priority area.
>
> The Government of Canada and the provincial/territorial governments will agree on an accountability framework for such new social initiatives and investments.
>
> All provincial and territorial governments that meet or commit

to meet the agreed Canada-wide objectives and agree to respect the accountability framework will receive their share of available funding.

With regard to direct federal expenditures, the agreement provides:

> When the federal government introduces new Canada-wide initiatives funded through direct transfers to individuals or organizations for health care, postsecondary education, social assistance and social services, it will, prior to implementation, give at least three months' notice and offer to consult. Governments participating in these consultations will have the opportunity to identify potential duplication and to propose alternative approaches to achieve flexible and effective implementation.

Although the Government of Quebec did not sign the agreement, its official reaction was somewhat muted and it did not officially denounce the agreement. It was reported that Quebec Premier Bouchard could not accept the agreement because it did not curb the federal government's power to mount unilateral programs like the Millennium Scholarship Fund and it would not allow Quebec to opt-out of future cost-shared programs, like homecare or pharmacare (*The Province*, 1999). The leader of the Quebec Liberal Party, Jean Charest, supported the decision of the Quebec government and said that he would not have signed the agreement as it was concluded.

It is clear that the provincial consensus position had collapsed, with the provinces other than Quebec abandoning their demand for the ability to opt-out of any new Canada-wide social program with full compensation. Some have argued that the provincial consensus position was merely a negotiating position, but Quebec Premier Bouchard was correct when he referred to the provincial position on federal spending power and opting-out as "essential." The Communiqué from the 1998 Premiers Conference, which was the negotiated and formal expression of the interprovincial understanding, referred to the provincial position on opting-out as "an essential dimension of the provincial/territorial consensus negotiating position" (APC, 1998b).

Initial reaction to the signing of the SUFA centred largely on whether or not it was a mechanism for centralization or de-centralization. Some commentators claimed that the framework shifted power to the federal government through provincial acknowledgement of federal spending power and by formalizing the means for its application. From this perspective, the provinces had approved the right and established the mechanism for the federal government to become increasingly involved in areas of provincial jurisdiction. Others argued that the framework restricted the ability of the federal government to establish national social programs and maintain national criteria and standards. Manitoba Premier Filmon observed that the agreement provided a greater restriction on Ottawa's spending power than had been proposed under the Meech Lake Accord. Similarly, Alberta Premier Klein was reported to have said, "The feds have less power than they had three hours ago" (Orchard, 1999).

In a February 4, 1999, press release, the National Association of Women and the Law, the Charter Committee on Poverty and the Centre for Equality Rights in Accommodation, expressed concern that the framework contained no "agreement on common standards for social programs and services that will give effect to our commitment to, and our shared responsibility for, the individual and collective well-being of all Canadians.... Instead it provides a statement of vague 'principles' which are meaningless and certainly unenforceable" (National Association of Woman and the Law et al., 1999). Similar reaction was expressed in a February 5 statement by the Alberta Federation of Labour, which noted that under the social union agreement "the federal government has given up its right to withhold transfer payments from provinces that violate federal law or regulations.... disputes over jurisdiction and the proper administration of programs will be settled through a yet-to-be-determined mediation process" (AFL, 1999). It was clear that the provincial and territorial governments had not yet succeeded in winning the confidence of advocacy groups, or likely the public, that they could more effectively secure the adequacy of social programs by acting collectively with the federal government than could the federal government acting unilaterally.

On February 5, 1999, the federal Minister of Intergovernmental Affairs, Stéphane Dion, and the Minister of Justice, Anne McLellan, issued a paper entitled *Collaborative Use of the Spending Power for Intergovernmental Transfers: The Race to the Top Model*, which provided an interpretation of the spending power provisions of SUFA (Dion and McLellan, 1999). The paper outlined the new approach that the federal government would take for new Canada-wide initiatives for health care, postsecondary education, social assistance and social services. The new approach would include the following elements:

- Federal and provincial/territorial governments will seek agreement on priorities and objectives and the initiative would not proceed unless the federal government and a majority of provinces agree.
- The design of programs and policies to achieve the agreed objectives would be the responsibility of each province and territory.
- The federal and provincial/territorial governments will also agree on an appropriate accountability framework.
- The distribution of funds would be determined as if no provincial programs were in place.

- Provincial/territorial funding for similar existing programming would be reinvested in the same or related programming area, subject to the agreed objectives and the accountability framework.

In a February 10, 1999, statement to the House of Commons, the federal Minister of Intergovernmental Affairs praised SUFA and noted that it established constraints on the federal government that "go beyond the provisions on limiting the federal spending power contained in the Meech and Charlottetown agreement" (Dion, 1999).

On February 8, 1999, the C.D. Howe Institute issued a critical assessment entitled *The Social Union Agreement: Too Flawed to Last* (Robson and Schwanen, 1999). This commentary stated, "The lure of money swayed the nine provinces that signed the deal away from their previous unanimous stance in favour of restraining the spending power" even though the amount and distribution of new health transfers was not specified. There seems to be general agreement on this point. Harvey Lazar noted: "To many observers, the final SUFA deal was only made possible when the federal government agreed to put more federal money into the CHST… the immediacy and the lure of the additional federal cash transfers, in the face of serious financial strains among most of the provinces, led provincial governments to sign what is now SUFA" (Lazar, 2000). It is worth noting that the 1999 federal budget provided "a significant increase in transfers to the provinces to support health care and a number of other initiatives which strengthen the federal government's contribution to Canada's health system." The budget proposed an increase in transfers to the provinces of $11.5 billion over five years, to be delivered through the CHAST (Canada, 1999). The C.D. Howe paper identified the following problems with SUFA: the agreement formula that required only 50 percent of provinces representing as little as 15 percent of the population, to implement a new Canada-wide program; increasing federal involvement in areas of provincial jurisdiction; insufficient specification of the conditions that would provide for opting-out; the disengagement of Quebec; and asymmetrical treatment especially regarding mobility and non-discrimination commitments.

SUFA has not had much of an impact on federal-provincial relations in the development of social programs. The federal government has continued to use its spending power and to design and implement social programs in areas of provincial jurisdiction without consulting with the provinces. Examples include the national initiative on homelessness, the national action plan for children and families, a federal strategy on disabilities and pilot labour market projects for older workers and youth. In addition, the federal government has refused to recognize the F/P/T Council on Social Policy Renewal as having the lead responsibility for implementation of SUFA.

The Social Union Framework Agreement has not stimulated federal-provincial cooperation in the development of new Canada-wide cost-shared social programs. Nevertheless, perhaps the agreement does provide a potentially useful mechanism for future initiatives. In any event, the NCB, which was developed and implemented without the benefit of SUFA, continues to function well and to provide the model for the kind of cooperation that the framework was intended to generalize.

Note

1. One of the odder pieces of intergovernmental communiqué language, written in an attempt to address conflicting positions on this issue, came from the communiqué of the May 1998 meeting of federal, provincial and territorial ministers responsible for Aboriginal matters and national Aboriginal leaders. Two paragraphs of that communiqué stated:

> All parties agree that effective solutions require a comprehensive, co-ordinated, and cooperative strategy. Without prejudice to the position of any party who holds a contrary view, Provincial-Territorial Ministers and National Aboriginal Leaders restated to the Federal government the issue of its treaty, constitutional and fiduciary responsibility to Aboriginal peoples. For its part, but without prejudice to the position of any party who holds a contrary view, the Federal government restated its longstanding position that it has primary but not exclusive responsibility for First Nations on reserve and Aboriginal peoples north of 60°, and that provinces have primary, but not exclusive, responsibility for off-reserve Aboriginal peoples.
>
> Without compromising these positions, the comprehensive approach proposes a process of cooperation between the federal government, provinces and territories and Aboriginal Peoples in developing a cross-sectoral action plan to identify strategic ways of improving the social, economic and environmental conditions for Aboriginal peoples. (Canadian Intergovernmental Conference Secretariat, 1998)

Reflections

Joseph Facal

Joseph Facal was a member of the National Assembly of Quebec from 1998 to 2003 and Minister for Intergovernmental Affairs from 1998 to 2002. He is currently visiting professor at Hautes Études Commerciales, University of Montreal.

I was Quebec's Minister for Intergovernmental Affairs, in charge of SUFA file, from 1998 to 2002. Let me briefly outline why Quebec chose in 1998 to join the SUFA negotiations already under way, why we decided not to sign the agreement and why I still think after all these years that our position was the correct one.

For decades, provinces in Canada have argued for the necessity to constrain the unbridled federal spending power in areas of exclusive provincial jurisdiction, to ensure stable and sufficient federal funding and to clarify responsibilities in the field of social policy. Quebec has always been the most vocal of all provinces on those issues. From our perspective, the 1995 and 1997 federal budgets were two watershed moments in the history of federal-provincial relations in Canada.

The replacement of traditional transfer mechanisms with the new CHST in the 1995 federal budget was accompanied by funding cuts of six billion dollars over two years for health care, social services and postsecondary education. The provinces were thus forced to assume a much larger share of the cost of these programs at a time when most were already saddled with severe deficits and exploding health-care expenditures. As Ottawa gradually regained control of its finances, it used its new spending muscles to launch one controversial initiative after the other in areas all under provincial jurisdiction. The 1997 federal budget gave birth for instance to the Canada Millennium Scholarship Fund, the Canadian Foundation for Innovation, the National Child Benefit and the Health Transition Fund. Others were to follow. In other words, the federal government decided to make itself more visible and influential through programs of direct funding to individuals and institutions in areas of provincial jurisdiction, instead of simply restoring funding to pre-1995 levels or vacating room through tax-point transfers to allow provincial governments to raise more revenues through tax increases.

We did not participate actively in interprovincial talks from 1995 to mid-1998 because other provinces were not yet ready to agree to our basic demand: recognition of the unconditional right to opt-out with full financial compensation for any province wanting to fully assume its responsibilities in areas of exclusive provincial jurisdiction. This had always been a demand of all previous Quebec governments, irrespective of their political obedience and based on a strict reading of the division of powers enunciated in the 1867 constitution. At a key meeting of all provincial and territorial leaders held in Saskatoon in August 1998, other provinces finally agreed to this fundamental Quebec demand. Thus was born a provincial common front based on what came to be known as the Saskatoon consensus.

Just four days before the fateful signing of SUFA by Ottawa and all provinces except Quebec, another crucial meeting of all provinces took place in Victoria on January 29, 1999. It reaffirmed the provincial common front born in Saskatoon in August 1998. During the Victoria meeting, we drafted a document, *Securing Canada's Social Union into the 21st Century*, which supposedly reflected what was still the common position of all provinces. It highlighted among other points:

- recognition that provinces have primary constitutional responsibility for social programs;
- recognition of the importance of clarifying the roles and responsibilities of each order of government and of avoiding overlap and duplication;
- recognition of the right to opt-out with full financial compensation for all new or modified Canada-wide programs and to submit the launching of any of these programs to the consent of a majority of provinces;
- recognition of the importance to ensure stable, predictable and adequate financial arrangements restored at the pre-cuts levels and valid for a five-year period;
- recognition of the commitment to eliminate unreasonable barriers to interprovincial mobility while also maintaining the ability of governments to pursue legitimate public policy goals; and
- recognition of the necessity to establish a dispute-resolution mechanism involving when necessary recourse to a third party.

As it turned out, during unofficial negotiations with the federal government in the days prior to the February 4, 1999, meeting at 24 Sussex Drive, all provincial governments except Quebec made a number of key concessions, most notably on the opting-out provision, and finally signed an agreement that was much closer to the federal position than to the provincial one born in Saskatoon and reiterated in Victoria. It was thus without the signature of the government of Quebec that SUFA came into existence.

All along, we knew that participation in a fragile provincial common front was a risky course of action for Quebec, but we reasoned that non-participation would not have been a better option. It would have left us with no possibility to influence the process and vulnerable to political attacks on the home front that we were practising a futile and irresponsible empty-chair policy. As for the outcome, I do not recall Premier Bouchard having the slightest hesitation. The SUFA document simply could not be signed as it stood. We were not surprised at all by the way the talks ended because we had seen it all coming in the previous days, as soon as the federal government began insisting it wanted a separate deal on health-care funding. Did we feel betrayed? Of course we did, but we never uttered the word in public. Betraying others is always shameful. Betraying yourself means you have also lost your self-respect. There was no need to overstate the obvious.

SUFA was seen in Quebec at the time as a major breakthrough for the federal government. Not only did it break the Saskatoon interprovincial consensus and isolate Quebec, but it clearly recognized most of the fundamentals principles and goals held by the federal government during the negotiation process. Most crucially from a historical point of view, it was to our knowledge the first time ever the provinces officially acknowledged and therefore gave political legitimacy to the federal government's spending power in areas of exclusive provincial jurisdiction, without succeeding in limiting its use in any significant way nor obtaining any other substantial concession in return. Basically, it consolidated even more the ongoing centralization of power in Ottawa.

In SUFA, the federal government pledges not to initiate new transfers to provinces without the consent of a majority of provincial governments, but a majority can now mean as little as six provinces accounting for 15 percent of Canada's population, well below the traditional constitutional threshold of seven provinces representing 50 percent of the general population. Even more important, these minimal self-imposed constraints only apply to new transfers to provinces, which have not been Ottawa's preferred vehicle for years. Direct transfers to individuals and organizations, which by-pass provincial governments, are now Ottawa's basic approach to social policy funding, and SUFA makes sure these can go on unabated. Almost all other provisions in SUFA either fall short or are a complete logical reversal of the positions elaborated by the provinces since December 1995 and laid out in the Saskatoon and Victoria documents. This was also the general conclusion reached by seven of Quebec's most reputed scholars in constitutional law and political science when asked to evaluate SUFA. (See Institute for Research on Public Policy, 2003). We felt vindicated when we realized that no credible observer in the rest of Canada had concluded that the provinces had gained anything, not even a precise federal commitment for additional health-care funding.

How can one explain the rapid collapse of the provincial common front and the endorsement by their governments of positions they had strongly rejected up to then? Just days before the signing of SUFA, the federal government had opened a second front, insisting it wanted to sign a separate agreement on health-care funding. Cash-strapped provinces were swayed by the lure of money, purely and simply. Also, provincial common fronts in Canada have always been marriages of convenience between very unequal partners. Poor provinces have historically supported centralization since it generally means more federal money. Public opinion in English Canada also tends to favour a strong central government. All this drastically reduces provincial bargaining power and makes it easy for the federal government to pit the smaller provinces against the larger ones.

To many observers, particularly in English Canada, the refusal of Quebec to sign SUFA was directly linked to the sovereigntist stance of its government at the time. This conveniently overlooks the fact that the two other parties in the Quebec National Assembly, the Liberal Party and the Action Démocratique, also rejected it. Liberal Party and Official Opposition leader, and now Quebec Premier, Jean Charest, said precisely that had he been at the head of the Quebec government at the time, he would not have endorsed SUFA either. Rejection of SUFA was almost unanimous in Quebec.

The position of the government of Quebec during SUFA cannot be fully grasped without an understanding of the common reading all Quebec governments have had of how and why the Canadian federal system came into being in 1867. As Alain Noël has pointed out, intergovernmental relations are a policy area like foreign affairs for Quebec governments. There is a strong continuity in positions from one government to another with only little variations. This is so because Quebec is the only society with a French-speaking majority and a well-defined territorial base on the North American continent, and it was so well before modern Canada was founded. Quebec was already distinct in 1867, with its French-speaking majority, its culture, its civil law tradition and its own institutions. It was as this kind of society that Quebec agreed to join Canada, on the basis of what it saw as a pact between two founding French and English-speaking nations, thereby establishing a federal system in which the two orders of government would be, so it was thought, sovereign in their respective areas of jurisdiction. Quebec felt it would then have the leverage it needed to preserve its identity. This desire to maintain and strengthen its identity was then asserted even more intensely during the early 1960s, when a modern Quebec state emerged during the period of the Quiet Revolution.

Meanwhile, another vision of identity emerged in the rest of Canada during the 1960s and since, promoted among others by Pierre Elliott Trudeau and ultimately entrenched by him. This is the vision of "one state, one nation," based no longer on the dual vision of the 1867 pact between two founding nations but on multiculturalism and the primacy of individual rights.

This vision of Canadian identity has given the federal government and the federal courts an ever-expanding role and has driven Canada into becoming an increasingly less federal and more unitary state. The fundamental problem lies in the fact that these two visions have progressively become more and more incompatible and have experienced growing difficulty in cohabiting within the same political system.

Quebec's view of itself implies a quest for more political autonomy based on a status and special responsibilities relating to its identity within an asymmetrical federal system. The Trudeau view based on individual rights and multiculturalism implies a strong central government and strict equality between the provinces, thus ruling out any kind of a special status for Quebec. The unilateral repatriation of the 1982 constitution without Quebec's approval was the most dramatic episode of the clash between these two irreconcilable visions of identity. The government of Canada imposed on Quebec a substantial reduction in the powers of Quebec's National Assembly and an amending formula that has turned out to be a constitutional straightjacket. This was viewed in Quebec as a rupture of the dual pact of 1867 between the two founding nations. No Quebec government, either federalist or sovereigntist, has since signed the 1982 constitution nor seems close to signing it.

Since this episode, all attempts at constitutional reform to bring Quebec back into the constitution fold have ended in failure. All shared the same central point: recognition of Quebec's distinct character. The failures of the Meech Lake and Charlottetown accords in the early 1990s can be explained by Canada's incapacity to recognize the distinctiveness of Quebec in the constitution. Even a symbolic recognition of Quebec's specificity has become unacceptable in the rest of Canada. Even more taboo is the idea that Quebec should be granted special powers that relate to its distinctiveness.

This lack of recognition of the national character of Quebec society has led to an almost complete absence of flexibility by the federal system with regard to Quebec. Indeed, the principle of equality between the provinces implies an impossibility of any kind of recognition of special status for Quebec because such an opening would be perceived in the rest of Canada as preferential treatment for Quebec. Even at the administrative level, the principle of equality means that any opening to one province must be offered to all provinces. Because the other provinces do not wish as much decentralization or as many new responsibilities, Quebec is trapped by this levelling down to the lowest common denominator. It cannot hope to get more responsibilities than whatever the other provinces want and Ottawa has agreed to give. I can hardly think of a clearer example of this kind of rigid federalism than the outcome of the SUFA talks.

In no way, shape or form can one conclude that SUFA has stimulated fruitful federal-provincial collaboration in social policy nor is indicative of a new era of cooperative federalism on any other count. The federal government has continued to introduce social policy initiatives in areas of exclusive provincial jurisdiction through the use of its spending power and without consultation or approval of the provinces. One can cite here the National Action Plan for Children and Families, the National Initiative on Homelessness, the Federal Strategy on Disabilities and the pilot projects for older workers among many others. As for the 2000 and 2003 health accords, they did not even refer to SUFA and came out of a process which ended with a "take it or leave it" stance from Ottawa.

In April 2003, Quebeckers elected a new federalist government, headed by Jean Charest, which has promised to revise SUFA and initiate negotiations on fiscal imbalance. Ottawa countered by simply denying the existence of fiscal imbalance. Six years after the adoption of SUFA without Quebec, the same issues lead to the same disputes using the same rhetoric. Only some of the protagonists have changed. As for Quebec, its core principles and historical demands of respect for provincial autonomy and recognition of the founding dualism of Canada are more marginalized than ever. It should therefore come as no surprise that recent public opinion polls indicate support for sovereignty has climbed back up to somewhere in the 45 to 50 percent range in Quebec, higher than it was before the launching of the 1995 referendum.

Chapter Eight

Conclusion

If we want peace and security for our children, then we must build, not only a humanitarian society in Canada and in this western hemisphere, we must play our part in building it all around the world. (T.C. Douglas, 1999)

Intense economic competition associated with internationalized production and trade will continue to present serious economic and social challenges. There will be ongoing pressure undermining wages and working conditions, and the number of people and families with insufficient incomes will continue to be unacceptably high. The need for social programs to address the impacts of economic and social adjustment will continue, and governments will need to improve programming in the areas of health care, social security, welfare, education and labour market training. Although such domestic measures will be required to respond to immediate and pressing circumstances, they do not address the underlying source of the problem and, in the longer term, they may not be sustainable. It may not be possible for governments to find the resources necessary to offset the decline in wages and working conditions and maintain living standards through income supplementation and the subsidization of services. It will be necessary to implement an effective international policy initiative to address the issues of globalization. This chapter addresses both domestic and international policy.

Domestic Policy

The implementation of the NCB, commitment to the NCA, negotiation of SUFA, and federal reinvestment in the CHST marked the end of what might be regarded as an initial phase of a larger project of social policy renewal that is required to facilitate adjustment to continuing economic restructuring. This initial phase of social policy renewal included development of the conceptual framework and approach, establishing structures and processes, setting objectives and priorities, mobilizing commitment and resources, and demonstrating success and potential

The next phase of social policy renewal will need to build on the achievements of the preceding stage, expand support and involvement through consultation and consensus, review and revise objectives and priorities, and design and implement new social policy initiatives. Future initiatives could include development of the following initiatives:

- intergovernmental mechanisms for social policy development, including measures for implementing SUFA;
- full implementation of the NCB;
- further consultations on the NCA and the development of a comprehensive national strategy on child care and early learning;
- a national initiative on homelessness and social housing;
- a comprehensive national strategy for labour force adjustment; and
- mechanisms to increase the involvement of Aboriginal people in identifying and addressing social policy priorities.

Structures and Processes

The machinery of collaboration, the particular structures and processes established to facilitate intergovernmental cooperation, was critically important and necessary for the development and implementation of the Social Policy Renewal initiative of 1995 to 1999, and beyond. The model for this approach was the establishment of intergovernmental ministerial councils of social services, health, education, labour market matters and other social policy sectors. Based on this general approach to intergovernmental collaboration, Premiers created the Ministerial Council on Social Policy Reform and Renewal, which reported directly to the Premiers. Its success in developing a framework and strategy for social policy renewal was largely related to its role as an instrument of the Premiers. Through the Premiers' mandate, the council was able to compel the involvement and cooperation of the various sector councils in the development of specific policy proposals.

Following from the success of this approach, the First Ministers established the federal/provincial/territorial Council on Social Policy Renewal to facilitate and manage overall intergovernmental collaboration on social policy objectives through the sector councils. In the course of implementing the social policy renewal strategy, the council was assigned specific responsibilities for fast-tracking work on the National Children's Agenda. In addition, it mandated the ministerial committee responsible for negotiations on the social union framework.

In order to coordinate provincial/territorial involvement in the federal/provincial/territorial council, and to monitor and report on the progress of sector council initiatives, Premiers established the provincial/territorial Council on Social Policy Renewal. The P/T Council was directly responsible to the Premiers and ensured that action was taken on Premiers' directives. Accordingly, the P/T Council compiled information on the social policy initiatives being undertaken by sector councils and prepared annual reports and recommendations for consideration at Premiers' Conferences. Intergovernmental officials exercised significant influence in ensuring that sector councils and their respective officials provided the necessary information on their social policy initiatives.

The council structure and process facilitated communication and continuity. The activities undertaken by the sector councils and their respective working groups were regularly reviewed at meetings of the P/T Council on Social Policy Renewal and the F/P/T Council on Social Policy Renewal. Representatives to the councils included Intergovernmental Affairs ministers and ministers who were also representatives on the Social Services Council and the Health Ministers Council. Similarly, federal representatives included the Minister of Human Resources Development and the Minister of Health Canada. As a result, there was a significant capacity for intersectoral and cross-sectoral communication and continuity.

Throughout the Social Policy Renewal initiative, provinces and territories have consistently endeavoured to develop consensus on issues prior to advancing a position with the federal government. Accordingly, the provincial/territorial ministers regularly met in advance of meetings with federal ministers. In addition, provincial/territorial officials held meetings and conference calls as required, to develop a collective understanding and maintain initiative on issues.

With the introduction of the Social Union Framework Agreement and, later, the creation of a Council of the Federation to supersede APCs and improve interprovincial collaboration, and the intended shift toward a more collaborative environment for intergovernmental relations, it is appropriate and necessary to revise the nature of the Social Policy Renewal structures and processes. The coordination of social policy initiatives, including the establishment of objectives and priorities and the reporting on progress, should become a more collaborative, intergovernmental responsibility.

Social Policy and the Social Wage

The subsistence needs of individuals and families (essentially food, clothing and shelter) are provided for through a combination of private means (wages from employment and other income) and social benefits, sometimes referred to as the "social wage" (welfare, education, health care). The Canadian Policy Research Network identifies the sources of well being (or welfare) as market income (employment earnings), family support (parental child care, housework and other care giving), public services (child care, health care), and community services (volunteer activities) (Jenson, 2004). The degree to which the support of individuals and families is shared between market and non-market measures, and the specific arrangements by which this division is accomplished, is determined by social, economic and historical circumstances. Issues related to wages and social benefits are highly contentious and subject to continuous public debate. Employers and workers contest and negotiate wage rates, but, in general, average employment incomes have been sufficient to provide for most of the basic, subsistence requirements of workers and their families. However, low wages are generally not sufficient to provide for subsistence needs of families, and public measures are required to supplement employment incomes. In this regard it has been observed that the problem is not unemployment, but low-wage employment (Maxwell, 2004).

Employers that pay wages that are less than what is required for subsistence are essentially being subsidized. From this perspective, income support measures can be understood as wage subsidization, or specifically, the partial socialization of the wages system. In general, public measures for wage subsidization are increasing in response to declining employment incomes. The trend in social policy is toward increasing the social wage through income support and social services, and away from universal programs and toward targeted benefits. With regard to specific program directions, governments will probably continue to increase funding for programs such as child benefits, child care and early education, housing subsidization and labour force adjustment. Current initiatives and directions include the following.

The National Child Benefit

The main objectives of the NCB are to reduce the level of child poverty by supplementing the incomes of low-income families with children, to enhance equity by subsidizing the incremental costs of raising children and to encourage labour force participation by decreasing the "welfare wall." The Canada Child Tax Benefit has become an effective mechanism for providing significant income support to families with children, but benefit levels are still not sufficient to fully meet the needs of children in low-income families. In addition, there is an increasing need to provide more financial assistance to middle-income families with children. Accordingly, there is general agreement that the CCTB should be increased, but there is no clear and definitive understanding on exactly how much the maximum benefit should be or how benefits should be structured in relation to income levels.

Policy analysts are currently considering these issues. In a paper that investigates and discusses the methodological issues involved in determining the appropriate level of child benefits, Michael Mendelson concludes that an adequate child benefit will be "sufficient to pay the average incremental cost of an additional child for a family living just above a poverty-level standard of living" (Mendelson, 2005: 60). Based on existing information, Mendelson estimates this amount at about $4000+, depending on the structure of the family, noting that an accurate estimate will require the development of credible poverty lines for various family structures. It is important to note that the child benefit provides only a base level of support for an average family living at the poverty line. Additional supports will be required for different needs based on family size, gender mix, children's age, geographic location, special health requirements and other special circumstances. Mendelson suggests that benefits should decline as the number of children increases, and be higher for older children and newborns. Mendelson concludes that an adequate child benefit can serve as a platform for the reform of the income security system for adults in that it provides a base of income support for families with children and establishes an approach to income subsidization that can be generalized to address the basic subsistence needs of workers.

While the determination of child benefits is subject to ongoing negotiation influenced by social, economic, cultural and historical factors, it is clear that development of a consensus on child benefits would be assisted by a better understanding and general agreement on the concept of the subsistence or poverty-level standard of living. It is also clear that, whatever the structure of child benefits, it should remain an income-related benefit and avoid creating employment disincentives.

Child Care and Early Education

The objective of child care and early education programs is to ensure the well being and safety of infants and children, contribute to early childhood development and learning, and support the economic and labour market needs of families with children. In part, child care and early learning programs and services can be considered as a social investment in the development of human resources, and in part they can be regarded as the partial transfer of child-rearing services from families to other arrangements in order to facilitate the increased labour market activity of parents. In this respect, increased government support for child care and early learning programs and services can be regarded as an increase in the social wage.

There are a wide range of private and public programs and services providing various forms of child care and early development. However, there is no overall system of child care and early learning, quality and standards vary widely, government funding is insufficient, and regulation is limited. With regard to early childhood education and care, Martha Friendly has observed that public policy is "incoherent, shifting and poorly developed" and public financing is "severely inadequate" (Friendly, 2004). In particular, the issue of quality is central to the discussion on child care and early education. It has been argued that the social and economic benefits of child care and development programs are directly related to the quality of the services that are provided, and that the establishment of government standards is the appropriate means for ensuring the provision of quality services (Battle and Torjman, 2002b; Friendly 2004).

Governments are increasing their support for child care and early education, and there is considerable interest in rationalizing the existing services and creating a comprehensive and regulated system. However, it has been difficult to achieve consensus on the features of a comprehensive national approach.

There has been a series of major initiatives that have contributed to the incremental development of what may eventually become a national system of child care and early learning. The National Child Benefit included provincial/territorial "reinvestment" initiatives for children, and the National Children's Agenda report, *The National Children's Agenda: Developing a Shared Vision*, provided a shared policy framework and identified objectives for future investment including early childhood development. Other important intergovernmental initiatives have followed from the consultations on the National Children's Agenda, including the First Ministers' initiative on Early Childhood Development (ECD, 2000), the Multilateral Framework on Early Learning and Child Care (ELCC, 2003) and the Early Learning and Child Care Agreement (ELCC, 2005).

The agreement on Early Childhood Development was concluded at the September 11, 2000, First Ministers' Meeting. Through this agreement, the federal government committed $2.2 billion over five years to supplement provincial and territorial expenditures for early childhood development services, including promoting healthy pregnancies, births and infants; improving parenting and family supports; strengthening early childhood development, learning and care; and strengthening community supports for families with children. This agreement built on existing programming and provided a national context for the new provincial/territorial child development initiatives that had been made possible through the NCB reinvestment commitments. The agreement recognized the primary responsibility of provincial/territorial governments for early childhood development programs and services and provided that each government would determine its priorities within the agreed framework. Although the agreement encourages increased government support for child care and development programming, it does not require specific investments in child care, nor does it provide the level of funding or prescribe the program criteria required to meaningfully contribute to the establishment of a national system for child care and early childhood development.

In March of 2003, federal and provincial/territorial ministers responsible for Social Services concluded the Multilateral Framework on Early Learning and Child Care. The Minister of HRDC referred to the framework as "the first step to a national child care program" (Friendly, 2004). In accordance with its 2003 budget, the federal government committed an additional $900 million over five years to support further provincial/territorial expenditures to improve access to affordable, quality, regulated early learning and child-care programs and services in child-care centres, family child-care homes, preschools and nursery schools. Eligible expenditures include capital and operating funding, fee subsidies, wage enhancements, training, professional development, quality assurance and parent information. The framework endorsed a set of principles that addressed key issues for effective early learning and child care, including availability and accessibility, affordability, quality, inclusiveness and parental choice. The 2004 federal budget committed an additional $150 million over two years to support programs and services under the framework, and the 2005 budget committed $5 billion over 5 years toward a national Early Learning and Child Care initiative (referred to in the Liberal platform for the 2004 federal election).

In negotiating this agreement, it is the federal intention that provincial and territorial governments will agree that funding will be available only for child care and early learning programs and services that adhere to the QUAD principles: *quality* — each facility must be regulated by the province or territory to ensure safety and an appropriate complement of professionally qualified child development staff; *universality* — the program will be open, without discrimination, to pre-school children, including children with special needs; *accessibility* — the program will be affordable to parents; and *developmental* — the program must include a component of development/learning that is integrated with the care component. However, provinces and territories have been resisting these criteria, arguing that the program should be flexible enough to support whatever programs are approved by provincial/territorial governments, subject to commitment to general objectives and a requirement for public reporting.

Consequently, although negotiations are ongoing, there is currently no national program for child care and early learning, and it is unclear what kind of arrangement will emerge. Nevertheless, there is, at least, a consensus among organizations advocating development of a national child-care and early learning system that a system for child care and early learning should ensure high quality programs and services that are universally available, accessible and developmental.

Housing Policy

Adequate housing is a fundamental determinant for the maintenance of health and well being (WHO, 1986). The importance of adequate housing is acknowledged in discussions in such social policy fields as population health, child development, disability issues, community development and social cohesion. Housing provides a platform for the success of other social policy initiatives, and expenditures on housing can reduce the cost of health care and other social programs (Carter and Polevychok, 2004: 2–6; and Battle and Torjman, 2002a: 15). Yet, inadequate housing, including homelessness, remains a serious social policy issue in many parts of Canada, particularly in northern and Aboriginal communities.

In 1996, the federal government decided to "clarify jurisdiction" with regard to social housing by phasing out its role and transferring management of the existing federal social housing stock to provincial governments. Accordingly, the federal government concluded bilateral devolution agreements through which provinces were given flexibility in managing social housing resources in their jurisdictions, but with declining federal funding. However, housing needs are increasing, the housing stock is aging and long-term funding for social housing remains an issue. The Premiers have directed ministers responsible for social housing to consider options for long-term funding of social housing initiatives (APC, 1997; 1998).

The most visible aspect of the housing issue, homelessness, has become a matter of heightened public concern and increasing government attention. In March 1999, the Prime Minister appointed a Minister of the Homeless to address the issue, and in November 2001 federal and provincial/territorial ministers responsible for housing agreed on a framework for initiatives to make housing more affordable. The Housing Framework Agreement included a federal commitment of $680 million over five years to be matched by provincial/territorial contributions. In 2003 the federal government committed almost $1 billion to address homelessness, enhance affordable housing agreements with provinces/territories and extend the housing renovation program. Nevertheless, government housing initiatives remain far too limited to achieve meaningful results, and the affordable housing initiative, in particular, has been criticized for its inability for address the main issue of affordability (FCM, 2004).

Housing policy is an obvious approach to increasing the social wage in support of low-income families and individuals and an important component of a low-wage, competitive economic strategy. In this regard the Federation of Canadian Municipalities (FCM) has observed that affordable housing is key to achieving a globally competitive economy and that "the economic success of cities is reinforced by a supply of affordable labour which in turn is linked to the availability of affordable housing" (FCM, 2004).

While there is support for a cooperative intergovernmental initiative for the development of a national housing policy, such an endeavour is complicated by issues related to equity and fairness, market effects and distortions, availability and affordability, and housing quality and maintenance. In particular, social housing requires very large financial commitments and is not really a cost-effective solution to inadequate housing, although there may be a role for social housing for special needs populations and it may be useful to build the public housing stock over time. However, social housing is not a sufficient response to the more general issue of housing availability and adequacy, which is largely related to low-wage employment and income insufficiency. This income assistance and shelter allowance programs to directly address the issue of housing affordability may prove to be more beneficial (FCM, 2004). In the current circumstance, it would be more effective to establish a national housing supplement through the federal tax system that provides an income-related benefit to low-income individuals and families. It would be necessary to coordinate and integrate such housing benefits with the NCB and other federal and provincial programs.

Labour Force Adjustment

Labour force adjustment refers to the transition of the labour force — the change in skills, location, employment status and other characteristics — in response to the human resource requirements of economic development and restructuring. Adjustment policies are needed to ensure that individuals, families and communities are able to cope with changing circumstances and do not suffer because of economic dislocations. Effective adjustment programs promote the income and employment security of workers.

Economic restructuring and structural change is uneven and disruptive. While some individuals benefit from economic restructuring, there are many others who are negatively affected through displacement, unemployment and loss of security. Governments facilitate social and economic restructuring and have a social obligation to ensure that the benefits of these changes are balanced and shared. It is the role of government to provide for the social security, labour force adjustment and human resource development mechanisms necessary to facilitate successful economic and social transition.

The objective of a labour force development strategy is to assist workers, employers, families and communities address the employment, financial, training and relocation implications of economic, structural and technological changes that result in business rationalization/expansion, plant closures and layoffs, organizational and technological change, union jurisdiction issues, rural decline and community centralization. Specific objectives include identification of adjustment needs, creation of adjustment partnerships, coordination of adjustment programming, facilitation of training and re-training, provision of re-employment assistance and provision of retirement assistance. Measures facilitating adjustment include education and training, mobility assistance, employment creation, counselling and retirement.

The Canadian Labour Market Productivity Centre has concluded that effective and equitable restructuring must promote the following economic and social objectives: high and rising standard of living marked by full employment; reduced structural unemployment and low inflation; wealth creation to ensure economic and social progress; societal equity to provide a sharing of the costs and benefits of change; and economic development that is sustainable in environmental terms.

Measures to facilitate labour force adjustment must involve the active participation and cooperation of government, business, labour and communities. Government and private sector adjustment initiatives such as the Industrial Adjustment Service, which was provided by the federal government until the mid 1990s, have demonstrated that labour force adjustment can be effectively implemented through partnerships between government, business and labour. Employers and workers are well positioned to provide advice on employment demands and labour force training needs. Government adjustment services can facilitate business-labour cooperation on adjustment issues such as advance notice of layoffs, severance pay, priority placement in new positions, seniority and employee benefits transfers, bridging benefits to retirement, retraining, relocation assistance and counselling.

Aboriginal Involvement in Social Policy Renewal

The intergovernmental Social Policy Renewal Initiative included attempts to increase the involvement of Aboriginal people. Initially, provincial/territorial interest in Aboriginal participation in social policy development was related to concerns about federal offloading of the cost of services for Aboriginal people. In October of 1996, four Premiers met with the five national Aboriginal leaders and discussed the issue of federal offloading of social service responsibilities. The Premiers encouraged Aboriginal involvement in social policy renewal initiatives pertaining to (but not limited to) federal offloading of services to Aboriginal people. Subsequently, the F/P/T Council on Social Policy Renewal concluded that direct participation of Aboriginal leaders at that stage of the initiative would substantially complicate the federal-provincial process. Aboriginal consultation and participation on working groups for sectoral initiatives was gradually established as a desirable approach. In particular, Aboriginal involvement was encouraged in the development of the NCB, the NCA, and SUFA.

Aboriginal participation was facilitated primarily through the establishment of supplemental or parallel consultative structures because officials and ministers were not prepared to make Aboriginal leaders full participants in established intergovernmental processes. As Aboriginal leaders were not party to the First Ministers' Meetings, governments took the view that they could not be members of the intergovernmental councils of ministers that reported to First Ministers, nor could they directly participate within working groups that reported to the ministerial councils. Instead, intergovernmental officials would consult with representatives of the national Aboriginal organizations through special meetings that were technically outside of the intergovernmental reporting process. Similarly, ministerial councils and First Ministers held separate meetings with Aboriginal Leaders that were supplemental to the strictly intergovernmental processes. This was considered a practical and effective approach to involve national Aboriginal organizations in the process of social policy renewal.

At their 1997 conference, Premiers directed Aboriginal Affairs Ministers to begin discussions with their federal counterpart and national Aboriginal leaders on a "comprehensive approach" to ensure that the federal government would meet its constitutional and fiduciary obligations to Aboriginal peoples.

The federal and provincial/territorial Ministers of Aboriginal Affairs and leaders of national Aboriginal organizations met in May 1998 to discuss how they might develop a strategy to address issues of importance to Aboriginal communities. The provincial/territorial ministers and Aboriginal leaders stressed the federal government's constitutional and fiduciary responsibility to Aboriginal people, and the federal minister reiterated the federal position that it has "primary but not exclusive responsibility for First Nations on-reserve and Aboriginal peoples north of 60°, and that provinces have primary, but not exclusive, responsibility for off-reserve Aboriginal peoples." This presented the usual impasse and, accordingly, the participants agreed to a "comprehensive approach" that would not compromise their respective positions on the nature of federal responsibility but would provide for "a process of co-operation between the federal government, provinces and territories and Aboriginal peoples in developing a cross-sectoral action plan to identify strategic ways of improving the social, economic and environmental conditions for Aboriginal peoples." This vague and illusive proposal provided the appearance of agreement but it did not identify a practical approach to addressing the issues.

With the introduction of SUFA, and the experience of Aboriginal involvement in social policy initiatives through participation on sector groups, it has become increasingly possible and desirable to introduce further means of facilitating the involvement of Aboriginal communities and Aboriginal leaders. On March 22, 1999, the Premiers and national Aboriginal leaders renewed their call to the Prime Minister to hold a conference of First Ministers and Aboriginal leaders to discuss the Report of the Royal Commission on Aboriginal Peoples and agreed that the national Aboriginal organizations be engaged in the implementation of the SUFA wherever such implementation has implications for Aboriginal people. It was also agreed that a meeting of the Council on Social Policy Renewal, supplemented by Ministers of Aboriginal Affairs and national Aboriginal leaders, would be convened to start this process. Subsequently, national Aboriginal organizations participated in the three-year review of SUFA.

Notwithstanding commitments for increased Aboriginal involvement in social policy development, the general decline in intergovernmental activity on social policy issues combined with organizational and resource challenges in Aboriginal organizations has limited consultation with Aboriginal organizations in recent years. However, First Ministers have initiated discussions with national Aboriginal Leaders on measures to improve the health status of Aboriginal people.

This marked the renewal of consultations and presented the possibility of expanding the agenda to include discussions on other areas of social policy. Renewed Aboriginal involvement has resulted in the establishment of a unique, tripartite structure and process that will better enable the participation of Aboriginal Leaders, officials and communities. Essentially, the First Ministers and Aboriginal leaders have directed federal/provincial/territorial ministers and officials to work in partnership with Aboriginal leaders and their representatives to address health and related social policy issues and report back to a meeting of First Ministers and Aboriginal leaders. This requirement to report directly to a joint body creates an opportunity and obligation for Aboriginal involvement in a social policy development process that could be broadly interpreted to include a range of issues related to the determination of population health, including issues of particular concern to Aboriginal communities such as education and housing.

International Social Policy

The benefits and liabilities associated with globalization are unevenly distributed, resulting in substantial social and economic disruption. Governments can play an important role in facilitating adjustment to these conditions but it requires international collaboration. There is a growing appreciation that coherence among trade, financial, economic and social policy is necessary to further advance international economic development and integration. Economic activity is increasingly being conducted in an international context that is largely beyond the effective regulatory control of national authority. The drive for increased productivity and the competitive requirements of the global economy have weakened the ability of national governments to impose labour regulations and generally provide for social security. As international trade and investment and transnational corporate expansion have proceeded, international structures and arrangements, such as the World Trade Organization (WTO) and related trade agreements, have emerged to facilitate and regulate the increasing international integration. However, international bodies have not been effective in regulating working conditions or enforcing international labour standards. The multidimensionality of globalization and international integration requires increased capacity for global governance and a greater degree of coordination of international institutions than is currently the case.

Enhancement of international global governance structures will involve "substantial adjustment in the amount of political authority exercised by national governments and a re-alignment in the authority exercised through extra-national rules and institutions" (Hart, 1996). In particular, international cooperation is required to facilitate economic and social adjustment and improve international governance mechanisms. In this regard, governments could advance the following initiatives.

- Promote adherence to basic human rights and core labour principles (freedom of association; right to organize, bargain collectively and take strike action; prohibition of child labour, forced labour and discrimination in employment) by promoting human-rights and labour-rights initiatives by the United Nations (UN), International Labour Organization (ILO) and other appropriate organizations; supporting formal linkages between the ILO and WTO and other appropriate international institutions; promoting recognition in trade agreements of labour rights, including enforcement mechanisms; and consulting with labour and human rights organizations in support of improved labour standards internationally.
- Support the reform of trade rules and practices to advance sustainable economic and social development, and promote human rights and core labour standards.
- Support development and adoption of codes of industry ethical practice, including UN, ILO and Organisation for Economic Cooperation and Development (OECD) initiatives; and support the ongoing work of the Industrial Standards Organization and Council on Economic Priorities Accreditation Agency, in the development of industry standards relating to occupational health and safety and other labour relations practices.
- Advance economic and social adjustment initiatives, including income support and human resource development, and coordinate adjustment initiatives with economic development strategies.
- Consult with labour organizations and civil society organizations and facilitate public discussion on the economic and social implications of globalization and international marketization.

Advocates of international labour standards generally promote the following internationally recognized standards based on the provisions of the ILO conventions on basic human rights:

- freedom of association and collective bargaining (the right of workers to form organizations of their own choice and to negotiate with their employers);
- elimination of exploitive forms of child labour (such as bonded labour and forms of child labour that put the health and safety of children at serious risk);

- prohibition of forced labour (such as slavery and compulsory labour); and
- non-discrimination in employment (the right to equal respect and treatment).

In addition, there is recognition that the promotion of labour standards within the context of international trade agreements will require that these mechanisms ensure that the comparative advantage of low-wage countries is maintained, discourage protectionist objectives and restrict the application of trade sanctions.

In its Singapore Ministerial Declaration the WTO cautiously addressed the issue of labour standards:

> We renew our commitment to the observance of internationally recognized core labour standards. The International Labour Organization (ILO) is the competent body to set and deal with these standards, and we affirm our support for its work in promoting them. We believe that economic growth and development fostered by increased trade and further trade liberalization contribute to the promotion of these standards. We reject the use of labour standards for protectionist purposes, and agree that the comparative advantage of countries, particularly low-wage developing countries, must in no way be put into question. In this regard, we note that the WTO and ILO Secretariats will continue their existing collaboration. (World Trade Organisation, 1996: section 4)

The ILO took an unprecedented measure on labour standards at its conference in June 1998. A declaration was ratified by the members specifying that:

> "all members, even if they have not ratified the Conventions in question [core labour standards], have an obligation arising from the very fact of membership in the Organization, to respect, to promote and to realize, in good faith and in accordance with the Constitution, the principles concerning the fundamental rights which are the subject of the Conventions, namely: a) freedom of association and the effective recognition of the right of collective bargaining; b) the elimination of all forms of forced or compulsory labour; c) the effective abolition of child labour; d) the elimination of discrimination in respect of employment and occupation." With this new declaration, countries will be required to report annually on the progress they have made in meeting these four fundamental rights. The ILO will in turn issue an annual report on global progress. (ILO, June 1998: Section 2)

Conclusion

The International Confederation of Free Trade Unions proposed that the WTO and ILO should establish an advisory committee to specify the minimum labour standards, including those regarding freedom of association and the right to collective bargaining, the minimum age of employment, discrimination, equal remuneration and forced labour, that WTO members would agree to enforce. Similarly, the Canadian Labour Congress proposed that Canada support the establishment of a joint WTO-ILO working party on a workers' rights clause that would be endorsed and implemented through WTO agreement. The European Union employs the Generalized System of Preferences, which provides trade incentives to benefit developing countries and includes special incentives to countries respecting fundamental ILO conventions on the prohibition of forced labour (ILO conventions 29 and 105), trade union rights (ILO conventions 87 and 98) and the prohibition on child labour (ILO convention 138). The Generalized System of Preferences is formally recognized by the WTO and has been implemented by the majority of industrialized countries.

Employers have generally resisted state regulation of the production process, but they are more willing to accept regulation that applies equally to all competing enterprises. Employers prefer rules that create a "level playing field" rather than regulatory anarchy. Within national markets, governments can establish and enforce labour standards. However, there are no international governance structures with sufficient authority to impose and enforce adherence to an international code of labour standards. This does not mean that there could not be an effective means for the international regulation of employment. The main problem with the implementation of labour standards is *not* that they are not adopted by governments, but rather that there is insufficient political commitment and/or economic capacity to ensure their enforcement. However, there are relatively effective means for regulating other aspects of international competition, for example, international trade agreements, such as those under the WTO. These agreements enforce compliance to rules through the ability to impose economic sanctions, essentially trade sanctions. Arguably, it would be possible for international labour standards agreements to be devised with the authority of economic sanctions.

In addition to the importance of labour standards in maintaining social well being, there are trade-related reasons for the establishment of universal labour standards. The objective of trade rules is to restrict unfair competition. Trade agreements seek to eliminate economic subsidies that interfere with market competition or provide unfair trade advantage and to ensure that there are no barriers to the free trade of equivalent goods. There are a few rules related to labour, such as the restriction on the trade of goods produced with prison labour. However, there is no recognition in trade agreements that the absence or non-enforcement of labour standards provides competitive and trade advantages at public expense and is tantamount to subsidization. Trade rules do not recognize that apparently similar goods produced under widely different labour practices are not equivalent goods.

Products contain socially important qualities related to the conditions and relations of production, and the differences in these qualities can be, and ought to be, regarded as a legitimate basis for discernment. A soccer ball made using child labour or under highly exploitive conditions is not the same as a soccer ball produced using unionized adult labour under recognized labour standards. This social content of products causes consumers to boycott goods that are produced under unethical, exploitive or environmentally harmful conditions.

Trade arrangements should permit preferential treatment that represents the legitimate collective expression of social concern. While WTO trade agreements acknowledge the rights of countries to pursue "legitimate domestic objectives," including the protection of human health or safety, animal or plant life or health, or the environment, the interpretation of these provisions by dispute panels has been so restrictive as to completely negate them.

The promotion of basic labour standards through the international trading system would require the WTO to agree to ensure the fundamental right of collective bargaining and to promote a code of labour practices (Hart, 1996). Such an agreement would be similar to the agreement on the trade related aspects of intellectual property (TRIPS), which requires WTO members to establish and enforce patent protection legislation of a specified nature. A similar agreement on labour standards could require members to establish and enforce fundamental labour standards. It has also been proposed that the WTO Trade Policy Review Mechanism could be used to monitor labour standards that are directly related to trade, such as those that might apply in the export processing zones.

Alternatively, an approach might be adopted that is similar to that used by the International Standards Organization (ISO), has established standards for the production of various goods. In order to receive ISO certification, certain rules regarding the quality of production must be adhered to. The ISO has standards related to occupational health and safety and could develop standards that recognize adherence to other labour and employment practices. Trade rules could permit discrimination between goods produced with or without ISO certification.

This is a complicated issue. Advanced economies are already subject to labour standards and would welcome the imposition of similar regulations on their international competitors. Multinational corporations that take advantage of low cost labour in developing countries and regulation-free, export-processing zones could also accept universally applicable labour standards. However, local producers in less developed countries and their government representatives on international bodies have expressed opposition to measures to improve labour standards because their trade competitiveness is largely based on low wages and substandard working conditions. This is an issue that will have to be resolved, but it must be understood that super-exploitation is contrary to human and economic development. Perhaps it is true that, in the long term, the arbitrage associated with international trade liberalization will lead to improved wages and working conditions. Rather than wait for these market forces, there are measures that can be implemented sooner that would reduce or eliminate the needless continuation of human degradation.

Unless a super-national approach is established to implement and enforce adherence to labour standards, there will be continuing pressure to decrease wages and degrade working conditions. It is in the interests of Canadian workers, families and communities to support the enhancement of labour standards internationally. Canadian governments — federal, provincial and territorial — should take active roles advancing the proactive involvement of Canada in advancing international social policy initiatives particularly fundamental labour standards.

Conclusion

Like many things, social policy has its seasons. There was a good deal of interest and activity directed at several important social policy issues during the mid- to late-1990s. Priorities were identified, plans were made, structures were created, processes were initiated and objectives were achieved. All of this required effort, resources, cooperation and good will. By the time the Social Union Framework Agreement was concluded, the momentum for social policy renewal was on the wane. There are exceptions where inertia of established processes has carried forward certain initiatives, especially in the area of the National Child Benefit and services for children and families, but in general the activity on social policy has slowed.

So, the question must be asked, "where to from here"? What can be done to advance work on social policy priorities? In the current environment, objectives and priorities could be established more collaboratively. Continued progress on social policy renewal initiatives will need to expand support and involvement through consultation and consensus, review and revision of objectives and priorities, and design and implementation of new social policy initiatives. It is also important that, as an advanced country, we focus at least some of our energies at advancing social policy priorities at the international level.

In the course of writing this book, we have talked with people who are involved in public policy development. It seems that there is a growing interest in mounting a new national initiative on social policy. Social policy advocates want to talk about the next phase in social policy development. Several people have suggested that a national conference on the future direction of social policy in Canada would be a useful way to initiate this discussion. We agree, and we hope that this review of social policy reform can be a useful contribution to planning for the future of Canada's social union.

References

Government reports, communiqués, press releases, briefing notes and other documents are available from the Canadian Intergovernmental Conference Secretariat, 222 Queen Street, 10th Floor, Ottawa, Ontario, K1P 5V9 P.O. Box 488, Postal Station A, Ottawa, Ontario K1N 8V5, phone: (613) 995-2341, fax: (613) 996-6091); and through provincial government archives.

Achcar, Gilbert. 2002. "The Clash of Barbarisms: September 11 and the Making of the New World Disorder." *Monthly Review*. September.

AFL (Alberta Federation of Labour). 1999. "Social Union Marks 'The Beginning of the End' says AFL." Press release. February 5.

Amin, Samir. 2006. "Beyond Liberal Globalization: A Better or Worse World?" *Monthly Review* 58, 7 (Dec.).

APC (Annual Premiers' Conference). 1994. *Final Communiqué*. September 1.

_____. 1995a. *Final Communiqué*. August 25

_____. 1995b. *Canadian Social Policy Reform and Renewal: Challenges, Issues and Concerns*. August.

_____. 1995c. *Some Ideas for Follow-up to Premiers' Discussion on Social Policy Reform*. August.

_____. 1996a. *Issues Paper on Social Policy Reform and Renewal: Next Steps*. August.

_____. 1996b. *Communiqué*. August 23.

_____. 1997. *Communiqué*. August 8.

_____. 1998a. *Communiqué*. August 7.

_____. 1998b. *Communiqué*. August 6.

Archer, Margaret, Roy Bhaskar, Andrew Collier, Tony Lawson and Alan Norrie (eds.). 1998. *Critical Realism: Essential Readings*. London: Routledge.

Armstrong, Pat. 1997. "The Welfare State as History." In Raymond B. Blake, Penny E. Bryden and J. Frank Strain (eds.), *The Welfare State in Canada: Past, Present and Future*. Concord, ON: Irwin Publishing.

August, Rick. 2003. "The Development of Active Social Policy in Saskatchewan: A Discussion Paper." Draft paper. Regina: Saskatchewan Department of Community Resources and Employment.

Axworthy, Lloyd. 1994. (Ch 2)

Aylward, Joan Marie (Newfoundland Minister of Social Services and Chair of the Provincial/Territorial Ministers Responsible for Social Services). 1996. "Letter to Stockwell Day, Chairman, Provincial/Territorial Council on Social Policy Renewal." November 20. Available at <http://www.releases.gov.nl.ca/releases/1996/hre/1129n01.htm>.

Banting, Keith G. 1987. *The Welfare State and Canadian Federalism*. Kingston and Montreal: McGill-Queen's University Press.

Battle, Ken (under the pseudonym Grattan Gray). 1990. "Social Policy by Stealth." *Policy Options* 11, 2 (February).

_____. 1991. "Child Benefits Reform." In Lorna R. Marsden and Brenda Joan Robertson (eds.), *Children in Poverty: Toward a Better Future*. Ottawa: Standing

Senate Committee on Social Affairs, Science and Technology.

_____. 1993. "Thinking the Unthinkable: A Targeted, Not Universal, Old Age Pension." Caledon Commentary, October. Toronto: Caledon Institute of Social Policy, available at <http://www.caledoninst.org/Publications/PDF/521ENG%2Epdf>, accessed July 23, 2007

_____. 2001. *Relentless Incrementalism: Deconstructing and Reconstructing Canadian Income Security Policy*. Ottawa: Caledon Institute of Social Policy.

_____. 2003a. "The Role of a Think-Tank in Public Policy Development: Caledon and the National Child Benefit." *Horizons* 6, 1 (March).

_____. 2003b. *Sustaining Public Pensions in Canada: A Tale of Two Reforms*. Ottawa: Caledon Institute of Social Policy.

Battle, Ken, and Michael Mendelson. 1997. *Child Benefit Reform in Canada: An Evaluative Framework and Future Directions*. Ottawa: Caledon Institute of Social Policy.

_____. 1999. *From Integration to Income Security: A Bigger and Better National Child Benefit*. Ottawa: Caledon Institute of Social Policy.

Battle, Ken, and Leon Muszynski. 1995. *One Way to Fight Child Poverty*. Ottawa: Caledon Institute of Social Policy.

Battle, Ken, and Sherri Torjman. 1993a. "A Framework for UI/Welfare Reform." Paper prepared for the Honourable Lloyd Axworthy, Minister of Human Resources Development. Ottawa: Caledon Institute of Social Policy.

_____. 1995a. *How Finance Re-Formed Social Policy*. Ottawa: Caledon Institute of Social Policy.

_____. 1995b. *Lest We Forget: Why Canada Needs Strong Social Programs*. Ottawa: Caledon Institute of Social Policy.

_____. 2002a. *Social Policy that Works: An Agenda*. Ottawa: Caledon Institute of Social Policy.

_____. 2002b. *Architecture for National Child Care*. Ottawa: Caledon Institute of Social Policy.

Bettney, Julie (Newfoundland Minister of Social Services and Chair of the Provincial/Territorial Ministers Responsible for Social Services). 1997. "Letter to Premier Ralph Klein as Chair of the Annual Premiers' Conference." July 31.

Biggs, Margaret. 1996. *Building Blocks for a New Social Union*. Ottawa: Canadian Policy Research Networks.

Blanchard, James. 1998. *Behind the Embassy Door: Canada, Clinton, and Québec*. Toronto: McClelland and Stewart.

Boismenu, G., and J. Jenson. 1998. "A Social Union or a Federal State? Competing Visions of Intergovernmental Relations in the New Liberal Era." In L. Pal (ed.), *How Ottawa Spends 1998–99: Balancing Act — the Post-deficit Mandate*. Toronto: Oxford University Press.

Bouchard, Lucien. 1999. *Declaration by the Premier of Quebec, Mr. Lucien Bouchard on the Social Union*. January 27.

Brennan, Richard. 1998. "New child-benefit program ready for unveiling." *Ottawa Citizen*, June 18.

Bryden, Kenneth. 1974. *Old Age Pensions and Policy-Making in Canada*. Kingston and Montreal: McGill-Queen's University Press.

Burtless, Gary, Robert Z. Lawrence, Robert E. Litan and Robert J. Shapiro. 1998. *Globaphobia: Confronting Fears about Open Trade*. Washington, DC: Brookings

References

Institution.

Buxton, William. 1985. *Talcott Parsons and the Capitalist Nation-State: Political Sociology as a Strategic Vocation.* Toronto: University of Toronto Press.

Caledon Institute of Social Policy. 1996. *Roundtable on the Ministerial Report on Social Policy.* June 17.

Campbell, Murray, and John Gray. 1995. "Social reform not halted, PM says." *Globe and Mail,* February 3.

Canada. 1889. *Report of the Royal Commission on the Relations of Labour and Capital in Canada.* Ottawa.

_____. 1919. *Report of the National Industrial Conference.* Ottawa: King's Printer.

_____. 1987. *Strengthening the Canadian Federation: The Constitution Amendment, 1987.* Ottawa: Government of Canada.

_____. 1996. *Speech from the Throne.* Ottawa: Government of Canada.

_____. 1995. *Budget Speech.* Ottawa: Government of Canada. Available at http://www.fin.gc.ca/budget95/speech/speech.pdf, accessed June 25, 2007.

_____. 1997. *Budget Speech: Building the Future for Canadians.* Ottawa: Government of Canada. Available at http://www.fin.gc.ca/budget97/speech/speeche.pdf, accessed June 25, 2007.

_____. 1998. *Working Together for Canadians: A Federal Proposal for a Framework Agreement to Strengthen Canada's Social Union.* July 15.

_____. 1999. *Budget Speech.* February 16. Available at <http://www.fin.gc.ca/budget99/speech/speeche.pdf> (accessed May 2007).

Canadian Intergovernmental Conference Secretariat. 1992. *Draft Legal Text, October 9, 1992.* Ottawa: Canadian Intergovernmental Conference Secretariat.

_____. 1998. "Federal-Provincial-Territorial Meeting of Ministers responsible for Aboriginal Matters and Leaders of National Aboriginal Organizations, Québec, Quebec — May 19 and 20, 1998." News release. ref: 830-616/04.

Carter, Tom, and Chesya Polevychok. 2004. *Housing is Good Social Policy.* Ottawa: Canadian Policy Research Networks.

Chrétien, Jean. 1997. "National Child Day Statement." November 19.

_____. 1999. Letter to Saskatchewan Premier Roy Romanow. January 25. Regina: Government of Saskatchewan Archives.

Courchene, Thomas J. 1994. *Social Policy in the Millennium.* Toronto: CD Howe Institute.

_____. 1996. *ACCESS: A Convention on the Canadian Economic and Social Systems.* Toronto: Ontario Ministry of Intergovernmental Affairs.

_____. 1997. "Chaste and Chastened." In R.B. Blake, P. Bryden, and J.F. Strain (eds.), *The Welfare State in Canada: Past, Present and Future.* Concord, ON: Irwin.

_____. 2004. "Social Policy and the Knowledge Economy: New Century, New Paradigm." *Policy Options* 25, 7 (August).

Cunningham, Dianne. 1998. "Ontario's Approach to Improving Canada's Social Union." *Policy Options* 18, 9 (November).

Danermark, Berth, Mats Ekström, Liselotte Jakobsen and Jan Ch. Karlsson. 2002. *Explaining Society: Critical Realism in the Social Sciences.* London: Routledge.

Department of Finance Canada. 1997. *Towards a National Child Benefit System.* Ottawa: Canadian Government Printing Office.

Department of Intergovernmental Affairs, Government of Saskatchewan. 1996.

Meeting Note: P/T Council on Social Policy Renewal. November 26.

Department of Labour, Government of Canada. 1919. *The Labour Gazette.* Ottawa: King's Printer.

Dion, Stéphane. 1999. *Statement in the House of Commons.* February 10.

Dion, Stéphane, and Anne McLellan. 1999. *Collaborative Use of the Spending Power for Intergovernmental Transfers: The Race to the Top Model.* Ottawa: Government of Canada.

Doherty, G., M. Friendly and M. Oloman. 1998. *Women's Support, Women's Work: Child Care in an Era of Deficit Reduction, Devolution, Downsizing and Deregulation.* Ottawa: Status of Women Canada.

Douglas, T.C. 1999. "Speech to the Saskatchewan Social Studies Teachers Association, October, 1978." In *Tommy Douglas in his Own Words* (documentary video production). Birdsong Communications.

Echenberg, Havi. 2004. "Back to the Future: The Rear-View Mirror Provides Glimpses of What Lies Ahead for Income Security in the 21st Century." *Policy Options* 25, 7 (August).

Facal, Joseph. 1998. "Pourquoi le Québec a Adhéré au Consensus des Provinces sur l'Union Social." *Policy Options* 19, 10 (November).

Federal/Provincial/Territorial Advisory Committee on Population Health. 1996. "Report on the Health of Canadians." Prepared for the Meeting of Ministers of Health, Toronto. September. Available at <http://www.phac-aspc.gc.ca/ph-sp/phdd/report/1996/cont-e.htm> (accessed May 2007).

_____. 1998. *Building a National Strategy for Healthy Child Development.* March. Cat. No. H39-424/1998E. Ottawa: Federal/Provincial/Territorial Advisory Committee on Population Health.

Federal/Provincial/Territorial Council on Social Policy Renewal. 1996. *Communiqué.* November 27. Ottawa: Canadian Intergovernmental Conference Secretariat.

_____. 1997. *News Release: Meeting of the Federal/Provincial/Territorial Council on Social Policy Renewal,* Ref: 830-575/005. January 29, 1997, available at http://www.scics.gc.ca/cinfo/8305755_e.html, accessed June 25, 2007.

_____. 1998a. "Co-Chairs Letter to Ministers Stewart and Wiens." April 29.

_____. 1998b. "Common Briefing Note for the March 13, 1998 Meeting of the F/P/T Council on Social Policy Renewal." March.

_____. 1998c. "Co-Chairs Letter to Chairs of Sectoral Ministerial Committees." April 29.

_____. 1998d. *News Release: Council on Social Policy Renewal Takes Next Steps on National Children's Agenda - Developing a Shared Vision.* Ref: 830-619/012, June 18, 1998, available at http://www.scics.gc.ca/cinfo98/83061912_e.html, accessed June 25, 2007; *News Release: Federal, Provincial, and Territorial Ministers Discuss Progress on Framework Agreement for Canada's Social Union,* Ref: 830-618/004, June 18, 1998, available at http://www.scics.gc.ca/cinfo98/83061804_e.html, accessed June 25, 2007

_____. 1998e. *News Release: Council on Social Policy Renewal Launches Work on Framework Agreement for Canada's Social Union,* March 13, 1998, available at http://www.socialunion.gc.ca/news/98mar13e.html, accessed July 5, 2007.

_____. 1999. *News Release: Federal, Provincial and Territorial Governments Launch Dialogue Process for National Children's Agenda,* Ref: 830-649/04, May 7, 1999, available at

References

http://www.scics.gc.ca/cinfo99/83064904_e.html, accessed July 5, 2007

Federal/Provincial/Territorial Deputy Ministers of Health. 1998. *Common Briefing Note.* May 20.

Federal/Provincial/Territorial Health Ministers. 1997. *News Release: Health Ministers Pledge Collaboration and Openness,* Ref: 830-588/06, September 12, 1997, available at http://www.scics.gc.ca/cinfo/83058806_e.html, accessed July 5, 2007.

_____. 1998. *Common Briefing Note for the Conference of F/P/T Health Ministers.* February 17.

Federal/Provincial/Territorial Health Officials. 1997. *Common Briefing Note for the September 10–12, 1997 Meeting of Health Ministers.* September.

Federal/Provincial/Territorial Ministers Responsible for Social Services. 1997a. *The National Child Benefit: Building a Better Future for Canadian Children.* Ottawa: Government of Canada, available at http://www.iigr.ca/pdf/documents/1345_Building_a_Better_Futur.pdf, accessed July 5, 2007.

_____. 1997b. *The National Child Benefit: Building a Better Future for Canadian Children.* Ottawa: Government of Canada, available at http://www.iigr.ca/pdf/documents/1345_Building_a_Better_Futur.pdf, accessed July 5, 2007.

_____. 1997c. *News Release: Meetings of Ministers Responsible for Social Services,* Ref: 830-574/004, January 13, available at http://www.scics.gc.ca/cinfo/8305744_e.html, accessed July 5, 2007.

_____. 1997d. *Report on the National Child Benefit.* January.

_____. 1997e. *News Release: Federal/Provincial/Territorial Ministers Responsible for Social Services get to work on National Child Benefit,* February 19, available at http://www.nationalchildbenefit.ca/ncb/news/97feb19e.shtml, accessed July 5, 2007.

_____. 1997f. *News Release: Federal/Provincial/Territorial Ministers Responsible for Social Services Continue Progress on National Child Benefit System,* Ref: 830-580/004, April 18, available at http://www.scics.gc.ca/cinfo/8305804_e.html, accessed July 6, 2007.

_____. 1997g. *News Release: Federal-Provincial-Territorial Ministers Responsible for Social Services Move Forward on Initiatives for Children and Persons with Disabilities,* Ref: 830-594/01, October 7, 1997, available at http://www.scics.gc.ca/cinfo/83059401_e.html, accessed July 6, 2007.

_____. 1998a. *NCB Governance and Accountability Framework.* March 12. Available at <http://www.nationalchildbenefit.ca/ncb/geston3_e.shtml> (accessed May 2007).

_____. 1998b. *News Release: Federal-Provincial-Territorial Ministers Responsible for Social Services Take Next Steps to Enhance Social Programs for Children and Persons with Disabilities,* Ref: 830-604/05, March 12, available at http://www.scics.gc.ca/cinfo98/83060405_e.html, accessed July 6, 2007.

_____. 1998c. *Record of Decisions, Meeting of March 12, 1998.* May 6.

_____. 1999. *National Child Benefit Progress Report.* Available at <http://www.nationalchildbenefit.ca/ncb/NCB-99/toceng.html> (accessed May 2007).

_____. 2000. *National Child Benefit Progress Report.* Available at <http://www.nationalchildbenefit.ca/ncb/NCB-progress2000/toceng.html> (accessed May 2007).

_____. 2001. *National Child Benefit Progress Report.* Available at <http://dsp-psd.communication.gc.ca/Collection/MP43-395-2002E.pdf> (accessed May 2007).

Federal/Provincial/Territorial Ministers Responsible for the Negotiation of a Social

Union Framework Agreement. 1998. *Meeting of April 17, 1998: Key Outcomes.* April 21. Government of Saskatechewan Archives.

Federal/Provincial/Territorial Social Services Officials. 1997a. "Social Services Status Report." November. Government of Saskatechewan Archives.

_____. 1997b. "Final Record of Decisions." March. Government of Saskatechewan Archives.

_____. 1997c. "Common Briefing Note for the October 6–7, 1997 Meeting of Social Services Ministers." October. Government of Saskatechewan Archives.

FCM (Federation of Canadian Municipalities). 2004. Big City Mayors Call for "New Deal" Partnership to Solve Housing. Available at <http://72.14.253.104/search?q=cache:Cu62ukJV_RcJ:www.newswire.ca/en/releases/archive/November2004/05/c9333.html+FCM+(Federation+of+Canadian+Mu nicipalities)+2004+%22affordable+housing+initiative%22&hl=en&ct=c lnk&cd=1>.

FMM (First Ministers' Meeting). 1997a. *Joint Communiqué First Ministers' Meeting* Ottawa, December 12, Ref: 800-036/06, available at http://www.scics.gc.ca/cinfo/80003606_e.html, accessed July 6, 2007.

_____. 1997b. "Scrum with Premiers." Unofficial transcript. December 12. (Copy in author's files.)

_____. 1997c. "Prime Minister's Press Conference." Unofficial transcript. December 12. (Copy in author's files.)

Foucault, Michel. 1980. *Power/Knowledge: Selected Interviews and other Writings, 1972–1977.* Brighton, Sussex: Harvester Press.

Frank, A.G. 1967. "Sociology of Development and Underdevelopment of Sociology." *Catalyst* 3.

Friendly, M. 2002. "Is This as Good as it Gets? Child Care as a Test Case for Reviewing the Social Union Framework Agreement." *Canadian Review of Social Policy* 47.

_____. 2004. "Strengthening Canada's Social and Economic Foundations: Next Steps for Early Childhood Education and Care." *Policy Options* 25, 3 (March).

Gilbert, Bentley B. 1966. *The Evolution of National Insurance in Great Britain: The Origins of the Welfare State.* London: Michael Joseph.

Government of Canada. 1994. "Lloyd Axworthy Announces Strategy for Social Security Reform." News release. Ottawa. January 31.

Greenspon, Edward. 1998. "Tearing down Canada's 'welfare wall.'" *Globe and Mail,* June 19.

Grinspun, Ricardo. 1993. "The Economics of Free Trade in Canada." In Ricardo Grinspun and Maxwell A. Cameron (eds.), *The Political Economy of North American Free Trade.* Kingston and Montreal: McGill-Queen's University Press.

Guest, Dennis. 1991. *The Emergence of Social Security in Canada.* Vancouver: University of British Columbia Press.

Hart, Michael. 1996. "A Question of Fairness: The Global Trade Regime, Labour Standards, and the Contestability of Markets." *Occasional Papers in International Trade Law and Policy.* Ottawa: Centre for Trade Policy and Law, University of Ottawa.

Hoselitz, Berthold F. 1960. *Sociological Aspects of Economic Growth.* Glencoe, IL: Free Press.

References

HRDC (Human Resources Development Canada). 1994a. *Improving Social Security in Canada: A Discussion Paper.* Ottawa: Minister of Supply and Services.

_____. 1994b. *Social Security Reform: Working Document for Discusssion with Provinces and Territories.* June. Ottawa.

_____. 1994c. *Improving Social Security in Canada: The Context for Reform: A Supplementary Paper.* October 5. Human Resources Development Canada.

_____. 1995. *Income Security for Canada's Children: A Supplementary Paper.* Ottawa: Minister of Supply and Services.

_____. 1998. *Summary: NCB Reference Group Meeting.* November 18

Institute for Research on Public Policy. 2003. *The Canadian Social Union Without Quebec: Eight Critical Analyses.* Montreal.

International Labour Organization(ILO). 1998. "ILO Declaration on fundamental principles and rights at work." June 18, available at http://www.ilo.org/public/english/standards/relm/ilc/ilc86/com-dtxt.htm, accessed July 23, 2007

Intergovernmental Officials. 1995. *Discussion Paper on Concerns with the Federal Approach to Social Policy Reform.* Prepared for the 1995 Annual Premiers' Conference. August.

Jameson, Frederic. 1991. *Postmodernism, or the Cultural Logic of Late Capitalism.* Durham: Duke University Press.

Jenson, Jane. 2004. *Catching Up to Reality: Building the Case for a New Social Model.* Ottawa: Canadian Policy Research Networks.

Kell and Ruggie. 1999. *Global Markets and Social Legitimacy: The Case of the 'Global Compact.'* csmworld.org

Kennedy, Mark. 1995. "Axworthy shelves social policy overhaul." *Ottawa Citizen*, February 1.

Kitchen, Brigitte. 1987. "The Introduction of Family Allowances in Canada." In Allan Moscovitch and Jim Albert (eds.), *The "Benevolent" State: The Growth of Welfare in Canada.* Toronto: Garamond Press.

Labour Commission. 1889. *Report of the Royal Commission on the Relations of Labour and Capital in Canada.* Ottawa: Royal Commission on the Relations of Labour and Capital in Canada.

Laurent, Stephen, and Francois Vaillancourt. 2004. *Federal-Provincial Transfers for Social Programs in Canada: Their Status in 2004.* Montreal: Institute for Research on Public Policy.

Lazar, Harvey. 2000. *The Social Union Framework Agreement: Lost Opportunity or New Beginning.* Kingston: Queens University, School of Policy Studies.

Liberal Party of Canada. 1993. *Creating Opportunity: The Liberal Plan for Canada.* Ottawa: Liberal Party of Canada.

_____. 1996. *Securing Our Future Together.* Ottawa: Liberal Party of Canada.

Marchildon, Gregory P., and Brent Cotter. 2001. "Saskatchewan and the Social Union." In Howard A. Leeson (ed.), *Saskatchewan Politics: Into the Twenty-First Century.* Regina: Canadian Plains Research Centre.

Marsh, Leonard C. 1975 (1943). *Social Security in Canada.* Toronto: University of Toronto Press.

Martin, Paul. 1995. *Government of Canada Budget Speech.* Ottawa.

Maxwell, Judith. 2004. *Beyond EI.* Presentation to the House of Commons Human Resources Committee. May. Available at http://www.cprn.com/documents/31277_en.pdf, accessed July 12, 2007.

———. 1996. "Social Dimensions of Economic Growth." Eric John Hanson Commemorative Conferences, Vol. VIII. University of Alberta. Available at http://www.cprn.org/documents/28965_en.pdf, accessed July 23, 2007.

McCarthy, S. 1999. "Ottawa urged to keep promise on daycare." *Globe and Mail.* April 13.

McLellan, Anne. 1998. "Modernizing Canada's Social Union: A New Partnership Among Governments and Citizens." *Policy Options* 19, 10 (November).

Mencher, Samuel. 1967. *Poor Law to Poverty Program.* Pittsburgh: University of Pittsburgh Press.

Mendelsohn, Michael. 1996. *The Provinces' Position: A Second Chance for the Social Security Review.* Ottawa: Caledon Institute of Social Policy.

_____. 2005. *Measuring Child Benefits: Measuring Child Poverty.* Ottawa: Caledon Institute of Social Policy.

Moscovitch, Allan, and Glenn Drover. 1987. "Social Expenditures and the Welfare State: The Canadian Experience in Historical Perspective." In Allan Moscovitch and Jim Albert (eds.), *The "Benevolent" State: The Growth of Welfare in Canada.* Toronto: Garamond.

National Association of Woman and the Law, the Charter Committee on Poverty and the Centre for Equality Rights in Accommodation. 1999. "Social Union Framework Heartless Say Social Justice Groups." Press release. February 4.

National Children's Agenda Steering Committee. 1998a. *Briefing Note: National Children's Agenda Strategic Considerations.* Prepared for the June 18, 1998 meeting of the F/P/T Council on Social Policy Renewal. June.

_____. 1998b. *The National Children's Agenda: A Framework for Discussion.* Draft. June.

National Forum on Health. 1997. *Canada Health Action: Building on the Legacy. Volume 1. Final Report.* Ottawa: Government of Canada.

O'Hara, Kathy. 1997a. *New Institutions for the Social Union: A Canadian Policy Research Networks Roundtable Discussion Paper.* Ottawa: Canadian Policy Research Networks.

_____. 1997b. *Securing the Social Union: Next Steps. Ottawa:* Canadian Policy Research Networks.

Orchard, David. 1999. "Still time to stop Meech 3 in its tracks." *Saskatoon Star Phoenix,* February 26.

Parliamentary Standing Committee on Human Resource Development. 1995. *Security, Opportunity and Fairness: Canadians Renewing Their Social Programs.* Feburary. Ottawa.

Parsons, Talcott. 1951. *The Social System.* Glencoe, IL: Free Press.

Peters, Suzanne. 1995. *Exploring Canadian Values: A Synthesis Report.* Ottawa: Canadian Policy Research Networks.

Pettigrew, Pierre. 1996. "Notes for an Address to the Canadian Club." November 6. Toronto.

Pettigrew, Pierre, and Stockwell Day (co-chairs of the Federal/Provincial/Territorial Council on Social Policy Renewal). 1997. *Letter to Prime Minister Chrétien* February 17.

Phillips, S. 1989. "Rock-a-bye Brian: The National Strategy on Child Care." In K.A Graham (ed.), *How Ottawa Spends: The Buck Stops Where?* Toronto: Oxford

References

University Press.

Polanyi, Karl. 1957. *The Great Transformation: The Political and Economic Origins of Our Time.* Boston: Beacon Press.

Premiers and National Aboriginal Leaders. 1996. *Communiqué.* October 28.

Premiers and Territorial Leaders. 199). *News Release: Premiers Agree to Consult Canadians on Unity,* Ref: 850-065/04, September 14, available at http://www.scics.gc.ca/cinfo/85006504_e.html, accessed July 23, 2007

———. 1999. "Letter to Prime Minister Jean Chrétien." January 22. (Copy in author's files.)

Privy Council Office, Government of Canada. 1996. "Minister Dion Outlines Vision for Social Union." Press release. November 18. Available at <http://www.pco-bcp.gc.ca/aia/default.asp?Language=E&Page=archive&Sub=pressrelease&Doc=19961118_e.htm> (accessed May 2007).

The Province. 1999. "Bouchard's Odd Man Out: Only Quebec won't sign the county's social-union deal." February 5.

Provincial/Territorial Council on Social Policy Reform and Renewal. 1995. *Ministerial Council on Social Policy Reform and Renewal: Report to Premiers.* December. Available at http://www.exec.gov.nl.ca/exec/PREMIER/SOCIAL/download/english.pdf, accessed July 16, 2007.

———. 1997a. *Progress Report to Premiers.* July. Available at <http://www.scics.gc.ca/pdf/85006109_2e.pdf > (accessed May 2007).

———. 1997b. *New Approaches to Canada's Social Union: An Options Paper.* April 29. Available at <http://www.scics.gc.ca/pdf/85006109_e.pdf> (accessed May 2007).

———. 1997c. *News Release: Provinces and Territories Stress Urgency of Social Policy Renewal,* Ref: 860-365/01, October 6, available at http://www.scics.gc.ca/cinfo/86036501_e.html, accessed July 16, 2007.

———. 1998a. *Report #3: Progress Report to Premiers,* available at http://www.scics.gc.ca/pdf/85007022_e.pdf.

———. 1998b. *Record of Decisions for the January 19 meeting of the P/T Council on Social Policy Renewal.* January 28.

———. 1998c. *Provincial-Territorial Consensus on Collaborative Approaches to Canada's Social Union.* June 12.

———. 1999. *Report #4: Progress Report to Premiers,* August, available at http://www.scics.gc.ca/pdf/report4e.pdf, accessed July 16, 2007.

Provincial/Territorial Deputy Ministers Responsible for Social Services. 1998. "Common Briefing Note for the Meeting of February 17." February 12.

Provincial/Territorial Ministers of Health. 1997. *A Renewed Vision for Canada's Health System.*

Provincial/Territorial Ministers Responsible for Social Services. 1996a. *Annual Meeting, September 16–17, 1996 – Record of Decisions.* October 10.

———. 1997. *Status Report on the National Child Benefit.* July.

———. 1998. "Common Briefing Note for the Meeting of February 17, 1998." February 12.

Quebec. 1996. *Position of the Government of Quebec at the Provincial-Territorial Meeting of Ministers Responsible for Social Services.* Canadian Intergovernmental Conference Secretariat, Document 860-336/004.

Rice, James J., and Michael J. Prince. 2000. *Changing Politics of Canadian Social Policy.* Toronto: University of Toronto Press.

Rimlinger, Gaston V. 1971. *Welfare Policy and Industrialization in Europe, America and Russia.* New York: John Wiley and Sons.

Robson, William B.P., and Daniel Schwanen. 1999. *The Social Union Agreement: Too Flawed to Last.* Toronto: C.D. Howe Institute.

Rodrick, Dani. 1997. *Has Globalization Gone Too Far?* Washington, DC: Institute for International Economics.

Romanow, Roy. 1995. Press release. August. Regina.

_____. 1996a. "From Federal Standards to National Standards." *Standard and Poor's Canadian Focus.* New York: Standard and Poor's Rating Group. November.

_____. 1996b. *Notes for Remarks to the Canadian Council on Social Development.* May 24.

_____. 1996c. *Address to the "Canada's Children: Canada's Future" Conference.* November 27.

_____. 1996d. "The Inequality Crisis: The Need for a New Agenda of Progressive Change." Presentation at the Federal-Provincial-Municipal Summit. Montreal, May 14.

_____. 1996e. "Renewing Federalism: Why Social Reform is Necessary." Presentation to the Canadian Council on Social Development. Montreal. May 24.

_____. 1997a. *News Release: Child Poverty, Youth Unemployment, Medicare Top Romanow's Agenda at First Minister's Meeting,* December 9, 1997, available at http://www.gov.sk.ca/news?newsId=9bd8bd4d-5895-44c7-9554-02a6bbe420e1, accessed July 18, 2007.

_____. 1997b. *Letter to Prime Minister Jean Chrétien.* November 26.

_____. 1997c. *Letter to Prime Minister Jean Chrétien, with attachment "Outline of a Federal/Provincial/Territorial Framework Agreement on Managing Canada's Social Union."* December 9.

_____. 1998. "Reinforcing 'The Ties That Bind.'" *Policy Options* 19, 10 (November).

Ryan, Claude. 1999. "The Agreement on the Canadian Social Union as Seen by a Quebec Federalist." *Inroads: The Canadian Journal of Public Opinion* 8 (June).

Saskatchewan and New Brunswick. 1997. *Status Report on Preparations for the December 12 First Ministers' Meeting.* November 10.

Saskatchewan. 1994. "Briefing Notes." May/August.

_____. 1994–95. "Briefing Notes."

_____. 1995. "Briefing Notes."

_____. 1996. "Briefing Notes."

_____. 1996b. "Briefing Notes." November.

_____. 1996c. "Meeting Note." December.

_____. 1997a. "Briefing Notes." June.

_____. 1997b. Briefing Notes." January 29.

_____. 1997c. "Briefing Notes." January/February.

_____. 1997d. "Briefing Notes." April.

_____. 1997e. "Briefing Notes." June.

_____. 1997f. "Briefing Note." October.

_____. 1997. "Briefing Notes." December.

_____. 1998. "Briefing Note." June.

References

_____. 1997. *Annual Report, 1996–97.*

Scott, K. 1999. "Moving Forward on the National Children's Agenda." *Perception* 23, 2.

Senior Provincial/Territorial Child Welfare Officials. 1996. *Report on Child Welfare.* August.

Shillington, Ned (Minister of Intergovernmental Affairs, Government of Saskatchewan). 1996. *Memorandum to Saskatchewan Premier Roy Romanow.* October 18.

Social Assistance Review Committee. 1988. *Transitions.* Toronto: Queen's Printer for Ontario.

Special Joint Committee of the Senate and the House of Commons on a Renewed Canada. 1992. *Report of the Special Joint Committee on a Renewed Canada.* Ottawa: Queen's Printer for Canada.

Splane, Richard. 1987. "Further Reflections: 1975–1986." In Shankar Yelaja (ed.), *Canadian Social Policy.* Waterloo: Wilfrid Laurier Press.

Standing Committee on Human Resource Development. 1994. *Interim Report, Concerns and Priorities Regarding the Modernization and Restructuring of Canada's Social Security System.* Ottawa: House of Commons.

_____. 1995. *Security, Opportunity and Fairness: Canadians Renewing their Social Programs.* Ottawa: House of Commons.

Stapleton, John. 2004. *Transitions Revisited.* Ottawa: Caledon Institute of Social Policy.

Stewart, Edison. 1998. "Martin says child poverty is a disgrace." *Toronto Star,* November 20.

Ternowetsky, Gordon, W. 1987. "Controling the Deficit and a Private Sector Led Recovery: Contemporary Themes of the Welfare State." In Jacqueline S. Ismael (ed.), *The Canadian Welfare State: Evolution and Transition.* Edmonton: University of Alberta Press.

Thériault, Camille. 1998. "New Brunswick's Perspective on the Social Union." *Policy Options.* November.

Tibbetts, Janice. 1997. "Ottawa plugs child-poverty plan as model of cooperation." *The Gazette,* February 24.

Timpson, A. M. (2001). *Driven Apart: Women's Employment Equality and Child Care in Canadian Public Policy.* Vancouver, UBC Press.

Torjman, Sherri. 1997. *The New Handshake Federalism.* Ottawa: Caledon Institute of Social Policy.

Toughill, Kelly. 1996. "Social program proposal called grab for power." *Toronto Star,* February 8.

Ursel, J. 1992. *Private Lives, Public Policy: 100 Years of State Intervention in the Family.* Toronto: Women's Press.

Western Finance Ministers. 1994. "Report to Western Premiers." May.

_____. 1996. "Seventh Annual Western Finance Ministers' Report." June 4.

WPC (Western Premiers' Conference). 1994. *Communiqué.* May.

_____. 1995. *Communiqué.*

_____. 1998. "Common Briefing Note." June 19.

_____. 1998. *Communiqué.* July 4.

World Health Organization. 1986. *Ottawa Charter for Health Promotion.* Geneva: World

Health Organization.

Wyatt, Mark. 1997. "Budget help inadequate: Romanow." *Regina Leader Post*, February 19.

World Trade Organization. 1996. Singapore WTO Ministerial Declaration. 18 December, available at <http://www.wto.org/english/thewto_e/minist_e/min96_e/wtodec_e.htm>.

Yalnizyan, Armine. 1993. *Defining Social Security, Defining Ourselves: Why We Need to Change Our Thinking Before It's Too Late.* Ottawa: Canadian Centre for Policy Alternatives.